AF352734

Patriots in Exile

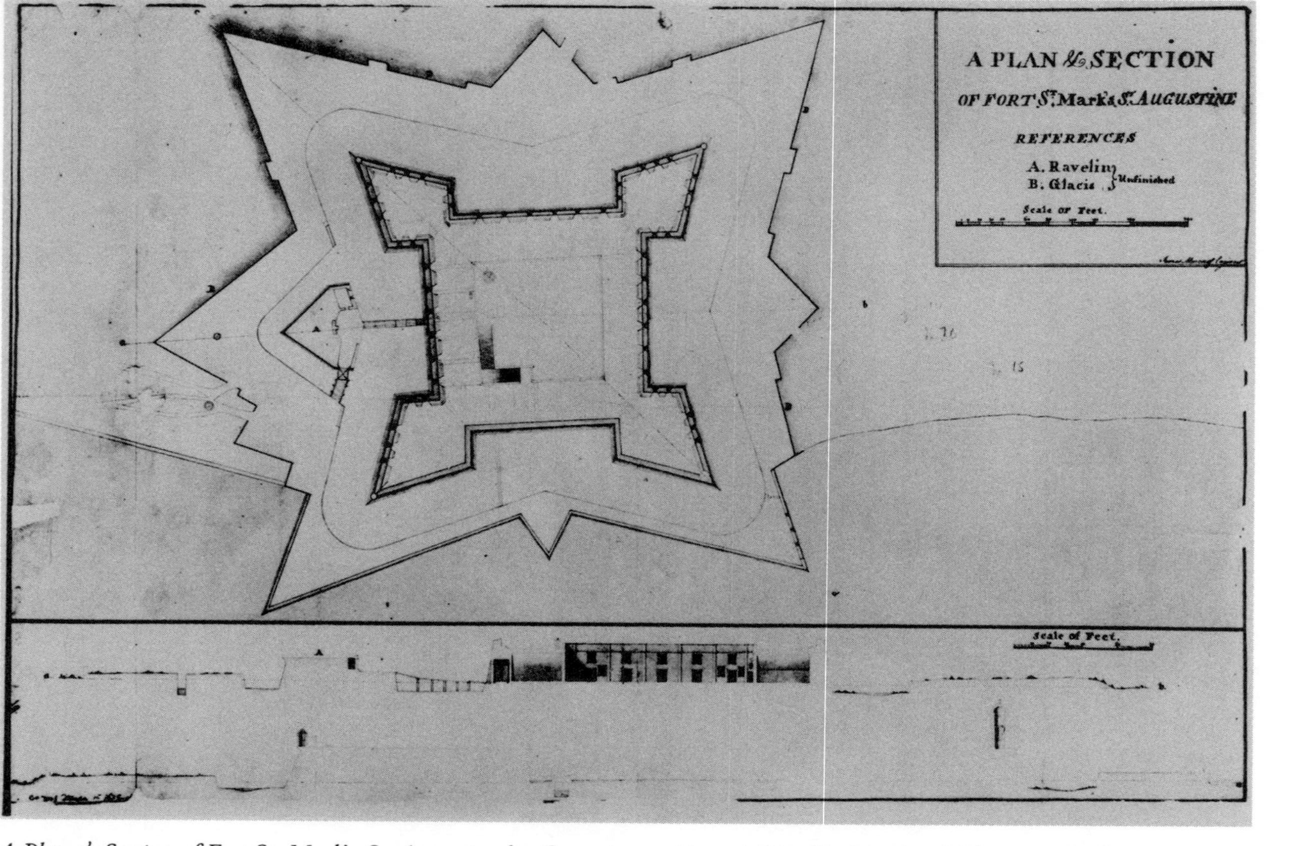

A Plan & Section of Fort St. Mark's, St. Augustine, by Capt. James Moncrief (n.d.). Prints and Photographs Division, Library of Congress, Washington, D.C.

Patriots in Exile

Charleston Rebels in St. Augustine during the American Revolution

James Waring McCrady
and *C. L. Bragg*

Published by the University of South Carolina Press
Columbia, South Carolina 29208

www.uscpress.com

Manufactured in the United States of America

29 28 27 26 25 24 23 22 21 20
10 9 8 7 6 5 4 3 2 1

Library of Congress Cataloging-in-Publication Data
can be found at http://catalog.loc.gov/.

ISBN 978-1-64336-079-9 (hardback)
ISBN 978-1-64336-080-5 (ebook)

This book was printed on recycled paper with
30 percent postconsumer waste content.

History affords no example of magnanimity,
that can surpass the firmness and patient suffering of
THE INTREPID ASSOCIATES,
who, selected as objects of peculiar severity, and more refined persecution, were
ACCUSED OF IMAGINARY CRIMES,
and, in violation of the capitulation of Charleston,
and every principle of good faith, torn from their families, and
EXILED TO ST. AUGUSTINE....
To find them, therefore, firm in duty, and meeting their fate with
that intrepid assurance
which could alone result from greatness of soul,
and a consciousness of correct and irreproachable conduct,
must,
as long as mankind possess
sense to perceive, and virtue to approve,
the beauty of patriotic worth and excellence,
secure to them
THE GRATITUDE AND VENERATION OF THEIR COUNTRY.

Alexander Garden, *Anecdotes of the*
Revolutionary War in America (1822)

Contents

Illustrations

Preface

As a child Waring McCrady occasionally heard a rich family story about the Revolutionary War. Unfortunately the passage of time, combined with forgotten specifics, diminished the tale to the status of little more than a curious "family fact," namely that two of his forebears (whose children later married) had been arrested by the British in Charleston during the Revolutionary War and, along with some others, were taken as prisoners to St. Augustine in East Florida for the war's duration. He never knew the particulars of when or why this occurred, exactly how it came about, who else was involved, or how long the exile lasted.

In the early 1950s, McCrady made a pilgrimage to St. Augustine and was shown the town's old fort with its windowless stone cell where Charleston patriots ("traitors" or "troublemakers" to their captors) had been imprisoned in the early 1780s. Sobered by the view, he dutifully tried to sense the suffering presence of his grandfathers Edward McCrady and William Johnson in the now tidy but still dark space.

If he did conjure such a presence, it was only that: a conjuring. When he returned home and reported his pious brush with ancestral suffering, he was told that he had it all wrong. Grandfathers McCrady and Johnson had never been in such a cell. Rather, during their entire stay in St. Augustine they were respected as gentlemen, allowed housing, were attended by their enslaved servants, and were given a certain liberty of the town. Obviously there was more to the story than he had been told, though at the time further details were not forthcoming.

Now in retirement two-thirds of a century later, McCrady has undertaken the challenge of rediscovering what he could of the story of the Charleston patriot exiles, details of which lay buried in scattered primary and secondary sources. For a while he was selfishly pleased that he would be the first to assemble a unified account of the St. Augustine exile.

But Waring McCrady was not alone in his interest in the Charleston exiles. Chip Bragg had been a student of South Carolina's colonial and Revolutionary War history for only a single decade, but that decade had produced a biography of William Moultrie and a book about the execution of patriot Col. Isaac Hayne by the British in 1781. Along the way Bragg noticed that the exile of a number of Charleston's "most respectable gentlemen" had received attention by most authors writing about the Revolutionary War in South Carolina, beginning with David Ramsay (one of the exiles) in 1785 and continuing up to the present (Bragg himself).

Some of the attentions are merely cursory mentions, others slightly more expansive, while more detailed treatments are found in the few existing full biographies of exiles, namely those of Christopher Gadsden, Edward Rutledge, and David Ramsay. The amount of coverage of the banishment in historical works seems to parallel the experience of Waring McCrady's family history in which as time passed detail decreased, two notable exceptions being Carl Borick's *Relieve Us of This Burthen* (2012) and Gwenda Morgan and Peter Rushton's *Banishment in the Early Atlantic World* (2013).

Whether the abovementioned treatments of the exile are brief or lengthy, all of the South Carolina historians past and present are tremendously indebted to Josiah Smith Jr. (1731–1826), a Charleston, South Carolina, merchant and importer, financial agent, plantation manager, and patriot. He served in the South Carolina General Assembly, which elected him to be one of several commissioners of the South Carolina navy, a post he held until 1780. During the siege of Charleston, Smith served as a militiaman in the battle lines in front of the town and so became a prisoner of war on parole at the capitulation. In 1758 he married Mary Stevens, with whom he had twelve children, six of whom (three boys and three girls) were living at the time of his transport to St. Augustine.[1]

Smith was a committed diarist. His journal was edited by historian Mabel L. Weber and published piecemeal over eight issues of the *South Carolina Historical and Genealogical Magazine* in 1932–33. Smith's diary is the sine qua non primary source concerning the patriot exile and documents the banishment in his own voice and from his own perspective. McCrady and Bragg, who learned of each other's work from a mutual friend, decided to join together and take Smith's excellent but singular view and pull in other available sources to tell a more complete story, one that begins well before Smith's diary opens and ends beyond its closure.[2]

The words *banishment* and *exile,* used synonymously and interchangeably in this narrative, have slightly different connotations, but both meanings are applicable in the context of the Charleston patriots who were transported to St. Augustine. *Banishment* carries more punitive undertones of wrongdoing and has an implication of permanence, whereas *exile* is often applied for political reasons, may be imposed for a restricted period of time, and can be voluntary.

Such transportations were not uncommon occurrences during the Revolutionary War. The patriots had already expelled individual loyalists for refusing to sign oaths of abjuration and allegiance. Nor was the banishment of groups unheard of—prominent disaffected Philadelphia Quaker men were exiled to

Winchester, Virginia, for seven months in September 1777. In the Charleston case, women and children also became exiles in 1781 when British authorities ordered the families of the St. Augustine exiles and others to "quit the province."[3]

Exactly who were these exiles, sixty-three of them, and what made them more odious to the British than other patriots residing in Charleston in 1780? Why did the British precipitously arrest and deport these prominent civilians and military officers who vociferously claimed they were adhering to the terms agreed upon at the surrender of Charleston on May 12, 1780? Their demographics are more fully explored in appendix A, but fourteen of them served on one or more of the extralegal councils or committees that functioned as a pre-Revolutionary shadow government of South Carolina prior to the formal rejection of royal authority.

Forty served in some military capacity during the war. Forty-three had or would serve in the colonial, provincial, or state legislature. Four had or would hold the office of lieutenant governor of South Carolina, two had been or would be elected governor of South Carolina but did not serve, and another would later be elected governor and would die in office. Three exiles signed the Declaration of Independence, and one signed the Articles of Confederation. Nine served or would serve in the Continental Congress, the Confederation Congress, or the U.S. Congress, and eighteen would vote for or against ratification of the U.S. Constitution. These are the kinds of men of which the British ridded themselves while they occupied Charleston from May 1780 until December 1782.

As to how and why, the notion of a sudden decision on the part of the British to set into motion the arrests, deportation, and prolonged exile will be dispelled early in the narrative. Given the scant evidence from both sides, it will be up to the reader to decide if the British made a fair decision. For such an analysis, a mere repetition of the details recorded in Josiah Smith's diary does not suffice; the justice of the exile merits examination from the standpoint of the British who governed occupied Charleston, the families left behind, the armies in the field, the Continental Congress, and finally, the Jacksonboro Assembly of January–February 1782.

To that end the authors present this account, written more than two and a quarter centuries after the event and begun as an attempt to reconstruct the banishment of grandfathers Edward McCrady and William Johnson. In doing so they chronicle the story of sixty-three patriots-in-exile, the British authorities who transported them, and, when evidence permits, the effect of the exile on their wives, their children, and their slaves—those silent exiles who were selected to accompany their masters.

But what of the two men who inspired Waring McCrady to search out the facts of their exile? Obviously if the exile had not occurred, there would be no story to tell. What is less obvious is that without the exile there might not have been a storyteller in the person of Waring McCrady. One can only guess what might have happened to the two families, eventually united by marriage, had Edward McCrady and William Johnson not sojourned in St Augustine. Lives might have taken entirely different courses.

Neither Edward McCrady (ca. 1750–94) nor William Johnson (1741–1818) became well-known or celebrated political or civic officers like their patriot counterparts who were signers, congressmen, state legislators, lieutenant governors, judges, or mayors (Johnson did serve in the prewar general assembly). Instead they represent the "everyman" patriots who were fervent in their beliefs and steadfast in their purpose and who went about conducting their business without calling particular attention to themselves (except of course while captive in Charleston, when they did indeed come to the attention of the British).

Both men came to Charleston from the state of New York. Johnson's family had already spent a century in Manhattan, whereas McCrady was a relatively recent arrival from Ulster, County Antrim, Ireland, via Jamaica who, at the urging of his wife's relatives, invested in Albany properties and considered establishing himself there. Something changed his mind in the early 1770s. He sold his New York holdings and restarted his American career in Charleston. It is possible that these two fathers of young families had been acquainted in the northern climes, where Johnson's mother still resided, but they certainly knew and liked each other amid the bustle of Charleston's conflicted revolutionary atmosphere.

McCrady and Johnson had fine houses near one another and overlooking the harbor from East Bay Street. Both had well-established households with large slaveholdings, and both had additional investment properties, including country farms that they referred to as plantations, and the necessary enslaved labor forces to run them.[4]

It is hardly inconceivable that Edward McCrady often personally greeted the guests at his popular McCrady's Tavern, which included dining facilities, inn accommodations, and after the war a "long room" that was at the time Charleston's largest ballroom and concert hall. The long room featured a curtained stage area for guest artists from abroad, lectures, poetry readings, and the like, as well as less formal entertainment for more mundane festivities. George Washington dined there as a guest of the Society of the Cincinnati while on his 1791 southern tour.[5]

As for William Johnson, it is known that he enjoyed lending a hand at hammer and anvil in the forge and ironsmith business that yielded a significant part of his income. He became a supporter of Christopher Gadsden's radical politics, voiced loud opposition to the Stamp Act, and helped organize the Liberty Tree Party in 1766. He made enough of a name for himself that he was elected to South Carolina's Provincial Congress in 1775.[6]

Both families attended St. Philip's Church in Charleston and integrated their lives with the best of the hundred-year-old city's upper classes, but their known tastes for serious literature, English silver services, and elegant mahogany furniture did not prevent them from being ardent revolutionaries when it came to the political, social, and commercial freedoms proclaimed by the budding United States. Each man had personal reasons for disliking the established colonial government, and as businessmen they both were heartily roused by the cries against taxation without representation.[7]

Editorial Note

The narrative often includes the actual words of the participants. The quoted matter retains the capitalization, punctuation, archaic spelling, and the occasional obvious misspelling of the original sources. Because of the variance in spellings and usage for the time in which our narrative is set, we have not employed "sic" to note departures from modern practices.

Acknowledgments

The authors are sincerely grateful to the individuals and institutional staff members listed below for their advice, encouragement, and editorial assistance: Charles B. Baxley of Lugoff, South Carolina, who introduced the coauthors to each other; Julian Victor Brandt III of Charleston; Nicholas Doyle, reproduction manager at the South Caroliniana Library of the University of South Carolina in Columbia; Mike Evans, living historian at the Castillo de San Marcos National Monument in St. Augustine; Ehren Foley, acquisitions editor at the University of South Carolina Press in Columbia; Lee Youngblood Green Jr. of Hartselle, Alabama; Molly Inabinett, librarian at the South Carolina Historical Society in Charleston; Caren M. Jones of Thomasville, Georgia; Renée LaHue Marshall, executive director of the Huguenot Society of South Carolina in Charleston; Wayne E. McFee, principal investigator at the National Centers for Coastal Ocean Science, NOAA National Ocean Service in Charleston; Angela B. McGuire at the Thomas County Public Library in Thomasville; Michele Lee Silverman, former research services librarian, and Emily Leto, library assistant at the Society of the Cincinnati in Washington, D.C.; Michele Wilbanks, coordinator of public and support services at the Department of Special and Area Studies Collections, George A. Smathers Libraries at the University of Florida, Gainesville; the Robert Manning Strozier Library at Florida State University in Tallahassee; the Library of Congress in Washington, D.C.; the New-York Historical Society in New York; the Society of the Cincinnati in Washington, D.C.; the South Carolina Historical Society in Charleston; and the Special Collections Department of the Marlene and Nathan Addlestone Library at the College of Charleston in Charleston. Special thanks go also to Phil Eschbach, of Winter Park, Florida, for his insistently warm and personal support.

Prologue

James Simpson's Charleston homecoming was bittersweet.

It was the middle of May 1780. A besieged Continental Army had surrendered Charleston only days before. The city was now occupied by British and Hessian solders who provided a heretofore unknown promise of safety to loyalist civilians such as Simpson.

The inhabitants of Charleston who maintained faithful loyalty to King George III had suffered terribly under the five years of patriot rule. Simpson himself had been absent since February 1777, having been banished from his home for refusing to swear fealty to the rogue province of South Carolina. His allegiance to the Crown had cost him valuable goods, acres of property, income, and status. He had endured transatlantic voyages and separation from family and friends. He had even tolerated life in an army encampment during the recent siege, though his friendship with the British commander, Lt. Gen. Sir Henry Clinton, certainly had made his existence tolerable.[1]

Now he was back. Home. As a victor. Not that there was much cause for celebration. War in general and a six-week-long siege punctuated by frequent bombardment had left their marks on Charleston, not to mention the recent explosion of four thousand pounds of ammunition in a storehouse that literally rattled the city, killed roundabout two hundred people, and started a fire that consumed six houses.[2]

"Nothing but the evidence of my senses would have convinced me that one half of the distress I am a witness to could have been produced in so short a time in so rich and flourishing a country as Carolina was when I left it," Simpson later wrote to Clinton. "Numbers of families, who, four years ago, abounded in every convenience and luxury of life, are without food to live on, clothes to cover them, or the means to purchase either. It hath appeared to me the more extraordinary, because until 12 months ago it had not been exposed to any other devastation of war except the captures made at sea."[3] Nonetheless he resolved to do everything within his power to bring about the restoration of royal government and prosperity to His Majesty's loyal subjects.

But first he would make sure that "those People whose persecuting spirit hath caused such calamities to their fellow subjects . . . receive[d] the punishment their Iniquities deserve."[4]

Introduction

Two Towns at Odds

In 1780 a surprise arrest and exile catapulted a group of energetic Charleston citizens out of their place of engaged action into a place of historic frustration. The British-imposed exile plucked them from a century-old colonial city once full of vigor, ambition, and promise and deposited them in St. Augustine, a colonial city twice that old yet still raw, confused, and directionless. The contrast must have provided them with steady subject matter for whiling away their imposed inactivity. How did these two towns come to be so different?

Charleston, at the time of its founding in 1670, was the southernmost point of English settlement in North America. But farther down the same coast, the similar-sized town of St. Augustine had already been alive for a century. In fact, the still charming little Florida outpost retains to this day its proud superlative for the continent: it is the oldest town north of Mexico to be founded and continuously inhabited by European stock.[1]

St. Augustine was established by the Spaniards in 1565, seventy-three years "after Columbus" and seventeen years before Spain settled Santa Fe in New Mexico (1582), twenty years before Raleigh's unsuccessful Virginia settlement at Roanoke Island (1585), forty years earlier than the French in Nova Scotia (1605), and forty-two years earlier than the first permanent English presence in the Americas (Jamestown, 1607). St. Augustine was settled forty-three years earlier than Champlain's Quebec (1608), forty-nine years earlier than the Dutch at New Amsterdam (1614), and fifty-five years earlier than the late-come Pilgrims at Plymouth Rock (1620). Why, after two centuries of existence and a century's head start, was it not bigger and more prosperous than Charleston?[2]

Spain had dreams of wealth when it laid claim to Florida in the heyday of far-reaching New World colonialism, but in the years before St. Augustine was established the area languished passively as an uncertain prize. Though history records a litany of struggles and activity in the western part of Florida (now known as the Panhandle, stretching along the Gulf of Mexico through Pensacola), the eastern part—the peninsula—remained basically wild and quiet, untroubled, and undeveloped during the first two centuries of Spanish dominion. The inhabitants of insecure little St. Augustine found no easy way to make their isolated lives productive and were warned that "good as their intentions may be, they are and will be helpless as long as His Majesty [King Philip] does not deign to arrange some class of commerce for the development of the province."[3]

Compared to the Spanish, the English were slow to take hold in the New World, and it was rather quietly that in 1607 they established Briton's first permanent presence in the Americas. This was Jamestown, more than six hundred miles up the coast from St. Augustine and not felt to be a particular threat to Spain's modest toehold. The French followed quickly but still further to the north, establishing their first North American town the next year at Quebec (1608). At its distance of almost fifteen hundred miles from St. Augustine, Quebec was even less of a threat to Spain. Then a period of fifty years passed without the planting of any further coastal town in the unorganized area between Virginia and Florida, the territory known after 1629 as Carolina (in honor of King Charles I). So St. Augustine had plenty of time to develop, but its only obvious incentive was to stand guard for the protection of Spanish trading vessels.

Other Atlantic coastal cities in the North American colonies were later established with conscious intent to become centers of immigration for permanent settlers and centers of commerce and culture for agricultural and industrial life. By contrast St. Augustine was founded by Spain as a presidio, or garrison town. The pious Spanish government officially fostered the outpost's incidental role as a missionary headquarters, but imperial concern focused primarily on establishing a military presence to fend off French encroachment. The real role of St. Augustine was to keep watch over the shipping routes funneling wealth to Spain from the Caribbean islands and Spanish-dominated lands of Central America and Peru.[4]

As for potential commercial development, it was noted as early as 1579 that orange trees brought to Florida from Spain seemed quite promising, yet the promise was not seriously pursued until 150 years later, and then not by the Spanish so much as by the British. More than oranges, the important sixteenth-century raison d'être for St. Augustine remained consistently the settlement's wooden fort, a primitive and relatively unthreatened protector of the town and area prior to the founding of Charleston about two hundred miles further up the coast (a few days away by sea). However, a distinct shadow of British threat was cast in 1665 when a new English map of Carolina rather ambitiously included the town of St. Augustine.

Fledgling Charleston actually appeared in 1670, and Spain took notice. Having the English in that close a proximity gave the presence of St. Augustine's fort greater significance from a military standpoint. Within two years the Spanish

Castillo de San Marcos; aerial view. Prints and Photographs Division, Library of Congress, Washington, D.C.

started serious construction on the Castillo de San Marcos, a coquina-stone stronghold that replaced St. Augustine's wooden fort.[5]

For strategic reasons Charleston relocated from its original site on the west bank of the Ashley River (a few miles northwest of its present location) to the more advantageous peninsula formed by the Ashley and Cooper Rivers. Charleston was at first comparable in function to the older little outpost in Florida, and it remained similar in size if not smaller for at least sixty years. There was, in fact, not much saber-rattling between the two settlements. St. Augustine continued its rather static role as an isolated Hispanic outpost with a largely defensive function and a great deal of jungle-like backdrop, but Charleston increasingly busied itself with a rapidly extending network of plantations and settlements and, thanks to its very accessible port, a bustling interaction with the English-speaking provinces to the north and with the West Indies. By the 1730s Charleston had its first newspaper and real bookstores and was on a path of steady growth in prosperity, refinement, and importance, with opportunities for expansion up its peninsula and across its rivers.[6]

By the mid-1700s, plantation trade, colonial government, and the activities of the Carolina port with its very active shipping industry had made Charleston the most developed town south of Philadelphia, both financially and culturally. Elegant steeples had appeared, with other permanent buildings residential, ecclesiastic, and civic; perfunctory St. Augustine, on the other hand, retained its basically two-story skyline. The military government of the Florida town had put

Castillo de San Marcos; southeast bastion. Prints and Photographs Division, Library of Congress, Washington, D.C.

all its architectural emphasis on the one grand fort, finally completed in 1756. As the imbalance grew between the two towns, they each increased in mutual suspicion. British analysts even argued that "Carolina must take St. Augustine, or St. Augustine would take Carolina."[7]

England and Spain contested one another's claim to the region, and half-hearted military operations were launched from Charleston against St. Augustine and vice versa. Smoldering enmity prevailed between the two towns until suddenly, almost by surprise, the British of 1763 found themselves in possession of all Florida, not by military conquest but rather as an unanticipated plum from the concluding arrangements of the Seven Years' War (French and Indian War). In a matter of months, St. Augustine's Hispanic population withdrew almost totally, and the town was reborn as a military outpost for British operations with attractive dreams of replicating the lifestyles of South Carolina and Virginia.[8]

Sad to say, those prospects faded seriously within a decade. Even with new government and a new (though minimal) population, the old problems of climate and isolation prevailed. To survive, English-speaking St. Augustine identified much more closely with England than with the increasingly independence-oriented populations of the colonies north of it, colonies with which Florida was now ostensibly identified but from which, dependent on London, it was politically isolated.

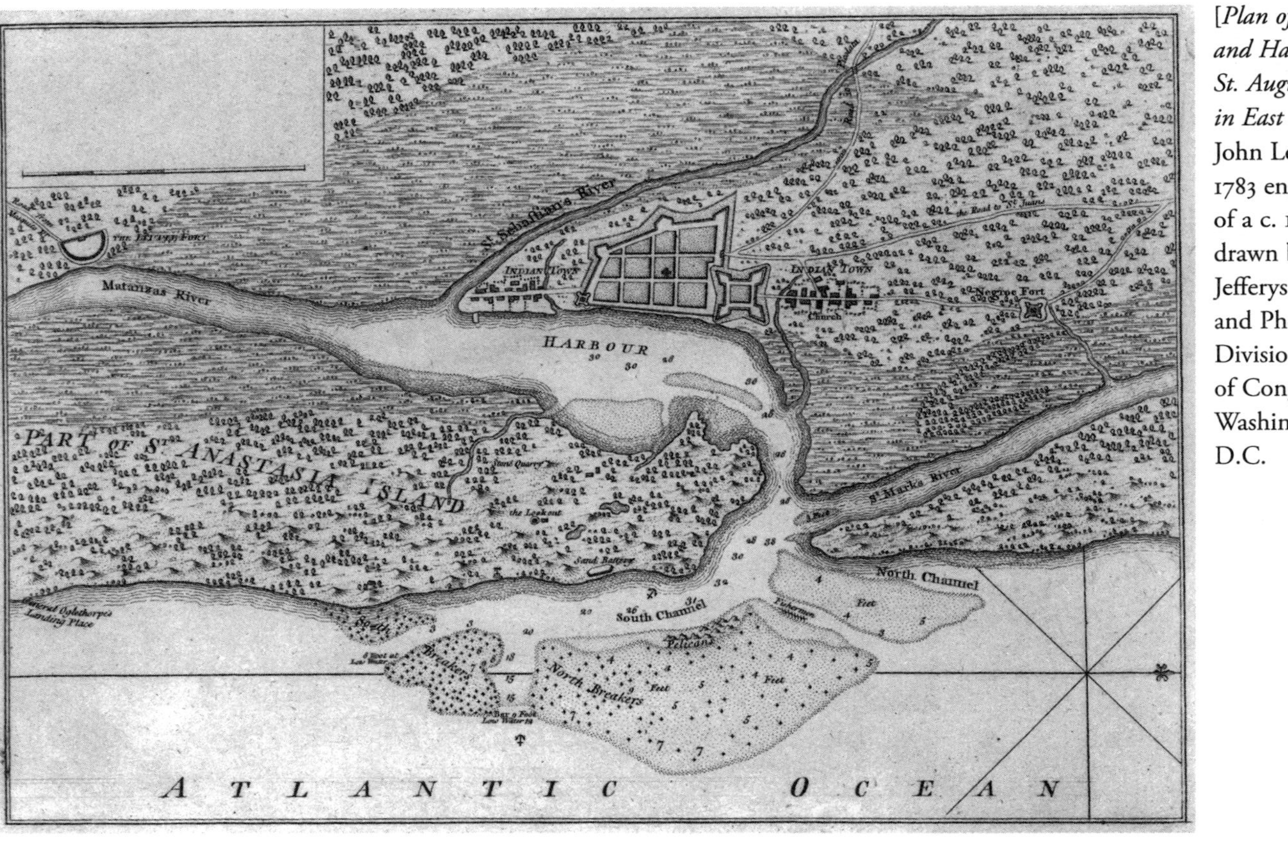

[Plan of the Town and Harbour of St. Augustine, in East Florida.] John Lodge's 1783 engraving of a c. 1762 map drawn by Thomas Jefferys. Prints and Photographs Division, Library of Congress, Washington, D.C.

The relationship between St. Augustine and Charleston became adversarial again when Charleston's revolutionaries ousted their royal government in 1775. Georgia served as a buffer between South Carolina and East Florida but could not be defended against British raiding parties. Many in Charleston and Savannah held a notion that the peace of Georgia and South Carolina therefore depended on the reduction of St. Augustine. Others were not so sure and doubted the ability of the British in St. Augustine to mount any meaningful incursions into Georgia—"their numbers being so few . . . they had better stay at home and take care of their own castle," opined William Moultrie.[9]

The Americans revolutionaries learned the hard way that East Florida would not be an easy prize. Between August 1776 and April 1779, three different expeditions were staged and mounted from South Carolina into Georgia for the purpose of taking St. Augustine, all of which were total failures on account of weather, disease, supply, and poor-to-nonexistent coordination between heterogeneous American commands (militia versus Continental, Georgia versus South Carolina). Otherwise, periods of inactivity were punctuated by quick forays instigated by both sides across the St. Marys River at the Georgia–East Florida border.[10]

From the outset of the Revolutionary War, the British found new and different uses for its isolated town and military outpost at St. Augustine. For one, an entirely separate influx of new arrivals took the form of loyalist sympathizers, colonials from all walks of life, from planter-merchant elites to illiterate seamen and farmers, all seeking to escape revolution and uneasily swelling the population of the East Florida town. The British found St. Augustine an obvious place to confine their prisoners, so that an unhappy population of royal-resisters increased there annually. The loyalist governor of Virginia sent Masons, Lees, and Hills to Florida when he deemed them dangerously seditious or outright rebellious. Two thousand is considered a conservative estimate of the French and American prisoners who were to do a stint there during the war. Most did not stay more than a few months, because it was in the interest of everyone concerned to effect speedy exchanges. But others were not so fortunate, among whom were to be counted the exiled Charleston patriots.[11]

How did it come to pass that out of Charleston's eleven thousand or more inhabitants, the conquering British selected sixty-three patriots for exile? It was not an arbitrary process.

Chapter 1

A Loyalist Embarks
on a Secret Mission

In most accounts the story of the banishment of South Carolina patriots to St. Augustine begins with British soldiers rousting certain gentlemen from their beds in the wee hours of the morning on August 27, 1780, almost as if the decision to take into custody and deport them was one that was made on the spur of the moment. Such was not the case. The episode actually began months earlier, germinating from events that had occurred nearly five years before, in 1775, when South Carolina transitioned from royal colony to self-governing province and began to prepare for the war that had already commenced in Massachusetts. The central figure leading up to the 1780 banishment was James Simpson, an attorney, a former resident of Charleston, and one of many who remained loyal to His Majesty, King George III.

Simpson, the man who arguably was South Carolina's preeminent loyalist, was born in Scotland in 1737. He was the oldest son of William Simpson, who served as South Carolina's chief justice in 1761 and 1762 and Georgia's chief justice from 1766 to 1769. Fifteen-year-old James came to America for the first time in 1752 with his father, an able but archetypical placeman (such royal appointees were sometimes purchasers of their political appointments) and a defender of the royal prerogative.[1]

In 1761 William Simpson published a very useful and exceedingly well-received handbook for justices of the peace, but as clerk of the Royal Council in 1762, he ran afoul of the Commons House of Assembly by becoming embroiled in the Gadsden election controversy. This dispute and war of words in the press over an election irregularity lasted more than two years and widened an already growing rift between the governor and the Commons House. The affair also put the elder Simpson (and probably James also) at enmity with Christopher Gadsden, whose special election to the Commons provoked the controversy.[2]

Soon after James Simpson arrived, he began a two-and-a-half-year apprenticeship in the law office of Charleston attorney James Michie, also a Scotsman, an associate of his father, and one of the most prominent legal and political figures in the colony. To complete his legal education he took Michie's advice and traveled to England in 1756 or 1757, where he clerked for two years in the office of barrister William Green. After finishing with Green, he continued in London for an additional two years "at a very Considerable expense consistently attending on the several Courts of Law & Equity and without any other View or intention than to become a Practitioner in the several Courts of this Province [South Carolina]." Whether he associated himself with any of London's Inns of Court during this time is unclear. He returned home in August 1763 and was admitted to the South Carolina bar on October 30, 1765.[3]

His peers saw in Simpson the potential to become a fine lawyer, and he quickly became a royal insider. In late 1763, at the age of twenty-seven, he was appointed clerk of the Royal Council of South Carolina, succeeding his father during the administration of acting governor Lt. Gov. William Bull II. The Royal Council was composed of twelve appointed members who were oftentimes professional politicians from England. These despised "placemen" served the governor in an advisory capacity as a part of the executive branch of a government modeled on the English system. In the colony the Royal Council acted as a provincial equivalent of the English House of Lords, and along with the governor, it was often at odds with the Commons House of Assembly, a popularly elected group that generally followed the procedures and customs of the British House of Commons. Having become clerk of the council, James was not nearly as controversial as his father.[4]

On May 5, 1769, Gov. Charles Greville Montagu selected Simpson to serve as acting judge of South Carolina's vice-admiralty court, replacing Sir Egerton Leigh. This court had been originally conceived in 1697 to have jurisdiction over local cases of maritime law, including war prizes, maritime contracts, and disputes between merchants and seamen. Judges of the vice-admiralty courts were Crown-appointed and empowered to issue rulings without a jury trial. The perception of a conflict of interest naturally arose, as the judges were paid no salary but instead received a portion of the funds arising from penalties and forfeitures imposed by the court. The Vice-Admiralty Court Act of 1768, one of the hated Townshend Acts that imposed customs duties on imports without the consent of the taxed, worsened the tensions by expanding the vice-admiralty courts' jurisdiction over customs violations and smuggling. This was bitterly resented by the colonists, who viewed the act and the court as yet a further infringement on their constitutional rights as British subjects.[5]

According to William Bull, Simpson accepted the position of vice-admiralty judge just at a time when that office was becoming seriously unpopular. The post that had once been a prestigious appointment had become an object of suspicion and criticism. There is no evidence, however, that Simpson conducted himself less than honorably during his tenure on the bench. He was not at all naive about the workings of the vice-admiralty court, as his mentor Michie had been vice-admiralty judge during the time of Simpson's apprenticeship a decade-and-a-half earlier. Simpson subsequently resigned this post in 1771 when he was chosen by Bull to be South Carolina's attorney general.[6]

Simpson would be the province's last royal attorney general. He served in office only until 1775, at which time the revolutionary provincial government superseded the royal government. Likewise Lord William Campbell, a Scotsman like Simpson, would be the last royal governor of South Carolina. Campbell arrived to take his post in Charleston on June 17, 1775, bearing instructions to restore royal authority in a colony that had been growing increasingly rebellious. Simpson was one of only fifteen people who greeted His Excellency on arrival.[7]

Campbell was too late: by the time he made landfall, the fires of revolution were burning hot, and he was unable to quench them. In fact by his own actions—his arrogant dismissiveness of the newly formed Provincial Congress, his efforts to incite backcountry loyalists and Indians against the patriots, and his requests for British reinforcements—he succeeded only in fanning the blaze. On September 15, 1775, Royal Governor Campbell boarded the sloop *Tamar* in Charleston Harbor and fled for his own safety.[8]

Simpson remained in Charleston despite a close relationship with Campbell. The royal governor had considered Simpson as one of the only three men in Charleston he could trust. Not long after he landed in Charleston, Campbell was overheard saying that "James Simpson was now Deputy [Lt.] Governor, but that it was not now to be declared, because it would ruin him; for the [rebels] now love him, but in a short time it would be otherwise, for the Town would be made level [by British reinforcements]."[9]

Indeed Simpson had not yet run afoul of South Carolina's revolutionary government and still enjoyed a reputation as "a very good friend to this Country, [who] has nothing at all to do with politicks." That was about to change. He saw firsthand what patriot radicals were capable of doing. A few weeks earlier a mob had tarred and feathered the gunner at Fort Johnson, George Walker, as punishment for his insolent speech. Walker was paraded around town in this pitiful and painful condition, halting in front of certain houses as a warning. Simpson's house was among them.[10]

On July 20, 1775, Simpson received a summons to submit himself to the province's General Committee. When he appeared two days later, the committee requested that he sign South Carolina's Articles of Association, in his words, "promising to support the Resolutions and obey the Determinations of the American Congress in opposition to the Authority of his Majesty and the British parliament." Not only did he refuse to sign, but he pointedly denounced the association, expressing his dissent "in a manly and proper way," and emphatically stated that he could not "subscribe it without Perjury and Perfidy."[11]

A notice from the General Committee, dated August 23, 1775, appeared in newspapers, advertising that Simpson and others like him were deemed "inimical to the Liberty of America" for refusing to subscribe to the articles of association. All persons were prohibited from having association or business with him beyond selling him such food and provisions as were necessary for the support of his family. At the same time, his liberty of movement was restricted, at first to the limits of Charleston, then later to his home.[12]

Notwithstanding his inability to travel or carry out his duties and the prevailing atmosphere of persecution that he felt, Simpson made it a point to learn virtually everything that was taking place in town and the surrounding countryside. He could not help but take notice of Charleston's rebel inhabitants as they fortified in anticipation of a British southern campaign to restore royal government in the southern colonies. The climax of this campaign was an attack that took place on the morning of June 28, 1776, when Cmdre. Sir Peter Parker's nine warships of the Royal Navy launched a ferocious but abortive day-long naval bombardment against a small, unfinished square palmetto-log-and-sand fort on Sullivan's Island at the northeastern entrance to Charleston Harbor. In the few weeks leading up to the battle, Simpson was held a close prisoner, and during the action he was taken from his house by an armed escort and forced to relinquish his money bonds, notes, and other valuable securities.[13]

A detailed rendering of the action of the battle of June 28, 1776, is beyond the scope of this narrative, but suffice it to say that while Parker's ships battered the fort's defiant defenders, British army troops commanded by Maj. Gen. Sir Henry Clinton rendered embarrassingly ineffectual assistance from nearby Long Island. The British strategy and tactics were flawed on several levels, and the South Carolinians led by Col. William Moultrie, who manned the fort's parapets, were resolute in their determination to hold their post. These factors combined to result in an unmitigated catastrophe for the British and a resounding victory for the Americans in what would be remembered afterward as the Battle of Sullivan's Island or Battle of Fort Moultrie.

In a highly critical twenty-page letter penned after the battle and sent to Lord George Germain, who as secretary of state for the colonies was responsible for prosecuting the war for the British side, Simpson itemized the recent failures of the British government and military in the southern theater. Demonstrating an acute comprehension of what had transpired in the colony and town over the preceding two years, he communicated to Germain the details of the rebels' preparation for the defense of Charleston and provided astoundingly accurate knowledge of the military situation in Charleston and the backcountry. Much of this information he may have gleaned from conversations and from the local newspapers, but his information was so detailed that he may actually have organized a network of informants around about the countryside. His narrative provides an excellent and concise history of the early days of the Revolution in South Carolina, and on its own merit is worth reading in its entirety.[14]

Simpson began by admitting "that it is easier to discover Errors after a Miscarriage, than to have foreseen and prevented them before it." And so he launched his frank dissection of what had gone awry in South Carolina. At first the revolutionary sentiments were tepid, but over time the moderates left town "and all power being now in the hands of the violent, Supported by Military force, every appearance of Discontent or dissention, received immediate punishment." This he knew from his own experience.[15]

Of the battle lost by the British on June 28, Simpson opined that it was "not less than to our subsequent mismanagement, that we owe our disgrace at Sullivan[']s Island. . . . Had the Conduct of the Commanders, equalled the Courage of their men, we should not have occasion at this day, to lament so disgraceful a disaster." He gave no credit to the raw but intrepid South Carolina patriots holding the unfinished palmetto-log fort against seemingly overwhelming British might, and his disdain for the American battle preparations only added to the shamefulness of the defeat.[16]

In his closing paragraph Simpson succinctly summarized everything that had gone wrong during the battle: the months wasted before the attack, the decision to bombard the fort on Sullivan's Island rather than attacking Charleston directly, the uselessness of Clinton's troops on Long Island, and the fact that the ships commanded by Sir Peter Parker did not get close enough to the fort to destroy it. As a matter of fact, Simpson was shocked that there had been no official inquiry "into the Causes which produced a miscarriage, as disgraceful to his Majesty[']s Arms, as it was fatal to his Government in the Southern Colonies."[17]

Simpson had wanted to leave the province as early as April 1776, but he knew too much—officials prevented his departure in the face of the impending invasion, and so he remained under house arrest for a time at the home of the deputy postmaster, George Roupell. Yet at other times he was allowed to move within the limits of town. It was during this time of restriction that he unsuccessfully attempted to publish a letter in the Charleston newspaper to state his perceptions of "the real Views of the principal promoters of the present Rebellion . . . [and] by publickly declaring his Suspicions of their Designs," consequently to convince his fellow Carolinians of "the fatal consequences of their Measures."[18]

However, on February 13, 1777, the South Carolina legislature passed an act establishing an oath of abjuration and allegiance. The oath required acknowledgement that South Carolina was now a free, independent, and sovereign state, that the people owed no allegiance or obedience to George III, and that they

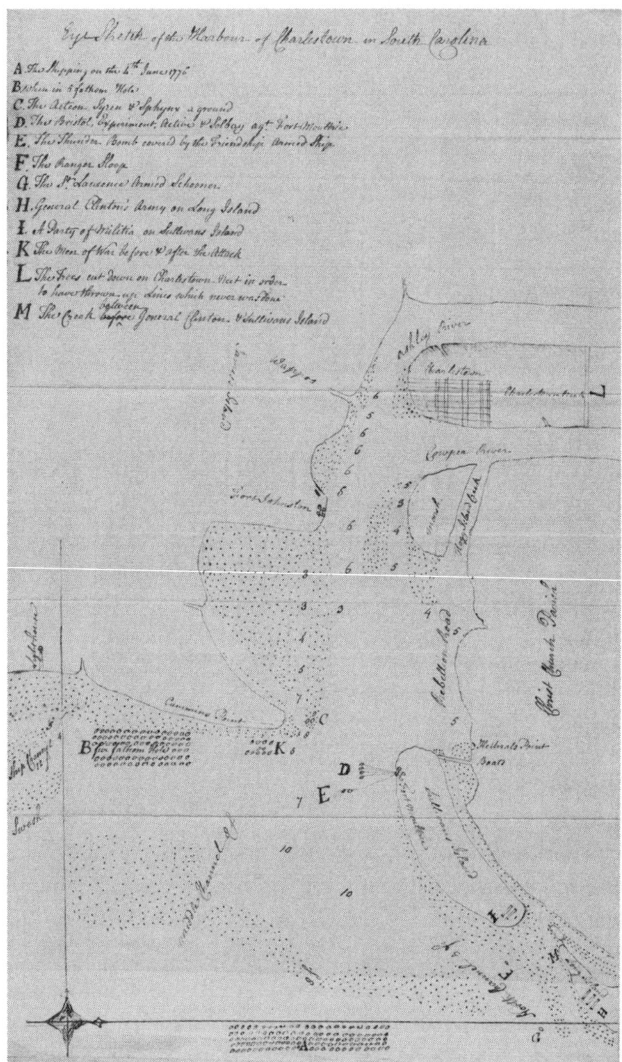

Eye-Sketch of the Harbour of Charlestown in South Carolina by James Simpson, 1776. Simpson included this map of the June 28, 1776, Battle of Sullivan's Island in his 1778 report to Lord George Germain. George Sackville Germain Papers, William L. Clements Library, University of Michigan, Ann Arbor, Mich.

must renounce allegiance to the king and swear allegiance to the state. Those persons refusing to take the oath were required to vacate the state within sixty days, and if they returned they would be judged guilty of treason and suffer death as a consequence. Simpson refused to take the oath. Instead he invested his wife with power of attorney, notified his debtors and creditors of his intention to vacate the province, and boarded the twenty-gun *Galetea,* which carried him off to Bermuda.[19]

From Bermuda Simpson traveled to British-controlled New York, bearing important intelligence that he hoped to transmit to the military authorities. In

New York he was able to secure interviews with Lt. Gen. Sir William Howe, who was commander-in-chief of British forces in North America, and with William Howe's brother Admiral Lord Richard Howe. Afterward, supposing that he could be of no further use in America, in September 1778 Simpson booked passage and returned to England.[20]

In England Simpson intended to resume the practice of law. On November 14, 1777, he had gained admission to the Honourable Society of the Middle Temple in London. He had long personal acquaintances with a number of other South Carolina attorneys who had been at Middle Temple: Edward Rutledge, Thomas Lynch Jr., Thomas Heyward Jr., Arthur Middleton, and Thomas Mc-Kean, all of whom had signed the Declaration of Independence. His eldest son, William, had been admitted to the same Inn on May 13, 1775.[21]

While in London, Simpson presented a memorial to Lord Germain explicitly detailing the hardships that he and his family had endured, as well as the monetary and property losses he had incurred as a direct result of his loyalty. He owned more than twenty-nine thousand mostly backcountry acres—he was quite the land speculator—and the value of his estate prior to his banishment, more than ten thousand pounds sterling, made him one of the colony's wealthiest men. William Bull and Charles Greville Montagu wrote letters on his behalf. These, combined with the letter Simpson had written to Germain in 1776 about the political and strategic situation in South Carolina, impressed Germain with the former attorney general's knowledge and mental acuity—all qualities his lordship decided to put to good use.[22]

In late 1778 the British launched a second expedition from New York for the reduction of Georgia and South Carolina, a revival of the southern strategy that had failed dismally in 1776. The reestablishment of civil government in Georgia was to be an important precedent to the opening of communications with South Carolina loyalists, and this was accomplished in part after Lt. Col. Archibald Campbell captured Savannah on December 29, 1778. The British subsequently failed to hold the Georgia backcountry but were still able to use Savannah to stage operations against Charleston.[23]

The recovery of South Carolina as an important second step in the restoration of royal government in the colonial south was a high priority for Germain. By sending civil officers such as Simpson, former clerk of circuit courts James Johnson, and former associate justice of South Carolina's supreme court Edward Savage, all of whom were well-known and had considerable influence among the backcountry inhabitants, Germain hoped to signal that he intended to restore civil government rather than governance by military law, even if the province was reduced by force.[24]

On January 19, 1779, Germain informed Simpson that the king's service required his presence in South Carolina and that he should immediately prepare to return to that province. A packet was making ready to sail from Falmouth to carry him to Georgia, which would be his base of operations. Germain had complete confidence in Simpson's ability to obtain information regarding the temperament and resolve of the inhabitants of the South Carolina backcountry. After putting in place a plan for loyalist cooperation when British troops returned to South Carolina, he was to proceed to New York and report to Lt. Gen. Sir Henry Clinton, who now commanded British forces in North America. He accepted the assignment without hesitation despite knowing that capture would likely subject him to imprisonment or even to a hangman's noose.[25]

After a series of delays, Simpson finally departed from London in April 1779 and arrived in Savannah fifty-one days later, the final leg of the journey aboard the fifty-gun *Experiment,* one of the men-of-war that had bombarded Moultrie's fort on Sullivan's Island three years earlier. In Savannah he found British troops commanded by Maj. Gen. Augustine Prevost returning to the city from an incursion into South Carolina. This foray had begun on April 29 and culminated in a brief and unsuccessful siege of Charleston that ended on May 13. The army's tactical retreat included a sharp rear-guard action at Stono Ferry on June 20 and occupied most of the rest of the month of June. On the way back to Savannah, Simpson later reported to Germain, the soldiers had plundered the countryside of foodstuffs, livestock and household furnishings and "carried away" a number of enslaved people. Not long after Simpson reached Savannah, messengers sent by the rebels arrived under flags of truce, requesting the return of property that belonged to widows, orphans, and others who had never participated in the rebellion.[26]

Despite Simpson's language that the slaves had been "carried away," most of them appear to have come voluntarily. These enslaved people brought to Savannah from the South Carolina countryside when the British army withdrew were certainly among those put to work on the fortifications surrounding Savannah and were possibly among those armed by Prevost to help resist the Franco-American siege of the town from September to October 1779.[27]

These inquiries and requests, Simpson told Germain, presented him with an unexpected and virtually effortless opportunity to gather intelligence: "As most of the persons who were sent were my former acquaintances, and desirous to see me on that account, as well as to inquire after Connections and Relations they had in Europe, my opportunities to gain the intelligence . . . were much better than I could have expected." There was more: "The most Violent of them without Scruple acknowledged their distress for want of both the conveniences & necesaries of life, and that their money was so much depreciated that it was almost of no value. Many of them exprest eager wishes for a Settlement and Peace, and mentioned with regret the remembrance of what they called the old times." He no doubt found highly satisfying these conversations that suggested discontent was likely festering in Charleston.[28]

But something else he learned disturbed him, namely that there were still many among his old acquaintances who were willing to use their influence to prevent the restoration of the "public tranquility" (his euphemism for the restoration of royal government). Simpson also surmised from reports gathered throughout the country that there was a general resentment against most of the current government officials and "those who have been active in enforcing their Tyrannical Edicts." These rebels were now apprehensive that the restoration of royal government would ruin them, and they were convinced that their own safety depended upon being able to retain the power of independence. This was the first time since Simpson had returned to the continent that he took specific notice of individuals actually in Charleston who were the driving force behind the rebellion. They were some of the same ones who were responsible for his own personal real estate forfeitures, financial losses, and removal from the province and the eventual expulsion of his family.[29]

About the same time that James Simpson was in transit between London and Savannah, his wife, Barbara, who had remained in Charleston at their fine home on Church Street, was informed that British prisoners of war being held in town were in distress. She privately went to their aid with a small monetary gift so that they could procure needed items. Her actions, when discovered, "were construed to be an offense of such enormity she was ordered immediately to quit the Province." She divested herself of the family's property and with her children—three daughters and two sons—sailed for New York, from where they planned to sail for England.[30]

The family's attempt to cross the Atlantic became an adventure fraught with hazard—Simpson wrote in his memorial that they were shipwrecked, then taken captive by a squadron of French men-of-war, and then carried to the island of Guadalupe in the Caribbean. From there the most expeditious route to England entailed a return to New York, which they apparently made. If a family reunion took place in New York, Simpson did not record it.[31]

Just how far and wide James Simpson was actually able to tour the backcountry to gather intelligence during the summer of 1779 is unknown, but he sailed for New York immediately after completing his assignment and arrived there on August 23, 1779. To Clinton he reported his interviews of several inhabitants from the South Carolina backcountry and a number of loyalist militia officers, all of whom consistently testified that since 1776 they had been the objects of unremitting persecution. Some backcountry loyalists had made peace with the rebels, some had fallen as martyrs, and others had simply fled. However, there were still great numbers of loyalists who had continued firm in their opposition to the rebellion and harbored enmity to their oppressors. It was these people the British would rely upon to rise up and join them when they attempted another invasion.[32]

The people with whom Simpson conversed repeatedly asked him about the likelihood of a fall campaign in South Carolina, and he gave them deliberately doubtful answers. By this they were very much affected, he said, "for they had been taught to believe that it would certainly take place, and were so confident of its success that it appeared to me their spirits rather required to be a little depressed than elevated." The most he would say was that measures were being considered, but that even if the king's troops were able to overrun the province and capture Charleston, unless royal government was firmly reestablished to render them secure without the protection of the army, any success would be incomplete. And if the army should be forced to withdraw, the loyalists' situation could become worse than before.[33]

Simpson told Clinton that he had been assured by the South Carolina loyalists that they were numerous enough to protect themselves, if only they were placed on equal footing with their opponents by being supplied with arms and ammunition. It was this lack of munitions they gave as being the sole cause of their present submission. They also said that "if they should afterwards suffer themselves to be overpowered they should think they were deserving everything they could suffer, and would never afterwards complain they were abandoned."[34]

In closing his report, Simpson stated that he was convinced that if the British moved into South Carolina early in the fall, the army could surely count on the assistance of considerable numbers of backcountry loyalists. This they could do, he thought, without risk of meaningful opposition, and by their success they would obtain "such a concurrence of many of the respectable Inhabitants in the lower Settlements . . . that a due submission to His Majesty's Government will be established throughout the country." Clinton, who was contemplating another Carolina campaign, was impressed with Simpson's findings and wrote to Germain of the "flattering hopes of assistance from the inhabitants held forth to us by Mr Simpson who ought to be acquainted with the temper of the people."[35]

Clinton did indeed launch a third campaign to capture Charleston in the spring of 1780. Savannah had been successfully defended against a combined Franco-American assault the previous October in one of the bloodiest battles of the Revolutionary War. The morale of the southern Continental Army was low, and its ranks had been depleted by battle loss and illness. Moreover a French fleet under Count D'Estaing that had been operating off the southern coast had recently departed. South Carolinians felt a growing sense of isolation, and political sentiment was increasingly divided.[36]

General Clinton was persuaded that conditions were right for an invasion, and accordingly he sailed from New York on December 26, 1779, bringing with him more than eighty-seven hundred British, provincial, and Hessian soldiers. The king's army made landfall some twenty miles southwest of Charleston on February 11, 1780, and advanced slowly inland. After crossing the Ashley River, the British broke ground on formal siege lines during the night of April 1. This campaign culminated in the Americans' most humiliating defeat of the war when Maj. Gen. Benjamin Lincoln surrendered to Clinton on May 12, 1780.

Simpson had accompanied Clinton to Charleston, and along the way a close bond developed between the two men—so close, in fact, that Clinton appointed Simpson to be his personal secretary. Clinton praised Simpson's assiduity and intelligence in a letter to Germain written soon after Charleston's surrender.[37]

Having thus returned to South Carolina in British triumph, Simpson again resumed gathering intelligence. Over time he was able to categorize the inhabitants of the province into four groups. First were "the people of the first fortunes in the province," who, lately convinced of their error "and feeling too late the miseries their fatal Politiks have produced," were favorably disposed toward the British. Next were some "who without reasoning upon the subject, or perhaps being incapable of it, but by being Tools to a faction, have been of great weight in keeping up the Flames of Rebellion." These were now ready to acknowledge that ruin was inevitable unless royal government was restored. The third group comprised those who still believed in their rebellious cause but realized that it could no longer be sustained.[38]

Finally came the recalcitrant rebels who held that their cause should never be relinquished. Simpson believed that the people of the first two groups greatly outnumbered the last two groups but that the peace of the province would be impossible to settle until "those People whose persecuting spirit hath caused such calamities to their fellow subjects shall receive the punishment their Iniquities deserve." He told Clinton that if the terror they excited was removed, perhaps meaning that if they themselves were removed, "a few months would restore this country to its former good Government."[39]

Simpson estimated that four-fifths of the people, particularly the inhabitants in the country, were ready to accept the king's rule. Then he got more specific, noting that in town "there are still some who associate in small parties and stimulate each other to continue in the rebellious principles which they have nurtured for some time past, and there is no doubt but that if they dared it would break out into practice." He advocated rigorous measures against these men "who are so infected with rebellious principles as to be ready on all occasions to give every disturbance to the King's government which is in their power." By mid-July he was devising a way to make an example of them.[40]

Clinton returned to New York in June 1780, leaving Lt. Gen. Charles, Earl Cornwallis to continue the subjugation of the southern colonies. Simpson remained in South Carolina at Clinton's behest, although the commanding general

The most Noble Marquis Cornwallis, K.G. Daniel Orme's 1794 engraving after the 1786 painting by John Smart. From the Anne S. K. Brown Military Collection, John Hay Library, Brown University, Providence, Rhode Island. Reproduced with permission.

came to miss his secretary and wanted him to come to New York as soon as possible. Simpson would be especially useful if a peace commission Clinton planned to establish gained traction. Cornwallis, however, had also become dependent on Simpson's services and would not consent to let him go until someone else surfaced who could take his place.[41]

Simpson filled other roles beyond intelligence gathering. When he inventoried the quantity of provisions remaining in the country beyond what was needed for local consumption, he found that there were considerable stores of rice, indigo, and tobacco that merchants badly wanted to export to Great Britain to cover their debts. As there were no export policies in place, Cornwallis delegated to him the responsibility for writing greatly detailed regulatory rules and regulations that would allow the reopening of trade between the province and England.[42]

Notwithstanding the occasional administrative duty delegated to him by Cornwallis, Simpson's primary function was to organize a civilian board of police. This was a difficult and arduous but necessary task, for which he told Germain he felt completely inadequate. The purpose of the board was to prevent anarchy and confusion, promote the good of the country, and demonstrate to

Charlestonians "that it is only by a restoration of the King's government that they can hope to regain the liberty and security which they before enjoyed under it." The board served as a civil court, mediated disputes between merchants and the British army, managed sequestered estates, enforced contracts, and regulated slavery.[43]

As the summer of 1780 wore on, ill health increasingly hampered Simpson's ability to conduct business. He grumbled to Clinton that he had time neither to eat nor to sleep and in exhausted terms complained to Germain that "the incessant fatigue which I have undergone since the reduction of Charleston in attending to the constant applications which have been made to me from all parts of the country, together with the extreme heat of the weather, hath so affected my health that I am very unfit."[44]

In August Simpson began to doubt his original assessment that tranquility would soon be restored and that the rebels would give up their cause. Instead he sensed a rise in the spirits of the rebellious faction, a change in their countenances. They were becoming increasingly optimistic that some upcoming great event would alter the status quo. Some of them were arrogant to the point of marking out those on the loyalists' side who would be the objects of their vengeance, and others had fixed the first day of September as the last day of British dominance in South Carolina. His doubt gradually gave way to certainty that some real plot was afoot. Perhaps it had to do with the arrival of Maj. Gen. Horatio Gates in North Carolina. Simpson's only recourse was to keep careful track of the ones he considered to be the most dangerous, hardened, and perverse rebels that he had ever come across.[45]

Simpson was soon convinced that it was indeed General Gates's approach that invigorated the Charleston patriots. Even without clear knowledge of the numerical strength and condition of Gates's force of Continental soldiers and patriot militiamen, or the tactical situations of the American and British armies, the rebels in town remained hopeful that Cornwallis would withdraw in the face of this oncoming threat. Following that, a general insurrection would liberate them all. It seemed to be a foregone conclusion. Gates, the "Hero of Saratoga," was believed to be unstoppable.[46]

Of course when the two armies met at Camden, the outcome was quite different. Both armies were making night marches on August 16, 1780, when they blundered into each other in the dark. In the confusion of the surprise, Gates wrongly deployed his most inexperienced militiamen to the left and center against Cornwallis's best regulars. The result was predictable—the American left collapsed in short order, while the Continentals on the right fought valiantly. Despite numerical superiority, the Americans suffered a humiliating rout, one of the worst defeats in American military history, rivaled perhaps only by Charleston's surrender three months earlier. Making matters worse, Gates's second-in-command, Maj. Gen. Baron Johann DeKalb, was mortally wounded, and Gates fled the scene on horseback.

Unbeknownst to Simpson, the battle's aftermath provided evidence that prisoners on parole in town were guilty of collusion, or at least that is what was alleged. According to Col. Charles Stedman, an officer who served on the staffs of Howe, Clinton, and Cornwallis, "by letters found upon some of the officers of general Gates's army, it was discovered that even persons of superior rank, prisoners upon parole in Charlestown, had held an improper correspondence with their friends in the country."[47]

Notorious British dragoon Lt. Col. Banastre Tarleton's recounting of the infractions is uniquely informative: "But accident now discovered how much the enemy's exceeded the King's friends in artifice. Perfidy and revolt had not been confined to the lower order of society. Some papers taken in the baggage of the American general officers, and other collateral intelligence, displayed the late opinions and conduct of many of the principal inhabitants of Charles town: Upwards of thirty of this description, since they had received pardon and protection from the British commanders, had held treacherous correspondence with the armed enemies of England, or had been indefatigably engaged in secretly advancing the interest of Congress throughout South Carolina."[48]

There was no question in Simpson's mind that something must be done with the perpetrators and that "their removal to a place where it will be out of their power to continue their mischievous and treasonable practices" was absolutely necessary. As long as they remained in the province, peace would be impossible to establish. Banishment, in short, was the only solution for those who "from the first moment of the surrender of the town [had] declared their fixed determination to adhere to the rebel cause as long as it had existence, and imputing the lenity with which they were treated to timidity [had] not only openly persuaded and exhorted but threatened and terrified others from submitting to the British government." Simpson did not have the authority to accomplish this himself. He would need the assistance of Charleston's military commandant, Lt. Col. Nisbet Balfour.[49]

Chapter 2

A Rude Awakening

The surrender of Charleston on May 12, 1780, ushered in a new era for the town's civilian population. The loyalist inhabitants were liberated, and the patriot residents faced an ironic role reversal: they were now subjected to some of the same oppressive measures that they had earlier inflicted on their loyalist neighbors. Under the ninth article of the articles of capitulation, civil officers and citizens who had borne arms against the British during the siege were considered to be prisoners on parole. Their property within the town's limits was at least theoretically secure so long as they abided by the terms of their parole.[1]

The term *parole* had a connotation quite different from its usage in modern criminal justice systems and described, in principle, an arrangement going back as far back as the Punic Wars during the third century B.C. As in other wars, during the Revolutionary War the victors in battle were usually left with far more prisoners of war than they were able to cope with in terms of confinement, housing, and subsistence. Such "prisoners" could theoretically be exchanged, but British and American negotiators would not agree upon an exchange cartel for the Southern Department until 1781. Thus the military officers and civilians captured at Charleston were officially still prisoners of war but, in fact, enjoyed a relatively liberal parole—at least at first.

Their "word" was indeed involved, as the patriot prisoners formally agreed, on their honor, to live peaceably at home until properly exchanged, to commit no actions detrimental to the success of the British army, and to refrain from communicating with His Majesty's enemies. Brig. Gen. William Moultrie believed that "[a] parole is a sacred act between parties which, if violated on either side, is void in itself." So even the staunchly patriotic South Carolinians remained at liberty to continue their lives and trades and to go anywhere about the town, even to the defensive lines and somewhat beyond if their business called for it, having given their word not to fight the occupation or insult the king.[2]

Ostensibly intending to facilitate the restoration of royal government in South Carolina, Clinton issued a series of proclamations before departing for

New York and leaving Cornwallis in command. The last of these edicts, dated June 3, 1780, unilaterally rescinded most paroles and stipulated that those now released from their paroles must choose between a full return to British allegiance with all the rights and duties of loyal subjects or be considered rebels and treated accordingly.[3]

Clinton's proclamations persuaded quite a few South Carolinians to join with the liberated loyalists by exchanging their paroles. It was complicated; a number of Charleston's inhabitants accepted Clinton's offer out of political and cultural loyalty (it had been comfortable to study in England, and many were still in correspondence with British cousins). Still others did so to ensure their ability to carry on trade and maintain financial security. And there were those who were intimidated, fearful that if they did not take British protection they would be informed against. But some inhabitants of Charleston remained resolute patriots, many more so than the British first anticipated, and they considered themselves among those who were exempted from the cancellation of their paroles by Clinton's proclamation.[4]

The occupiers felt that they had liberated the town and that inhabitants should naturally be glad to have normality restored. Such was not the case. Loyalists and collaborators in town thought the rebels were being treated too leniently. The loyalists certainly had not enjoyed similarly generous treatment under the few years of revolutionary patriot rule, and after the town's surrender to the British, they began clamoring for retributive justice. Circumstances would soon evolve to their better liking.

In order to encourage further loyalist allegiance to the king, the royal authorities gradually abridged the rights of the parolees through a series of additional measures. The rebels, considered captives, were denied the benefits of the courts—they could not sue, but they could be sued. They were greatly limited in their movement on land and water, being generally confined to town and required to have special permission to travel elsewhere, which was regularly and summarily refused. Merchants were constrained in the conduct of business, and mechanics and other artisans (acknowledged subsets of society) were eventually prohibited from plying their trades. One clause in the parole document, depending on interpretation, gave British authorities a right to require any recalcitrant patriot to move to another address. It was yet to be seen how far that authority would be applied as the situation in Charleston evolved.[5]

Meanwhile there was overt harassment as well. For example, militia captains George Abbott Hall and Thomas Heyward Jr. were assailed by a party of British officers while strolling one day on a public street. The bullies tore the cockades from the two men's hats and indignantly trampled them underfoot. It is not known whether or not the tormentors realized that Heyward was a signer of the Declaration of Independence who had been wounded in the arm while leading a detachment of the Charleston Artillery in the American victory at Port Royal Island on February 3, 1779.[6]

These constant irritations induced quite a number of citizens, by necessity, to submit and exchange their paroles for British protection. True loyalists reveled in the overthrow of the dejected and discouraged revolutionary party, many of whom were concerned that the Continental Congress might actually be planning to abandon South Carolina to the British. The British fostered this discouragement by concealing news of a June 25, 1780, congressional resolution specifically disavowing the rumor of abandonment. Yet in spite of the occupiers' efforts at restoring normality, there remained a core of influential revolutionaries, former leaders that were still considered prisoners on parole, who subtly and discreetly but nonetheless steadily continued to fan the glowing embers of liberty. Dr. David Ramsay, one of these influential revolutionaries, later recorded that "the silent example of men who were revered by their fellow-citizens, had a powerful influence in restraining many from exchanging their paroles as prisoners, for the protection and privileges of British subjects."[7]

Rebellious attitudes toward the British occasionally accounted for less serious but potentially awkward moments. Shortly after the capitulation of Charleston, one Sunday the Reverend Edward Ellington, rector of the parish of St. James, Goose Creek, read in the litany, "That it may please thee to bless and preserve his most gracious Majesty, our Sovereign Lord, King George." Dead silence ensued. Then, instead of the response from the congregation normally expected at that point—"We beseech thee to hear us, good Lord"—a muffled voice distinctly repeated the response from the previous section: "Good Lord deliver us."[8]

The sensitive British could view such a modest example of daring as an active encouragement of the spirit of resistance. General Cornwallis certainly was aware of James Simpson's opinion of the perpetrators and referred to them as "that set of villains who would never have allowed us to retain the peaceable possession of this province." Cornwallis apprised Clinton that the resistance was indeed significant and that, ever since the reduction of Charleston, "a number of the principal and most violent inhabitants have held constant meetings in town [in undercover places such as McCrady's still-thriving tavern] and carried on correspondence with the country to keep up the flame of rebellion and impose on the ignorant by spreading false reports throughout the whole province to encourage the disaffected and intimidate the others." They distinctly angered Charleston's new military commandant, Lt. Col. Nisbet Balfour, who proclaimed them ringleaders and abettors.[9]

Thirty-seven-year-old Balfour from Scotland was a battle-hardened veteran. He had been wounded at Bunker Hill in 1775 and had fought at Long Island, Elizabethtown, Brandywine, and Germantown. Earlier in the war he served as aide-de-camp on the staff of Lt. Gen. William Howe when Howe commanded all British forces in North America. He then was given charge of the Twenty-Third Regiment of Foot, the Royal Welch Fusiliers, and led his men into battle at Monmouth Courthouse in 1778.[10]

The Fusiliers came south during the Charleston siege, and after the capitulation Clinton dispatched Balfour to Ninety Six to help subdue the backcountry. When Clinton sailed north for New York in June and left Cornwallis in command, he also left behind Brig. Gen. James Paterson as military commandant of Charleston. Paterson, it seems, was overwhelmed by the complexity and oftentimes civil nature of the job and was on July 18 shipped to New York on account of illness. Cornwallis decided that Balfour, now one of his most trusted subordinates, would be of better use in town. Balfour thus returned to Charleston on August 6, 1780, and became the town's commandant. He was disappointed by Cornwallis's order and would have much preferred to have remained in the field at the head of his men, but Cornwallis, who was about to take the field himself, insisted on the change.[11]

Balfour was an excellent officer and well regarded by his peers, but he loathed the rebellious Americans and would provide them with ample reasons to hate him in return. Brig. Gen. William Moultrie, who was in charge of Charleston's Continental army prisoners and who had enjoyed an amicable working relationship with Paterson, described Balfour as a "proud and haughty Scot, [who] carried his authority with a very high hand; [with] his tyrannical disposition, [he] treated the people as the most abject slaves."[12]

Balfour had broad civil powers and absolute authority over virtually everything in Charleston, even the power to arrest and confine civilians without justifiable cause. To the patriots, he was a tyrant. His violent and arbitrary administration nourished an increasing desire among the populace for an American force to liberate them from ill treatment and oppression. It was in Balfour that James Simpson found a willing accomplice to join him in ridding Charleston of rebel agitators.[13]

To ensure that he was not perceived to be acting out of fear, Cornwallis had been waiting to take action until something decisive happened between the British and Continental armies. There was no better opportunity provided than his crushing defeat of General Gates at Camden on August 16, 1780. In short order he directed Balfour to apprehend those among the Charleston rebels who Simpson thought were the most dangerous.[14]

A particular term of the parole clause, "surrender myself to him at such time and place, as I shall hereafter be required," Cornwallis was pleased to interpret as giving him general authority to move parolees around. He explained to Clinton that "Simpson is clearly of opinion that the changing their place of residence on parole from Charlestown to St Augustine is no breach of the capitulation," and therefore he would be on solid legal footing. "I have intelligence of their corresponding with the enemy, of their propagating false reports, and receiving General Gates's proclamation [offering military assistance and amnesty to those who had taken British protection]," Cornwallis offered, adding that in his opinion there could be no doubt that the measure would appear as just as it was expedient. What Cornwallis meant by "intelligence," whether unsubstantiated rumor or hard evidence, is unknown.[15]

Simpson's success in surreptitiously identifying patriots for deportation to St. Augustine, and their total ignorance of his having drawn up such a list, is aptly illustrated in the postwar writing of Maj. Alexander Garden, a Continental officer and son of the prominent loyalist Dr. Alexander Garden. If Garden's text is completely sincere (and there is nothing to suggest he intended any sarcasm or irony), then his words reveal the extent to which the patriot elites were blinded to the threat posed by Simpson's secret sleuthing: "It should forever redound to the honour of Mr. Simpson . . . that the only use which he ever made of his power and influence, was to mitigate the sufferings of the unfortunate, and by generous attention, to free them from every taint of political animosity, and to reconcile them to a government which they appeared unable to resist. . . . He constantly opposed every arbitrary decree that issued from the higher authorities, and warned them of the inevitable results that would follow the tyrannical measures pursued."[16]

Perhaps Simpson did generally comport himself as Garden said, but it was definitely Simpson who made the list of violators who would be banished. It appears that they never realized that a man with whom they had been acquainted for decades and held in high regard was responsible for separating them from their homes and families. But alas, they had earlier done the same to him.[17]

Acting on Cornwallis's orders, in the predawn hours of August 27, 1780, Balfour sent armed redcoats under the direction of Maj. George Benson and Capt. John McMahon to the homes of twenty-nine civilian patriot prisoners on parole. Concerning Major Benson, there is little on record other than that he was commissioned an ensign in the Ninth Regiment of Foot in 1770, made lieutenant of the Forty-Fourth Regiment in 1771, attained the rank of captain in 1776, and served as brigade major and Balfour's assistant adjutant general in Charleston. He was highly esteemed by Balfour, who entrusted him with the most confidential matters.[18]

A single surviving anecdote given from a patriot perspective (which must be received accordingly) was meant to portray Benson's unsavory character. Alexander Garden related an episode during the occupation in which Benson is alleged to have placed a stick into the hands of an enslaved man and ordered him to chastise an elderly planter, because the latter had advised the slave's return to the service of his owner. It is a tale without beginning or end and conveys the swirling confusions of emotions and duties under Charleston's occupation. But more than that, it illustrates the shift in power dynamics by which the once power-ful had become impotent. The idea of being rendered powerless by an external authority, exercising power through the hand of an enslaved man, was truly a terrifying prospect to a slave owner. It made the war's consequences all the more dramatic and immediate.[19]

On the other hand, Capt. John McMahon (born ca. 1754) was a man whose ultimate reputation would make fascinating any account of his life. On the other side of the Atlantic, he was the natural son of an Irish butler and a chambermaid in a noble family. He escaped that identity by acquiring a number of various petty government jobs, the last being a treasury clerk employment, from which he was dismissed in disgrace after two years. He subsequently joined a company of strolling players before entering the service of a "gentleman" under whom he developed his genius for intrigue. He became so involved in the designs of his master on the wives and daughters of their neighbors that he was again dismissed. It was then that he volunteered for military service and was sent to America as a member of a company of the Sixty-Third Regiment commanded by Capt. Fran-cis, Lord Rawdon.[20]

Recognizing McMahon's gift for intrigue, Rawdon helped McMahon obtain an ensigncy in the Forty-Fourth Regiment, where he likely became acquainted with Benson. From that position he advanced to being a deputy commissary, a job in which he could and did pocket enough money eventually to be able to afford purchasing a lieutenancy and later a captain's commission. Such was his status when he appeared on the Charleston scene, given the job of barracks mas-ter by Balfour.[21]

It was later and back in England that McMahon's career became really no-torious, when an introduction to the Prince of Wales (later to be crowned King George IV) positioned him to operate as the chief pander and pimp of His Royal Highness—a function he fulfilled so well that he blossomed into new dignity as keeper of the privy purse, companion, and confidant of the heir to the throne. Such was the man who, under instructions from Balfour, set out with Benson on the morning of August 27 to round up the Charleston patriots—a former kitchen boy.[22]

Rousted out of bed, disoriented, and given only minutes to dress, the startled patriots were hustled down the streets of Charleston while their wives and chil-dren stood by helpless and frightened out of their wits. The soldiers escorted them to the upper floor of the Royal Exchange and Customs House, where they were held under guard in a reasonably spacious upper room until about ten o'clock. One of the prisoners, Josiah Smith Jr., remarked that they were treated like convicted felons. Back home their private papers were rifled, and guards were posted at their houses. Reports were circulated around town to give every impres-sion that they had been apprehended for violating their paroles, even suggesting

The Royal Exchange and Customs House where the exiles were first taken after their arrest. Photograph by Rick Rhodes, Charleston, S.C. Reproduced with permission.

that they had been concocting a scheme to burn the town and massacre loyal subjects. Of all of the gentlemen thus taken, it was Lt. Gov. Christopher Gadsden who probably received the roughest handling. He had always been a radical patriot, and at the time of the capitulation, he was the ranking civil official in town.[23]

Charleston's early risers observed the spectacle, some filled with dread and horror, others brimming with smug and hardly concealed self-satisfaction as the British went about their appointed rounds. A few sympathetic ladies gathered on the balcony of the home of Mrs. Ellis, who lived next door to physician-patriot David Ramsay. When Ramsay was brought out with a small bundle of clothing under his arm and surrounded by twelve armed soldiers, one of the ladies cried out, "Only look at that! Twelve armed British soldiers to carry one poor rebel across the street! You dastardly cowards!" The soldiers reportedly looked up at the balcony and cursed her.[24]

The arrested men in the Exchange knew each other well and could readily see that the British had made a thoroughly informed selection of the most influential patriots. Of the twenty-nine, nineteen were either members of the revolutionary government (the lieutenant governor of the state and his Privy Counsellors, members of the House of Representatives, the judge of the admiralty court, the attorney general, etc.) or officers in the revolutionary militia. Two were signers of the Declaration of Independence (Edward Rutledge and Thomas Heyward Jr.). In addition there were three physicians. (More demographic details can be found in the introduction to appendix A.)[25]

The remainder consisted of six ordinary citizens whose underground connections and activities most insidiously threatened the occupying authorities. Three years of building and running a tavern that was a hotbed of revolutionary sentiment and subversive grumbling, propaganda, and recruiting constituted a sufficiently qualifying crime for Edward McCrady. His great-grandson later commented that McCrady was one of the few who occupied no official civic or military position, "a fact which indicates that it was his personal character and influence which rendered him obnoxious to the British rule."[26]

No doubt as they congregated at the Exchange, the prisoners looked around, nodded to each other in recognition, spoke soft words of question or encouragement, and wondered exactly what had precipitated this violation of the articles of capitulation. So far they had been provided no explanation for their treatment and likely pondered whether or not their arrest was just another mean and capricious act of Balfour. The extent to which they openly protested is not reported—the guards may have enforced silence.

These men were all familiar with the Royal Exchange building. Many of them had transacted business there. The massive but elegant masonry edifice on the waterfront of the Cooper River where Broad Street meets East Bay had served as the center of Charleston's import-export trade. Completed only a decade earlier, the building already had a colorful history. Early revolutionary meetings had been conducted there, and the colony's delegates to the First Continental Congress had been elected in the Great Hall upstairs. Confiscated British tea had been stored in the cellar, and the Continental Army had hidden gunpowder within the cellar's walls during the siege (the British never discovered it). Since Charleston's capture, the occupiers had been using the Exchange as a barracks with the cellar serving as a jail (or "provost" as it was called).[27]

At the time of the arrests, the British separately collected the wives of the offending patriots and assembled them in the old market to consider how they were to be treated. Perhaps among them was Mary Stevens Smith, wife of Josiah Smith Jr., for whom the unexpected arrests was certainly an ordeal. The recent loss of her second son, a promising boy of thirteen who succumbed to smallpox, already burdened her spirit. And now she was also within weeks of the end of her twelfth pregnancy. Whether or not the British were so heartless as to compel her attendance is unknown, but being left at home without her husband was hardly better.[28]

Some cases of life under submission were less pitiful and more a question of outraged dignity. The officer assigned to 153 East Bay Street met with brief but haughty resistance from Eliza McCrady, wife of the aforementioned tavern keeper, who was nonetheless whisked to the marketplace assembly. The summary outing was so swift and unanticipated that her only recorded indignation was the humiliation of being forced to appear in public without a hat. British officers assigned to the marketplace questioned the arrested wives, in search of treacherous connections. A conversational exchange between Mrs. McCrady and one of the interrogators, no doubt each appreciating the other's accent, established that they were both Campbells and cousins in the old country. He thereupon "ordered her to be released and himself took up his quarters in her house to see that she was protected." Consequently Eliza seems to have received a degree of respect or at least was allowed a measure of independence throughout the British occupation.[29]

The captives were not moved to the dreaded Exchange cellar as expected. Instead at ten o'clock they were escorted from the rear of the building to small boats waiting at the dock on the Cooper River, and from there they were unceremoniously rowed to the armed ship *Lord Sandwich,* anchored in the harbor off the ruins of Fort Johnson on James Island. The pealing bells of Charleston churches going about their regular Sunday schedules became increasingly softer as the oarsmen drew the arrested patriots farther and farther away from the peninsula on a rather long but probably not unpleasant trip, rowing across the slightly choppy waves of the huge harbor to the waters near the abandoned fort.[30]

The captain of the *Sandwich,* William M. Bett, was completely surprised by his unexpected passengers, who arrived aboard with only half an hour's warning from town. Bett solicitously apologized to them for his unpreparedness and provided their dinner as best he could on the spur of the moment. Charlestonians, it will be remembered, were accustomed to having their principal meal (their "dinner") in the afternoon, and these particular sufferers had not even had breakfast.[31]

When Bett realized that the arrestees had not been furnished with bedding, he personally went ashore in mid-afternoon to call upon the commandant, from whom he obtained permission for friends of his passengers to visit and bring bedding from home and other items necessary for comfort. Bett's quest met with quick success. By evening all twenty-nine troublemakers had been furnished with bedding and supplies, and most had received visits from relatives or friends in town. The officers and men on the ship proved to be as civil as their captain, and the ruffled patriots could at least conclude that they were being acknowledged and treated more or less as gentlemen.[32]

Once they had recovered their dignity, after the rough manner in which they were taken into custody and the humiliating way they were conveyed from their homes, the prisoners gathered their collective faculties and prepared to articulate their objections. This they discussed with characteristic eighteenth-century prudence; they slept on it, and the next morning produced an elegant memorial to Lieutenant Colonel Balfour declaring emphatically that they were not conscious of having willfully broken their paroles. They were more than a little anxious to learn what they had done to merit such extraordinarily severe and scandalous treatment, especially as they began to suspect that they might be marked for quarters in the infamous prison ships or else possible transportation elsewhere.[33]

The memorial, signed by them all, requested a full and speedy inquiry so that they might know the exact nature of their supposed offenses and the names of their accusers. A cooperative Captain Bett took the signed document, set out for town, and delivered it in person to the commandant at noon on August 28. Balfour, who was not interested in due process, never directly replied to the captives' memorial.[34]

While inbound to town, Captain Bett likely passed in the harbor a boat that was simultaneously bringing out Major Benson. The latter was on his way to the *Sandwich* bearing an unsigned and undated notice, presumably dictated by Balfour, indicating that a summary judgment had already been rendered. General Cornwallis was "highly incensed at the late perfidious Revolt of many of the Inhabitants of this province." Papers that had fallen into his hands since the defeat of Gates at Camden had convinced him, he claimed, of the means by which "several persons" on parole in Charleston were fomenting a spirit of rebellion. He had therefore decided to change their place of residence from Charleston to St. Augustine, East Florida, "in order to secure the quiet of the province."[35]

One wonders what memories of personal shenanigans flashed through the feignedly innocent minds of McCrady and friends upon hearing that Cornwallis was well informed and reportedly in possession of actual papers that had fallen into his hands. And other questions were no doubt mulled: Just who were the "several persons" who were to be ordered to change their place of residence? Could it be all twenty-nine of the offended parties? They had yet to hear a direct reply to their morning's inquiry, but at last they had a clearer idea of what might lie ahead if their objections went unheard. While waiting, they instinctively held to and polished their posture of righteous indignation with protestations of innocence and allegations of injustice in the British betrayal of their oaths of parole.[36]

That evening Captain McMahon came out to the ship and delivered another message, this one verbal. McMahon said that Cornwallis acknowledged them to be Charleston prisoners on parole, but that for "reasons of policy" it was necessary to change their residence. In fact he was changing it from Charleston to St. Augustine, some two hundred miles to the south. Any of them who considered this to be an infringement of their rights under the articles of capitulation would be treated as close prisoners while onboard the ship and after their delivery to St. Augustine. Dissenters were requested to sign their names. The gentlemen on board were too perplexed to give McMahon a coherent answer, so he reboarded the small boat that carried him through the harbor and returned him to Charleston.[37]

If Cornwallis was incensed, then William Moultrie was astonished. General Moultrie, native of Charleston, former member of the colonial and provincial legislatures, and iconic defender of the fort on Sullivan's Island on June 28, 1776, had been General Lincoln's second-in-command during the siege of Charleston. In June, Lincoln had been allowed to travel to Philadelphia under the terms of his parole, making Moultrie the de facto commanding officer of the captive Continental Army in Charleston. He and Col. Charles Cotesworth Pinckney had established residence at Snee Farm, Pinckney's uncle's plantation five miles away in Christ Church Parish. They regularly received copies of the gazette published under royal authority, so it had taken the news a few days to find him.[38]

When Moultrie perused the pages of the August 29 issue of the *Royal South-Carolina Gazette,* he was shocked to find a paragraph listing the names of prisoners sent aboard the *Lord Sandwich.* He immediately wrote to Balfour, denying that these "most respectable gentlemen" with whom he was so well acquainted could have been guilty of a breach of their paroles or any article of capitulation or done anything to justify such harsh treatment. As the senior continental officer prisoner under the articles of capitulation, Moultrie perceived it his duty to call for the release of the unjustly arrested gentlemen.[39]

Many of these gentlemen were General Moultrie's close friends, and his half-brother Alexander Moultrie was among them. The general insisted that they be returned to their parole status forthwith and argued that their being aboard a prison ship violated the ninth article of the articles of capitulation, that civil officers and citizens who had borne arms during the siege as militia were prisoners on parole. He warned Balfour that failure to comply with his demands would result in a full report to Congress in Philadelphia, and that Congress would surely somehow intervene.[40]

After a few days of silence, the often dismissive and always caustic Balfour replied to Moultrie through an intermediary that he would not answer a letter written "in such exceptionable and unwarrantable terms as that to him from Gen. Moultrie . . . nor will he receive any further application from him upon the subject of it." Actually, when he read Moultrie's letter, Balfour knew something that Moultrie did not—that he had already arrested eleven more civilians and sent them under escort to the armed transport *Fidelity,* captained by William Pilmore and similarly moored in the harbor.[41]

The account of the apprehension of William Johnson, a gentleman-entrepreneur who was one of this second group of arrested patriots, provides insight into just how unsettling the experience was. On August 30, seventy-two hours after the first round of arrests, Johnson was removed from his house at 140 East Bay.

The accusations against him were not specified, and like the others he pled in vain that he was being unjustly taken away. He and the ten other newly arrested patriots were likewise escorted to the Exchange and from there marched to a little boat that would take them not to join the original group on the *Lord Sandwich* but to be placed separately on board the *Fidelity*.[42]

There were enough Tories in Charleston that an unsympathetic crowd gathered this time to mock the little boat-ward parade. As the prisoners, guarded by a file of soldiers, passed these ill-wishers, Johnson politely bowed to one he recognized, smiling at him in acknowledgement. Another of the onlookers called out to him, "You will soon laugh on the other side of your mouth!"—a sarcastic goading that Johnson was to recall with pleasure in postwar years when the foundry he owned was once again prosperous. The official publicity, like the ill-wishers, was not kind. The royal gazettes in all parts of the British dominions scorned the arrestees and "represented them as criminals, apprehended for being concerned in the most dishonourable and mischievous practices."[43]

But not all of the royal supporters were so rude. Manners, education, and social affinity resulted in many instances of friendship and harmony between British loyalists and American rebels, their social interests rising above their political differences. One young member of the occupying forces, Thomas R. Charlton, who later became a lieutenant colonel in the Royal Artillery, made a point of visiting William Johnson on the *Fidelity*, to see him and inquire what he could do to assist. Johnson gratefully asked him to maintain the blacksmith shop and workmen for the support of his family, a task that Charlton faithfully performed.[44]

It gradually became evident that a trip to St. Augustine could not be avoided. Another loyalist, Capt. Thomas Buckel, was very generous to Johnson and Edward McCrady. This dependable friend of Johnson's came out to the *Fidelity* bearing a letter of credit on a St. Augustine merchant good for two hundred pounds sterling. The gentlemen were embarrassed to accept charity when theoretically they were perfectly well-off, but they wisely decided to do so because managing family finances was going to be difficult without the cooperation of the British. There would be financial hardship enough to go around. Mary Cochran, wife of Capt. Robert Cochran, who was part of the second round-up, worried how she was to support her son Charles at his school abroad. She would no longer be able to send funds for his expenses in France, nor could she arrange payment for bringing him home.[45]

Whether the rebels were guilty of breaking their paroles depends on which side of the argument one believes. The soon-to-be exiles asserted emphatically that they were not conscious of having broken their paroles, and Moultrie fully agreed with them. But two centuries and more have preserved nothing in their defense other than their word and their indignation. Contemporaneous correspondence between Simpson, Cornwallis, Balfour, and Germain indicates that the rebels did violate the terms of their paroles, and, writing later as historians, Henry Clinton, Banastre Tarleton, and Charles Stedman furthered the claim. Yet none of the incriminating correspondence supposedly discovered by capture at Camden or elsewhere has been found, which is quite remarkable considering the number of alleged correspondents.[46]

The revolutionaries have two exculpatory arguments in their favor. First is the fact that Cornwallis had already demonstrated in the field that he was willing to punish unto death any inhabitants of the province who had taken protection and later participated in the revolt. A number of men were hanged at Camden and elsewhere. An exile's great-grandson, the historian Edward McCrady Jr. (1833–1903), argued that Cornwallis would not have hesitated to hang the Charleston exiles if he had possessed tangible proof that they were guilty.[47]

Second is the verbal message delivered aboard the *Sandwich* by Captain McMahon stating that Cornwallis considered the gentlemen on board to be prisoners on parole and that the change in the place of their residence from Charleston to St. Augustine was merely a policy decision made in accordance with the paroles they had given, which stated "that upon a summons from his Excellency, or other person having authority thereto, that I will surrender myself to him or them at such time and *place* [emphasis added], as I shall hereafter be required." In sum they were not being punished. Just moved. And such was the end of any semblance of negotiations, accusations, or explanations. The affected citizens, for the rest of their lives, would righteously consider the whole affair an affront to their honor and a violation of the articles of capitulation.[48]

Eventually two of the detained patriots were permitted to return to town. One was Dr. Peter Fayssoux (born 1745), an esteemed Edinburgh-trained Charleston physician of Huguenot extraction who was still serving the Continental Army as surgeon general of the Southern Department. Fayssoux had been behind the palmetto logs with Moultrie on June 28, 1776, and during the war had played an important role in caring for wounded and sick soldiers from both sides.[49]

At the time of his arrest, Fayssoux was in charge of the Continental hospital in Charleston, and if his transport to the *Lord Sandwich* was in error, it would not be surprising to learn that Lieutenant Colonel Balfour came to consider Fayssoux's return to Charleston an even greater mistake. Fayssoux became a thorn in the side as a loud and sharp critic of Balfour and the British treatment of American prisoners of war after the Battle of Camden, particularly their confinement aboard prison ships in the harbor, where they suffered extreme overcrowding, disease and pestilence, and debilitation, if not death.[50]

The other gentleman sent home to Charleston was Thomas Savage (born 1738), whose health was so precarious that he was deemed unable to withstand even a short ocean voyage. He had served in the Provincial Congress, and in 1776

Hon. Alexander Moultrie, from James Moultrie, "The Moultries, Part II: The Moultries of South Carolina," *South Carolina Historical and Genealogical Magazine* 5, no. 4 (1904): facing page 60.

the House members selected him to be one of several commissioners to superintend and direct the naval affairs of South Carolina. Family tradition long held that to demonstrate the ardor of his patriotism he once thrust a knife through the portrait of King George III hanging in his dining room. Despite his indisposition in August 1780, the British did not forget Savage. His health sufficiently recovered for him to make the voyage to St. Augustine a few months later.[51]

Alexander Moultrie (born ca. 1750) was the lone exception to those who were transported to St. Augustine on the *Fidelity.* A few days prior to departure, he, his wife, Katy (née Catharine Judith Lennox), and seven-year-old-daughter, Catharine, boarded Capt. John Clarke's schooner that would accompany the *Fidelity* southward to East Florida. Alexander, or "Sandy," as he was known, had been admitted to the Middle Temple in London to study law in 1768, had served his province and state in its legislatures, was the state's first attorney general, and had held the rank of captain in the Charleston militia.[52]

If he was afforded special treatment, it was not because one of his older half-brothers was Brig. Gen. William Moultrie, but because his other, oldest half-brother was Dr. John Moultrie Jr., the lieutenant governor of East Florida. Alexander and John had maintained cordial relations despite their political differences. After Charleston's surrender the loyalist was able to reopen correspondence with his rebellious brother, writing: "How unhappy & sad must that man be who dares not ask a blessing on the most public & interesting endeavors of his brothers, but on the contrary with deep sorrow & concern pray[s] to the Almighty to confound all their devices."[53]

Over the next few days, the two ships, *Lord Sandwich* and *Fidelity*, were provisioned, and during this time friends and family from town were granted permission to come aboard to bid the prisoners farewell. Josiah Smith summed up the mood of the ships: "A grievous sight it was indeed to see Husbands parting with their distressed Wives, Fathers bidding Farewell to their beloved Children, and Friends separating from Friend, perhaps many, never to meet together again." On September 3 the remaining twenty-six were transferred with their personal belongings and twenty-six slaves from the spacious (though "loathsome") atmosphere of the *Lord Sandwich* to the considerably smaller *Fidelity*.[54]

The number of exiles (now totaling 37), enslaved servants, the crew of the *Fidelity*, 15 British invalid soldiers, and additional seamen put on board to help defend the ship should it be attacked en route to St. Augustine in all totaled 106 souls. Adding to the calamity of separation and forced abandonment of their homes was the terrible overcrowding of the quarters belowdecks that could not be alleviated topside, where conditions were also exceedingly disagreeable on account of the sheep, hogs, and poultry that were put aboard to provision the passengers at their destination.[55]

On the morning of September 4, Capt. Thomas Henry Abbott and another officer, a Lieutenant Smith, came aboard the *Fidelity* at the behest of Balfour and called the prisoners together. He then presented them with a parole document to sign in affirmation that while aboard and while in St. Augustine they would not do anything prejudicial to His Majesty's service. If they should happen to be retaken by their countrymen, they would not return to a part of America under British control but would still consider themselves bound by their parole. The gentlemen all agreed to the terms of the new parole except for Mr Gadsden, the ever-recalcitrant lieutenant governor.[56]

Abbott and the prisoners then moved on to a more interesting review of the decreed rules and privileges. The exiles were assured of three weeks' provisions, to be followed by some sort of regular delivery service between Charleston and St. Augustine by which they could order from their families and legal representatives anything they desired (at their own expense), including the transfer of bondservants and family members, with transportation to be provided at British expense. James Fisher and John Blake had agreed to be financial agents in Charleston through whom expenses could be charged to family accounts.[57]

Balfour expected the "St. Augustine gentry" (as he called them) to sail on the night of September 4. They did not travel very far that day. After the decks were cleared, the *Fidelity* dropped down close to Sullivan's Island to await the next morning's fair winds and rising tide. The favorable wind and tide would enable a crossing of the Charleston Bar, a submerged obstruction of marine sand that ran from north to south just outside the harbor between Sullivan's Island and Morris Island. Prior to departure a passenger managed to send a last message home to his wife, saying, "I am quite easy, and doubt not but that God, in whom I trust, will still continue his care, and be my guide even unto death. God bless you and all the children, and cease not to pray for [me]."[58]

About seven o'clock on the morning of September 5, the seamen weighed anchor and set the sails, and by ten o'clock the *Fidelity* and the separate schooner carrying the Moultrie family were across the bar. Favorable winds and a passage of seventy-two hours brought the exiles to their Florida destination early on the morning of September 8.[59]

Chapter 3

The Reception at St. Augustine

St. Augustine was the southernmost British base of military operations against the southern colonies. Though it was oldest European settlement on the North America mainland north of Mexico, by 1780 the town had been in the hands of the British for only seventeen years. During the Seven Years' War (French and Indian War), the British captured the Spanish colony of Havana, Cuba, and a number of French islands in the West Indies. Under the terms of the Treaty of Paris signed in 1763, Great Britain returned Havana to Spain in exchange for all of Spanish Florida, which extended from the Atlantic Ocean to the Mississippi River.[1]

The British subsequently divided Spanish Florida into East Florida and West Florida. East Florida contained most of the Florida peninsula and a bit of the panhandle extending west to the Apalachicola River. Its capital was its only town—the garrison city of St. Augustine. West Florida's borders ran from the Apalachicola River west to the Mississippi River and had Pensacola as its capital. Spain's cession of Florida gave Great Britain control of Caribbean shipping lanes from Havana to New Orleans.[2]

East Florida had remained loyal to King George III. By the time of the Revolutionary War, the total population of the province, excluding the British garrison at St. Augustine, was only about three thousand inhabitants. About two-thirds of East Florida's citizens resided in and around the capital. In comparison to the capitals of the "thirteen colonies," St. Augustine was considerably smaller and far more primitive—by one estimation the town consisted of about three hundred houses sited in an area that measured only three quarters of a mile long and a quarter mile wide. The populace enjoyed few of the advantages enjoyed by their more northern counterparts; nonetheless the Church of England and most of the normal institutions of British government, excluding a legislature, were maintained, albeit on a smaller scale. No newspaper was printed in St. Augustine until 1783, and so most news came to town via the gazettes published in Savannah and Charleston.[3]

The ocean could not be viewed from the town, nor the town seen from the sea. The little fortified settlement sat on the western shore of a long north-south body of water (now incorporated into the Intracoastal Waterway) more or less parallel to the Atlantic but hidden by very large islands. Of these the principal one was Anastasia Island, standing directly between the town and the ocean with its orange plantations, shell-stone (coquina) quarries, and a nearly hundred-foot lookout-signal tower. The tower was of coquina and wood construction, and from it flags and a small cannon gave warnings when boats were sighted.[4]

A broad waterway opened between Anastasia Island and the next landmass to its north, an inviting entrance into the backwater of the Matanzas River on the hidden shore of which the town lay protected, but the view through the waterway from the ocean did not expose the town proper. Instead the viewer was faced by the massive coquina Castle St. Mark (Castillo de San Marcos, or Fort St. Mark, as the British called it) immediately at the north end of the town and perfectly positioned to discourage unwanted ships from approaching through the passage from the Atlantic.[5]

Most of the vessels that called on the port came on short coastal runs from Charleston, though occasionally there were arrivals directly from northern ports or from Europe. Adding to the safety of the town, though detracting considerably from its convenience as a port, was the fact that the waterway and the shallow section of the Atlantic on which it opened were treacherously strewn with huge sandbars that were often only a few feet below the surface, typically eight feet at low tide, perhaps twelve or thirteen at high tide. Ships that arrived and saw what appeared to be an attractively inviting entrance had to be warned that it was virtually impossible to get through safely, first, without knowledgeable local pilots and, second, without just the right combination of winds and tides to give maximum advantage over the hidden shallows.[6]

The schooner carrying Alexander Moultrie and his family was able to ease over the bar and reach town expeditiously. Captain Pilmore of the *Fidelity*, however, was aware of the hazards and held his ship at anchor while the flagmen in the watchtower on Anastasia Island informed the town of the vessel's arrival and the call for proper guidance into the port. After a two-hour wait, a pilot arrived and brought the ship somewhat closer in, during which time the exiles stretched their necks to view the Anastasia shore and the threatening solidity of the distant fort. They were also unnerved by the realization that the area was strewn with wrecks, testifying to any sailor's nightmare of the invisibly lurking bars. That afternoon Captain Abbott and Lieutenant Smith took the ship's yawl into town for dinner and to arrange for schooners to come out to transfer both people and cargo ashore, since lightening the ship was recommended for any attempt to cross the submerged sandbars.[7]

Because bad weather was threatening this already delicate transfer operation, a decision was made to wait until the next day—and the next, and the next, and the next, until the better part of a week had passed. Delays of this kind were not uncommon. When British governor of East Florida Patrick Tonyn arrived from England on March 1, 1774, his ship the *Britannia* had lain off the bar for sixteen days. It may have crossed the minds of the gentlemen prisoners that if it was so hard to get into St. Augustine by boat, there would probably be little chance of flight by sea.[8]

At last, on September 13 the offloading began. Supplies went first, on Captain Clarke's schooner, since the passengers could not be maintained ashore without them. St. Augustine was too small a community to absorb so many people without assistance. Indeed the new arrivals would soon learn that the economics of the already subsidized town were stressed by an increasing influx of other prisoners and loyalist refugees.[9]

Even before reaching town themselves, the exiled friends naturally wondered just how comfortable they were going to be. At least the climate would be familiar, virtually identical to that of Charleston. Palmettos and live oaks were all about, though the numerous orange trees indicated a more nearly tropical setting than Charleston could boast. There were also sprawling fig trees that the Spanish pioneers had brought, and lush grape arbors and tended herb gardens on virtually every city lot. A nineteenth-century travel book provides a description attuned to the exiles' concerns: "Malaria is almost unknown," it claimed (though this was not true in 1780), "and the constant sea-breezes moderate the cold of winter and mitigate the heat of summer. Frosts seldom occur, and the mean winter temperature is 58.08°. Nevertheless, cold northeasters are liable to make themselves felt in January and February, and this renders the place less desirable for consumptives than some of the inland resorts. The summer climate is delightful." To that extent, the Charlestonians could expect to feel at home.[10]

A full day was consumed transferring thirty-two barrels of rice and fifteen hogsheads of rum, plus cannon shot and other military supplies needed at the fort. On the morning of September 14, a different schooner came out from town, and by noon all the baggage, livestock, poultry, and other provisions were loaded from the *Fidelity* to the schooner. Four more hours were required to get the thirty-seven exiles and their twenty-six slaves aboard. At four o'clock began what was predicted to be a relatively uneventful trip to shore, but the usual complexities and narrowness of the ocean channels were exacerbated by unexpectedly rough seas.[11]

The schooner took on nine feet of water at about one-third of flood tide, and then in spite of qualified pilots, became grounded on a sand bank. Attempts to pull her off by drawing the anchor proved futile. The unfortunate travelers were forced to spend an especially disagreeable night among sheep, poultry, and hogs, so crowded and confused in the listing ship that some of them chose to climb into the sails or into lifeboats alongside in search of sleep.[12]

At long last, very early on the morning of September 15, two boats came out from town to take the weary Charlestonians to their new place of habitation. As the travelers rounded the northwestern tip of Anastasia Island, they could see for the first time the very modest skyline of East Florida's capital and its minimal urban development. The central square and its guardhouse were visible through a dip in the tree line, and a quarter mile to the south one could make out the old military barracks. Foliage largely concealed the rest, which was essentially a two-storied town. Only the handsome spire of the parish church, the eight-bell cupola of the State House, and the heavy square belvedere of the governor's house were otherwise discernable above the trees, a cityscape far different from that of their beloved Charleston and its skyline of belfries and spires.[13]

The British had indeed made improvements during the intervening seventeen years since the Spanish had gone. In particular they had built a stone seawall southward from the fort to the plaza at the center of town. From there the seawall turned out in into the bay at the point where the bay itself scooped inward to meet the plaza. This formed a small but neat breakwater and wharf at the very heart of town that served as a docking area for debarking and embarking. The water's end of the rectangular plaza had a stone guardhouse to oversee any landings.[14]

About half past eight in the morning, the Charleston patriots finally came ashore and stepped directly into the main town square (the plaza, which the British usually called the parade ground). They were escorted without guards to the State House at the far left corner of the same square. There they were offered a breakfast (coffee, tea, and hot buttered bread) at the hospitality of the commissary for prisoners, one William Brown, a gentleman who was to prove more friendly than most in Augustinian officialdom.[15]

The square, or plaza (which in modern times makes a lush central oasis for the historic section of St. Augustine, with its huge oaks and its well-tended grass, paths, and flower beds), was at that time a rather dusty open field—beaten by the heels and wheels of parades and formal ceremonies both urban and colonial, civil and political, military and religious (all powers being inextricably intertwined). All the same, it was graced by the facades of two of the only three buildings in town that could claim any architectural sophistication.[16]

One of these, facing the bay and occupying the entire west end of the parade ground, was the governor's "palace," a stuccoed, two-story residence that boasted a cantilevered and roofed second-floor wooden belvedere or balcony (suggesting a review of parades from on high or perhaps a blessing of the crowd by some ecclesiastical dignitary). Through the high garden wall, a handsome entrance door

Gen[l]. Tonyn, painted by Martin Archer Shee, engraved by George Clint. From the Thomas Addis Emmet, Collection of Illustrations Relating to the American Revolution and Early United States History, The Miriam and Ira D. Wallach Division of Art, Prints and Photographs: Print Collection, The New York Public Library.

opened onto the plaza, severely framed under a suggestion of classical entablature by flanked pairs of plain Tuscan pilasters. (This lot is now occupied by the twentieth-century municipal museum that recalls the old residence by a representation of the balcony but unfortunately omits the more elegant Tuscan entrance.)[17]

The other important building on the plaza, most impressive of all, was the State House to which the exiles had been led for breakfast. Unfortunately no drawing survives to preserve its effect, though it was supposed to be the city's finest example of architecture. The departed Spaniards had built the shell of the structure, which they had intended to be the bishop's palace. It was inherited unfinished by the British, who were obliged temporarily to remodel it for the use of soldiers while extended barracks were being built at the south end of town, then also for the use of the parish services while St. Peter's was being put into condition. Still unfinished, it had at least one room big enough for the colony's legislature to meet (though that modest body was not formed until 1781). Coincidentally, patriot exiles had been arrested and taken into the most elegant civil building of Charleston and thence transferred to its architectural equivalent in St. Augustine.[18]

As though by deliberate contrast to the cordial reception at the State House on the square, the exiles next encountered Commissary Brown's superior and foil, the governor himself. East Florida's royal governor was Ireland-born Lt. Col. Patrick Tonyn (1725–1804), who had been an army officer since the age of nineteen. He had seen action in Germany at Minden and Wetter with his father's Sixth (Inniskilling) Regiment of Dragoons in 1759 during the Seven Years' War, and in 1761 he became lieutenant colonel of the 104th Regiment of Foot, a post he held until the unit disbanded.[19]

Tonyn was appointed governor of East Florida in July 1773 and arrived to take office on March 1, 1774. A friend of General Clinton, he is generally considered to have been an able officer and governor, though he demanded strict adherence to class and rank and could be bellicose and autocratic with settlers and other government officials. Under his tenure East Florida had become a haven for southern loyalist refugees and a base of operations from which to harass patriots in Georgia and South Carolina. To this end he raised the East Florida Rangers (later known as the King's Carolina Rangers) and engaged the help of Florida Creek and Seminole tribes in support of the British.[20]

Tonyn had a persistent streak of mistrust and was ever ready to whiff the scent of insubordination. He had accused his own chief justice, South Carolinian William Drayton, of secretly sympathizing with the Revolution, and he did likewise to almost anyone else who dared to suggest amendment to his policies. There may have been some truth in such charges, if to criticize the governor was per se to be revolutionary, but on the whole there was little genuinely anti-British sentiment in Florida. Nonetheless Tonyn alienated people and stimulated criticism from all sides. Drayton described his autocratic rule as despotism completely enthroned.[21]

Tonyn had already formed a low opinion of his captives even before their arrival, one that seems to have been on a level with the sentiments of Simpson and Balfour. He expected the new arrivals to be wicked and vile promoters of "hellish rebellion." On September 9 he wrote to Balfour that he knew them to be "the most mischievous and flagitious [of subjects] and the very demagogues of sedition in South Carolina." Nor did he believe that they would honor their paroles; he preferred close confinement over "the indulgent permission of a district, which they have abused in Carolina and will probably do so again." Confinement, he said, would prevent "their pestiferous counselling being of any weight here in poisoning the minds of the people."[22]

Tonyn's view from the beginning was that a "proper use of hemp" (i.e., hanging) should be applied to what he referred to as an infernal disease, because "such deep and latent venom cannot be radically cured by more gentle remedies." He promised Balfour that he and the commandant of the army, Lt. Col. Beamsley Glazier, would keep a watchful eye over the prisoners.[23]

Such was the governor who now came to meet the exiles and give them a taste of his unqualified authority. His main business was to decree his decision that all of the Charlestonians were once again to swear formal agreement to the terms of parole. "Expediency, and a series of political occurrences," he condescended, "have rendered it necessary to remove you from Charleston to this place; but, gentlemen, we have no wish to increase your sufferings. To all, therefore, who are willing to give their paroles not to go beyond the limits prescribed to them, the liberty of the town will be allowed. A dungeon will be the destiny of such as refuse to accept the indulgence."[24]

The preceding quotation and the rendition of what happened next comes from the account published by Alexander Garden in 1822, and while his work was filiopietistic and trended toward the laudatory, Garden's biographical sketches are authentic, and his related incidents are factually consistent with other sources.[25]

Asked if they would accept the terms, the intrepid Christopher Gadsden, speaking on behalf of them all, raised his hand to propose a slight amendment and to complain of their harsh treatment since their arrest, to which the governor dryly informed him that this was not an occasion for discussion, only one for saying yes or no—he had not come there to argue. Whereupon, given that choice, Gadsden tersely and emphatically said no. Tonyn looked at Gadsden and said of the proposed new parole, "Think better of it, Sir. A second refusal of it will fix your destiny—a dungeon will be your future habitation." "Prepare it, then," said the inflexible patriot; "I will give no parole, so help me God!" He was escorted off to the "Castle" dungeon forthwith.[26]

Gadsden (1724–1805) was unique among his fellows, not necessarily in the ardor of his patriotism, for they were all fervent patriots, but perhaps for his brash outspokenness and the breadth of his revolutionary activities and experiences. Early in his career, the Charleston merchant had served briefly as purser aboard a British man-of-war from 1745 to 1748 during King George's War. In 1757 he helped to organize the Charleston Battalion of Artillery, of which he was captain during the Cherokee campaigns of 1759. He had served both on the Royal Council and in the Commons House of Assembly prior to South Carolina's rupture with England.[27]

In 1765 Gadsden was one of his province's three representatives to the Stamp Act Congress in New York. He attended the First and Second Continental Congresses (1774–76) but returned home to accept a commission as colonel of the First Regiment of South Carolina Provincial Troops, bringing copies of Thomas Paine's recently published *Common Sense* with him. He was disappointed to be consigned to Fort Johnson during the Battle of Sullivan's Island on June 28, 1776, and though he was later promoted to brigadier general in the Continental Army, he resigned from military service in 1778 over a variety of military and civil disputes. He remained active in civil government, however, and was South Carolina's lieutenant governor and ranking civil official in Charleston at the time

Christopher Gadsden, 1724–1805, half-length portrait after Joshua Reynolds. Prints and Photographs Division, Library of Congress, Washington, D.C.

of the capitulation. If there was a die-hard and recalcitrant patriot in the group of exiles, it was Christopher Gadsden.[28]

According to Alexander Garden, Gadsden considered the rejection of Tonyn's proposed new parole a point of honor. After all, as Charleston's ranking civilian official, he had signed the articles of capitulation himself. He firmly believed he had maintained the letter of their law, and just as firmly believed that the British had not. "With men who have once deceived me, I can enter into no new contract," he said. "Had the British commanders regarded the terms of the capitulation of Charleston, I might now, although a prisoner under my own roof, enjoy the smiles and consolations of my surrounding family; but even without a shadow of accusation proffered against me for any act inconsistent with my plighted faith, I am torn from them and, here in a distant land, invited to enter into new engagements. I will give no parole."[29]

Such stunning opposition to the arbitrary mandate of the British authorities, seen as impudent lack of submission, was esteemed a crime too flagrant to go unpunished. And thus Gadsden's residence became a stone cell in the fort, a dark, damp, windowless bombproof of about four hundred square feet that met the description of a castle dungeon as well as could any dank and ancient cranny in Europe. Why this, and not a simple restriction to the State House on the town square? Or the official jail that was quite nearby? Or the prison ship *Otter*, anchored in the harbor?[30]

The bombproof was by far the cruelest of the available choices. Yet Gadsden did not complain. "He uttered no sigh, he made no remonstrance, he did not deign to solicit a mitigation of the severities inflicted upon him." Tonyn, of course, saw the situation somewhat differently. To Lord Germain he wrote dismissively if not derisively, "Mr. Gadsden, the titular lieutenant-governor, an old man of a distinguished inflammatory disposition, is lodged in the fort because he refuses to be admitted to the liberty of a district on parole."[31]

Staunch patriot that he was, Gadsden felt sure that the Charleston capitulation agreements had not singled him out for special treatment, nor had the instructions for exile, but even so, the British knew he was an unusually important revolutionary and were out to humiliate him with a sharp vengeance. He later wrote to George Washington that their treatment of him "was much more severe and pointed [than] against any of my Friends, which appears to me more owing to the Station I was in [as a governor and a general] than as Mr. Gadsden (though I believe [I was] no Favourite as such)." Thus, in conformity to his own stubborn will and as a standing protest against what he believed to be outrageous tyrannical conduct, he was hauled off to a windowless, vaulted stone cell in the southeast corner of the old fort (the "Castle"), where he did without sunlight for the next ten months and more.[32]

Of the total time the exiles were in St. Augustine, Gadsden declared that he was confined in the Castle for forty-two weeks, during which time none of his friends were permitted to visit. As to paroles, "I told them I had kept the first as a Gentleman, defied (and do still defy) them to prove the contrary, and was determined never to take a second which would imply a breach of the first." The British officers were ordered not to converse with him, but many of them often did, and Gadsden later affirmed that they behaved with decency and that he was never insulted; in fact once when it was ordered that he could not light a candle and he was in total darkness for two or three nights, even his jailers admitted their shame at being party to the pitifulness of his situation.[33]

Garden recorded that some generous subaltern offered to supply Gadsden with illegal candles but that the prisoner declined the favor lest the officer should expose himself to the censure of his superior. He surely had better lighting than Garden's hyperbole suggests: "Sensible that activity of mind would increase its energies and better enable him to support the oppression, he diligently engaged in the study of the Hebrew language and was hourly increasing his reputation as a scholar, while his enemies vainly hoped that he was writhing under the penalties of his political offences."[34]

The Castle's officers found Gadsden to be a man they could admire. The lieutenant governor was arguably the most prominent individual ever to be

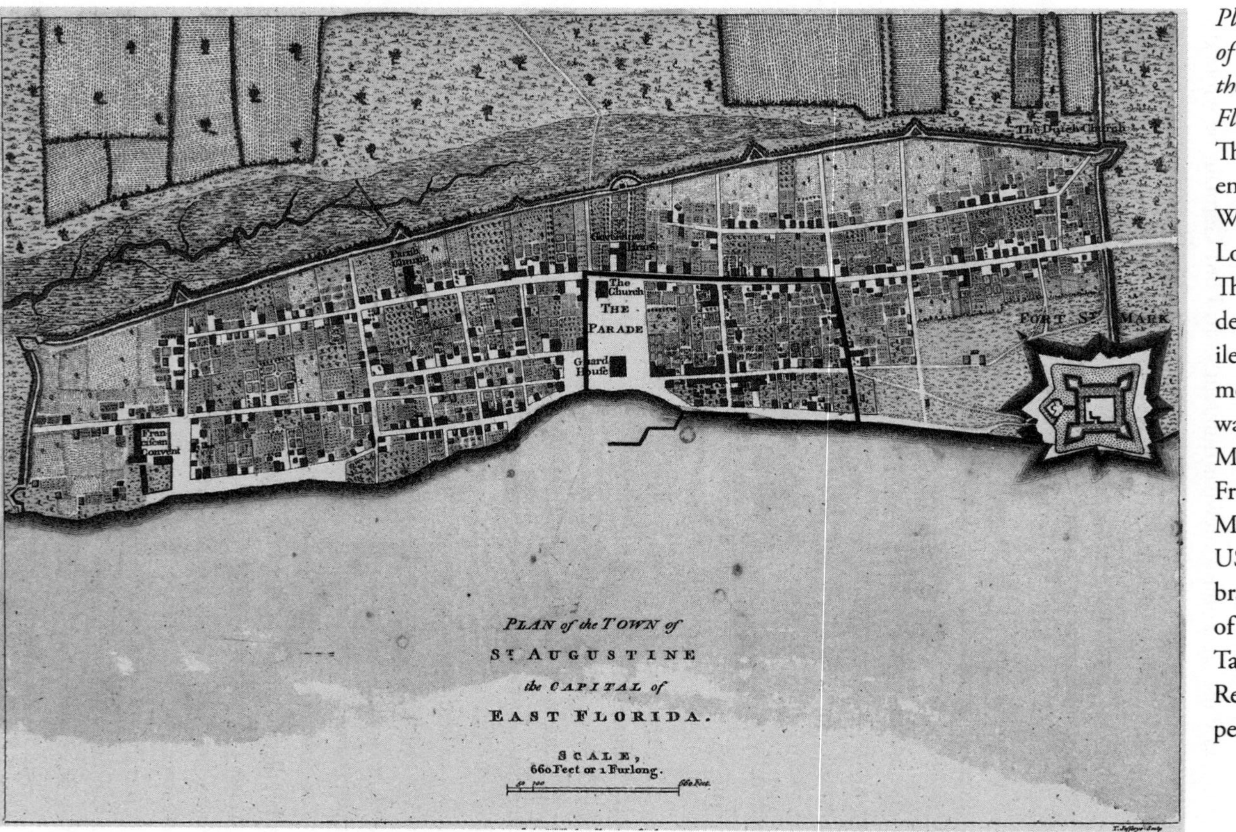

Plan of the Town of St. Augustine, the Capital of East Florida, map by Thomas Jefferys, engraved by William Faden, London, c. 1777. The heavy lines delineate the exiles' boundaries of movement. The waterway is the Matanzas River. From the Florida Map Collection. USF Tampa Library. University of South Florida, Tampa, Fla. Reproduced with permission.

incarcerated in that fort, before or since. Indeed, in the rather low-profile military history of St. Augustine, his fellow group of exiled South Carolinians were the best-known prisoners ever to be detained there.

Unquestionably awed by the staunch nobility of Gadsden's unyielding honor, the rest of the exiles were nonetheless struck by the immediacy of his disposition by Tonyn. The intimidated gentlemen abandoned any lingering scruples and said yes to the new oaths, so that "each for himself, severally, [took] Parole upon the Honour, & Faith of a Gentleman," thereby accepting commitment to a much more restricted range of freedom than they had enjoyed in Charleston. Of course there would be petty annoyances and small tyrannies to bear, but the exiles were all men of education and some fortune and would be able to pass the time without great physical suffering.[35]

Within the town of St. Augustine, the Charlestonians were required by their new agreement to stay inside the area limited on the south by the street (now called "Bridge Street") that went from the bay west to the fortification exit behind the parish church; on the west by Church Street (now called "St. George"), which went from the barracks grounds on its south end all the way up to the town gate at the northern limit of town; on the north by the lane that leads eastward from Church Street to the engineer's house (now called Hypolita Street); and on the east by the waters of the bay.[36]

These limits are in notable contrast to their having had full freedom of the city in Charleston. Why they should have had less in St. Augustine is not clear, but the restrictions may have been a precaution of keeping the prisoners a block or more away from St. Augustine's fortifications and thus away from any temptation to climb the walls. If so, it was an unnecessary device, first because of the exiles' genuine and much vaunted sense of honor, and second because it would have been suicidal to leap the walls and enter the snake-and-alligator-infested bogs to the west and south or the thoroughly patrolled open space to the north, peopled by armed guards and commanded by the indomitable fort itself. Swamp and jungle were not a tempting route for escape, and even if they could escape from the town, In all of East Florida there would be no place to go—not a single sympathetic community to provide sanctuary.

The only actual road out of town was the King's Road, a sixteen-foot-wide swath of danger that left from the guarded gate at the north end, passing right by the guarded fort, and was too regularly traveled by loyalists and threatened by Indians to accommodate a getaway. In fact the King's Road, an oyster-shell-encrusted mire, was so long, so bad, and so undependable that the exiles were later to refuse when the British authorities tried to get them to leave by it. As for escape by water, it likewise offered no temptation; the prisoners had seen firsthand the near impossibility of unguided access to the ocean.[37]

The imposed street limits also suggest that the British saw in the revolutionary gentlemen a potential for committing espionage and thus wished to keep them several blocks away from snooping about the guarded wall on the west, the fort on the north, or the barracks on the south. A third theory for the setting of the northern and southern limits derives from the concentrations of taverns near the fort and barracks at the two ends of town; the red eyes and sinister teeth of alligators lurked outside the western fortifications, but the red eyes and sinister weapons of drunken soldiers were equally to be avoided beyond the prescribed limits north and south.

After the gentlemen signed their new agreement, their slaves, exiles in their own right, perhaps doubly so, made verbal oaths to the same effect. There followed a little ceremony by which each Charlestonian was called by name and individually walked out onto the parade ground to exchange a tipping of hats with the governor. Innocent as that may sound, such a ritual was apparently grating on the pride of the exiles, who deemed it too insultingly close to "passing under the yoke," a classical Roman ritual used to humiliate captive enemies.[38]

The Exiles Settle In

Once the exiles' baggage finally arrived at the parade ground dock, their enslaved laborers were assigned to move it all to the State House where breakfast had been served. The gentlemen meantime arranged a three o'clock dinner at Dott's Tavern, each paying 6 shillings 3 pence for the meal, including liquor. A supper of coffee, bread, and butter preceded their all retiring to the State House, where mattresses were spread on the upstairs floors for them to spend the night. Notwithstanding the crowded conditions, they slept soundly, being exhausted from the loss of sleep the previous night aboard the schooner.[1]

The next morning, September 16, they received a gift of fifteen large pumpkins sent by one John Imrie. This disgruntled former Charlestonian was a shipwright and passionate loyalist who prior to the British occupation of South Carolina had been forced by patriots to flee Charleston. He subsequently took up residence in St. Augustine, where he was engaged in producing turpentine. Having little idea of what to do with Imrie's pumpkins, his fellow Charlestonians deduced that the gesture must have been intended as an insult, especially considering that the gift came from the same individual who had purportedly erected a large pair of gallows as a symbolic gesture to greet them on the day they were scheduled to arrive.[2]

Fortunately, during the complicated transition from ocean to port, the spectacle of the gallows had been taken down before the patriots ever had a chance to see it. But the message got through that there was a real possibility of being treated not as prisoners of war but as traitors to the king, an identity that could call for a death sentence. For this reason they missed no opportunity to remind their captors that they were men of honor who had signed pledges back in Charleston and had not broken those pledges. The insistence on their adherence to their paroles was not merely an honorable pose; it was a legalistic point to keep at bay any idea of more dire consequences.

Governor Tonyn was clearly not ready for his guests. The exiles were expected to reside in one fairly large upstairs apartment in the unfinished State House, and they did just that on their first night ashore—but they were most unhappy with the sleeping arrangements in a space that had temporarily served as barracks for British soldiers. Yet there was one whose night was even worse than that of the exiles, namely the *Fidelity's* captain. With passengers and cargo at long last safely on shore, and himself and his oarsmen warmly entertained in the city, Captain Pilmore set out on the evening of September 15 to return to his ship and his own bed. To his dismay he was not able to reach the ship, because his oarsmen were too intoxicated to be seaworthy.[3]

By the time Pilmore and his crew stumbled back to the plaza dock the next morning, the winds were contrary to his departure. Rather than testing the waters, he made arrangements for his crew to spend the next twenty-four hours sleeping off their incapacities while he awaited a calmer wind. By Sunday, September 17, clearer heads, favorable winds, and decent weather enabled the *Fidelity* to depart for Charleston, and it made port there four days later. Before leaving St. Augustine, Pilmore received letters onboard from the exiles, and he promised to deliver to them to families and friends when he reached Charleston. His word was good, and the families in Charleston thus obtained the first news that loved ones were as safe and as well as could be expected in St. Augustine. In his letter home, Josiah Smith grumbled about their insulting and circumscribed situation and informed his friends that he and his fellows would have to remain in this disagreeable town until the Continental Congress arranged their freedom through an exchange of British prisoners.[4]

Meanwhile the food was generally satisfactory—local seafood was abundant. Sleeping accommodations, however, were entirely unacceptable for such a large group. Alexander Moultrie, having relatives already in town, had arranged more personal quarters for his family, but the other men, with the advice and consent of Commissary Brown, found it desirable to work out other arrangements of shared lodging in the form of three separate living and eating groups or "messes." Seven of them, including Thomas Heyward Jr. and Edward Rutledge, went in with Moultrie to form a mess. They rented a stone house with a large orange-tree garden on the northwest corner of the parade ground (directly opposite the State House, where the cathedral and its garden are today). A second group of twelve men, including Edward McCrady and his friend William Johnson, decided for the time being to remain in the State House until something more to their liking could be found.[5]

The third and largest mess of seventeen, which included Dr. David Ramsay, Richard Hutson, and Josiah Smith, found a large wooden house one street back from the bay, on the northwest corner of the intersection of the streets now called Hypolita (officially their northern limit) and Charlotte, where, after a few days' preparations, they could sleep on the upper story four to a room and enjoy the southern porches both upstairs and down. The lower floor provided a living room, a dining room, and two service rooms, one of which housed their

Thomas Heyward, Jr.
Portrait by Thomas Sully,
1854, after Jeremiah
Theus. National Portrait
Gallery, Washington,
D.C.

gardener's quarters. The garden, in which they soon set about raising food to their liking ("for health, recreation, and fresh vegetables"), extended north behind the house—technically north of their restricted limits, but they received permission to use it.[6]

Since they were only two short blocks from the Castle St. Mark, this group of seventeen took on the burden of supplying food to poor Mr. Gadsden, who remained righteously alone in his private cell at the Castle. They could enhance his diet, but they could not visit him in person. Since he was officially considered a part of their mess, he would incur a seventeenth part of the table expenses but, of course, would not be charged rent.[7]

It made sense that Heyward (thirty-four years old) and Rutledge (thirty-one) would mess together. Both men studied law at the Middle Temple in London and were admitted to the South Carolina bar. Both were also planters, and both had been active in the revolutionary movement from the outset. They had served together in the royal assembly prior to the Revolution and in the provincial legislature. Rutledge was sent to Philadelphia as a South Carolina delegate to the First Continental Congress in 1775, and during the Second Continental Congress in 1776, Heyward, who replaced Christopher Gadsden, joined him. He and Heyward were two of South Carolina's four delegates who signed the Declaration of Independence on July 4, 1776.[8]

Edward Rutledge. Henry Bryan Hall's 1872 engraving after the c. 1794 painting by James Earl. From the Thomas Addis Emmet, Collection of Illustrations Relating to the American Revolution and Early United States History, The Miriam and Ira D. Wallach Division of Art, Prints and Photographs: Print Collection, The New York Public Library.

These two obviously had a great deal in common. Being members of the lowcountry planter aristocracy and leaders in the political arena did not preclude military service for either of them. As captains in the Charleston Battalion of Artillery, they aided in the defense of their town and, again together, were instrumental in General Moultrie's victory over the British at Port Royal Island, eighteen months before their St. Augustine exile. Captain Heyward had been wounded in the arm during the engagement. Heyward and Rutledge likewise served in the middle of the siege lines at the hornwork during the 1780 siege of Charleston. As militiamen they were subject to article 4 of the articles of capitulation, which permitted them to remain at their homes on parole until the British decided otherwise.[9]

Edward Rutledge was certainly distressed over separation from his wife, Henrietta, once he learned of the calamity that had befallen his family. Their two-year-old son, Edward Jr., described by Eliza Lucas Pinckney as a charming infant, had toddled too close to a fire in the nursery and sustained burns that proved to be fatal. Henrietta would never recover from the shock of her loss and would suffer memory lapses, deep depressions, perhaps even psychotic breaks—according to family lore, "at times she would lunge into a fire in an attempt to save the child she had lost." The exact date of the little boy's death is hard to pinpoint, but evidence suggests that it may have occurred while the exiles were sailing between Charleston and St. Augustine. If so there was probably a considerable delay before Rutledge actually learned of the tragic episode.[10]

Exile to St. Augustine hardly relieved the patriots from any British military presence. The Florida town was garrisoned by troops of the Sixtieth Regiment (the Royal American Regiment of Foot). Two hundred soldiers were once thought sufficient to maintain the entire colony of East Florida from their St. Augustine station, but in December 1779 the British augmented the military presence with an additional three hundred troops. Lt. Col. Beamsley Glazier was given command. He was a veteran officer who had taken a courageous part in the British repulse of the Franco-American assault on Savannah on October 9, 1779.[11]

Over time St. Augustine had become a regular domicile for prisoners, so that before the end of 1781 it would be home to some three hundred captives held in various degrees of incarceration, all of whom required housing and feeding by the British government. Governor Tonyn was hard put to find the two thousand pounds per year required to pay Brown, the commissioner of prisoners. Moreover he required a budget sufficient to purchase the rice, flour, beef, pork, medicine, and other supplies to fill all of those mouths, and even more funding to keep in repair the jails needed to house the most problematic of the inhabitants of St. Augustine. An influx of loyalist American refugees further strained his finances. Yet nobody starved, and the little town kept its reputation as an exceptionally healthful post.[12]

Of course there were "recurring diseases and pestilences," and now and then a prisoner would succumb to illness. The financially harried governor would then face still more expense—the costs incurred for the local carpenter to make a simple wooden coffin for the poor decedent, for the work of the gravediggers, and for the rector to preside over the interment. Small comfort it would be for a Carolinian, if the worst should happen, to be laid to rest gratis in the isolated wilds of this exotically foreign province.[13]

The Charleston exiles spent the first week in St. Augustine becoming familiar with the town. St. Augustine was a collection of nearly four hundred little buildings, quite modest architecturally but having a distinctive charm in a provincial Hispanic way, layered over by a decade and a half of British refurbishing. The buildings along the narrow, sandy streets had only one or two stories and reflected the necessities imposed by the clime and the financial limitations of a struggling economy. There was no clay in the area and therefore little use of brick. Since the town was built on a sandy site bordered by marshes, it had been assumed in its first century that the ground would not support stone structures. Wood was plentiful, and thus there were many structures with clapboard siding.[14]

Later on, quarries on Anastasia Island that had been excavated to provide material for the permanent fort made available the relatively light natural seashell composite called coquina, easily cemented by seashell mortar called tabby. Both materials could be poured into cast shapes on the site of construction. Because such materials were porous, walls were generally protected with lime-plastered surfaces, then sometimes painted red, green, brown, or ocher. Prior to the British occupation, a great majority of roofs had been thatched with straw or palm. In time boarded or cypress-shingled roofs became more common, though there were also a good number of flat masonry roofs, tiled or tarred. None of the old houses had chimneys, since, unlike Charleston, pre-British St. Augustine had virtually no fireplaces (except, of course, for the separately built kitchens). What little heat was needed in houses had normally been supplied by braziers (metal pans of hot coals).[15]

The largest of the three groups of exiles, the one that lived nearest the fort, rented its Hypolita Street property from Spencer Mann, who was genuinely sympathetic to their plight. Mann owned considerable property both within and without the city walls and was a respected attorney employed by the comfortably wealthy James Penman. Together Mann and Penman were considered St. Augustine's preeminent merchants, and they commanded more funds than the whole East Florida colonial government had at its disposal. When it was necessary for the British hierarchy to pay for black laborers to perform much-needed repairs of the town fortifications, it was Penman and Mann who supplied the money.[16]

The funding may be taken as an indication of genuine public spirit, though Governor Tonyn was always suspicious of Mann's liberal leanings. The previous commandant of the garrison, Lt. Col. Lewis V. Fuser, indicated as much in a letter written to General Clinton well before the Americans were brought to St. Augustine, a letter not kind to either Mann or the administration. The commandant said he could expect "very little assistance from this place; fine promises, pompous writing; and nothing done, is what I have experienced these three years past." He explained about being forced by Tonyn's lack of money to obtain funds for repairing the defenses from the Mann and Penman pair, who "belonged to the anti-Tonyn faction."[17]

It is known that Mann did not admire the governor, as he made clear in an epistolary report: "With respect to our settlement, we are going back every day, and I believe our ruler [Governor Tonyn] has neither ability to point out or interest to procure any good for us." Mann was clearly risking his own funds by signing for the commandant's military provisions, in spite of which loyal generosity Tonyn characterized both Penman and Mann as two of "the principal leaders of a desperate faction" who had "endeavored by every infernal artifice to dash this province into the same rebellious state with the other colonies." There is actually little evidence that Mann was seriously revolutionary, but he clearly was gracious in befriending the guests from Charleston.[18]

Not so gracious were the general orders approved on September 16, eleven days after the exiles had sailed out of Charleston and issued publicly the next day, the same day of the *Fidelity*'s departure back to that city. The gentlemen had signed their new agreement and the slaves had made their verbal oaths, but the commanding officer of the garrison, Lieutenant Colonel Glazier, remained distrustful of their sincerity. Now a new decree required the Charleston captives to appear at the State House twice daily for roll call: "at Gun Fire in the Evening and at Guard Mounting in the Morning."[19]

The order suggested once more the uncertainty of their legal status by giving them yet another identifying title: "The Rebel Prisoners." They were instructed to place "some badge of distinction on their Negroes and other domestics, so that they may be known," and they themselves were not allowed to wear any rebel uniform or coat that looked like a British or French regimental. And finally the garrison's soldiers were absolutely forbidden to attempt any personal association with the rebels, much less be seen with them, under threat of court martial for disobedience of orders.[20]

The righteous patriots took this decree as yet another insult. They had so recently given their pledges of honor, yet they were being treated "as if no dependence could be placed on these sacred ties." They added logic to their pride, complaining that standing for attendance at the State House in the heat of a Florida day was inconvenient and inappropriate when they might better be retired to their apartments and improving themselves by reading and other pursuits. The arguments of heat and the pursuit of literature were hardly persuasive. Given the area restrictions of the parole, it was impossible to be more than five minutes away from the State House, so temporal convenience was not an impressive complaint either. Realizing that their objection was as petty as the discipline objected to, the prisoners quickly gave in and decided it was wiser to comply, since "our Noncompliance might Induce [Glazier] to plague us more in some other way."[21]

The enslaved who had accompanied the exiles to Florida were not required to appear for roll call, but an order requiring all Charlestonian slaves to wear some badge of distinction called for a measure of creativity. It was already a law that St. Augustine black people who had proof of freedom were to wear an armband inscribed with the word *free*, and slaves belonging to rebellious masters, or those whose political status was uncertain, were to wear heart-shaped badges; so the exiles needed to take council only to agree on what would make a distinctive heart. Without overtaxing their imagination, they settled on a red heart to be suspended around the neck. Those enslaved subsequently took interest in personalizing their own various heart-badges, but the net effect in form and color was "not pleasing to the British Officers" and therefore suited the smug owners very nicely.[22]

Deprived of conversation with so many of their English captors, and resigned to the fact that they were definitively and ignominiously in "banishment . . . to the inhospitable shores of that barren country," the patriots spent two days figuring among themselves an equitable distribution of the supplies brought with them: quantities of clean rice, rough rice, corn, British flour, Carolina flour, Irish pork, beef, bacon, British butter, powdered sugar, rum, and coffee, as well as a number of sheep, hogs, "fowles" (meaning chickens), geese, and ducks. There were also cakes of British soap, tallow candles and candlesticks, wooden bowls, a metal stew pan, copper tea kettles, iron pots, and an iron griddle.[23]

Of course it was understood that the exiles could order more of anything from Charleston, but had they been counting on a convenient and regular supply, they would not have brought 294 pounds of flour and 66 pounds of bacon. Another curiosity of note is that the three groups took fairly distributed proportions of everything else (including geese and ducks), but one group alone got all seventeen of the chickens. Perhaps the back garden of their habitation at the State House was somehow a superior accommodation for "fowles."[24]

The next task was to settle the group's finances. Josiah Smith had been put in charge of the distribution of general stock and had kept exact records of anything anyone used prior to the September 15 subdivision into three groups. He informed everyone of how much each had expended. Thomas Heyward was the most parsimonious of the entire company. He had charged a mere 13s 8d, while the biggest debt was that of the rector of St. Paul's, John Lewis: £6/4/6 and seven-tenths of a penny. The average was more than three and a half pounds.[25]

On September 20 the commissary sent to the State House the first delivery of government rations due the Charlestonians as prisoners of war. Except for firewood, the rations consisted of food and were as good as could be expected in an area where almost every article had to be imported and was subject to the vagaries of war. A week's ration consisted of a pound of salted Irish beef per day (or a pound of fresh beef, or nine ounces of salted pork, if preferred), a mere ounce of butter per day to go on the daily one-pound loaf of bread, and the choice of a serving of rice, peas, or oatmeal each day.[26]

Given the diet's monotony, the exiles' chief gratification proved to be the local abundance of fish available, albeit at rates inflated by increased demand occasioned by their arrival. Since the regular rations were to be supplied on a weekly basis, the overall selection was enough that each person could vary his own diet from one day to another. However, they all agreed that the drinking water from local sulfuric wells was bad, making the palate yearn for other more agreeable beverages. Irritatingly there was no automatic portion of rum, and what could be bought in town—even with the fairly regular connections to Cuba—did not satisfy the South Carolinians, accustomed as they were to the use of table wines from France and Spain. They preferred Jamaican rum. Moreover the water could be made passable for drinking if turned into strong tea, and they regularly took that option.[27]

Had there been a source of higher-quality alcoholic drinks, the exiles would have found it. They were free to use the local taverns—of which tiny St. Augustine could boast some forty, not to mention a subgenre called "punch houses" that existed thanks to the military character of the town, its idleness, its isolation, and the large number of young unmarried men. A number of these taverns, located naturally near to the barracks south of the exiles' restricted zone or to the fort north of the zone, were off-limits to the exiles, and many others were more intimate affairs such as were often operated by citizens in the main rooms of their personal dwellings as an easy way to supplement household income.[28]

Such homey sources were in part the result of a deliberate attempt to discourage the proliferation of larger and noisier drinking establishments. The official solution had been to license almost anyone to sell spirits in quantities of less than two gallons, which raises the question of how lavishly alcohol was being served in the noisier places. The numerous intimate establishments that could seat only a few drinkers touched on another problem, namely that to attempt to socialize with any of the local citizens was to flout the rules. The tyrannical English governor intended to maintain close restriction.[29]

Governor Tonyn was serious about forbidding all military personnel from informal association with the exiles and threatened court-martial and punishment for breaches of his order. He also had the military authorities advise the inhabitants of the town to refrain from communicating with the Charlestonians. Tonyn's ego was large enough that he could assume such advice would be considered scarcely less than an order, and one that would be universally honored, given its lofty source. In fact he later bragged confidently in a letter to Lord Germain, explaining that "these incendiaries can do little mischief here; and [in order] that their opinions and principles may be confined to themselves as much as possible, and for their former conduct, they are treated at a great distance by me, and having a friendly intercourse with them is considered as disrespectful to His Majesty and displeasing to me."[30]

Ironically Tonyn's imperious tone actually increased the number of disaffected locals, especially the tavern keepers and other merchants whose business suffered, and it called attention to the South Carolinians as exotic and mysterious, even endowing them with a nuanced aura of forbidden fruit rather than exciting the inhabitants to acts of contempt against them. So the exiles did not necessarily have to stay at home; it was too small a town not to get to know people. In addition to the public houses, which often were a disappointment, there were skittle alleys, shuffleboards, billiard parlors, and even bawdy houses (though no record survives to indicate that any Charlestonian frequented the latter).[31]

John Moultrie, Jr., oil on canvas by Jeremiah Theus. Courtesy of Dr. J. Austin Ball II, Charleston, S.C.

Publicly, at least, the Charlestonians were ostracized by what little formal society the town could boast. There were nonetheless not a few cultured citizens who dared to receive them. Ordinary people could more easily afford to be kind, especially where money was to be made. For instance, and quickly enough, friendships developed with rancher Francisco Sanchez, who had long carried on a butcher business in St. Augustine and who could thus supply more and better meat than was provided by the official rationing.[32]

The exiles might have expected a sympathetic interest from one obvious Carolina connection. The lieutenant governor of East Florida, Dr. John Moultrie Jr., was the brother of Gen. William Moultrie and half-brother of exile Alexander Moultrie. Having been reared in Charleston, he had a lifelong acquaintance with many of the prisoners. Dr. Moultrie seems to have generally kept himself aloof, perhaps embarrassed at the treachery he presumably represented in the eyes of the revolutionaries. He was also aware of the stern nature of his superior's convictions. The governor had been quite clear about that. One witness, however, suggests that Moultrie did contribute oranges and other provisions to rebel prisoners and former friends.[33]

Josiah Smith received a breakfast invitation from the lieutenant governor on the morning of September 21. In his diary Smith stated that he had expected a warmer reception than what hospitality he actually received. For years he had been the executor of the estate of Moultrie's wife Eleanor's late father, Capt. George Austin of the Royal Navy, and had always worked hard to improve the Moultries' advantage. At breakfast Smith warned Moultrie that his (Smith's) detention and absence from Charleston was certain to damage the estate—could not the lieutenant governor use his influence with Lieutenant Colonel Balfour in Charleston to enable his homecoming?[34]

Moultrie was not at all helpful, and Smith was chagrined that the lieutenant governor declined to act on his behalf, instead offering only "his general invitation of calling at his house now & then to chatt with his family over a dish of Tea or Coffee." Giving up that hope, Smith would have to be content with "depending upon a kind providence alone, for a timely release from [his] present unjust confinement in the Town of St. Augustine."[35]

But in spite of that coolness in hospitality, it must be admitted that Lt. Gov. John Moultrie Jr. (1729–98) was an interesting character. He had earned his medical doctorate at the University of Edinburgh in 1749, becoming the first native-born American to graduate with a degree in medicine from what was then the best medical school in the English-speaking world. His highly acclaimed thesis on yellow fever, written in Ciceronian Latin, was subsequently translated into French and German. Moultrie's friendship with Col. James Grant, forged during the Cherokee campaign of 1761, led to his 1764 selection by Grant to the Royal Council of East Florida. As president of the Royal Council in 1771, he became acting governor of the province when Grant departed East Florida for England, and he was soon after appointed to the office of lieutenant governor.[36]

Moultrie had truly come from a family of divided allegiance. Three of his younger brothers were or had been patriots: Brig. Gen. William Moultrie, who was on parole in Charleston; Capt. Thomas Moultrie, who had perished during the siege of Charleston; and of course half-brother Alexander Moultrie, who was there in St. Augustine. Notwithstanding his brothers' politics, John was zealously loyal to the king and remained in the office of British lieutenant governor for the duration of the Revolutionary War.[37]

It is a curious coincidence that only five days after Smith's breakfast with Moultrie and his pointing out what a help he could be back in Charleston, a sloop arrived from Charleston bringing letters to most of the exiles. Smith learned that his family was well but remained resigned to his "cruel separation" from them. On the other hand, he also learned that George Austin, son of the aforementioned Captain Austin and brother of Eleanor Moultrie, had recently died intestate. Mrs. Moultrie, who was very much affected by her brother's decease, became heiress to what Austin had left behind, part of which was to be paid through accounts managed by Smith—three hundred pounds sterling "for the purchase of two valuable Negro Men, Quacko the Driver, and his Brother

Aleck a Cooper, at the Estate's Pedee plantation." The money for these transactions was to have been long since remitted through him but had, of course, been "prevented by the late commotions in Carolina." Smith could be of no help. He was stuck in St. Augustine.[38]

The momentum of the more refined social life of St. Augustine eddied about the lives of the British officers with whom the exiles were so specifically forbidden to converse. In the early 1780s, the British officers staged plays to relieve boredom and raise money for widows. The productions were presented in the State House, with officers playing both male and female roles, as was customary there and in other British-occupied cities. In addition prosperous merchants would partner with the officers to organize balls. And there were dinner parties and club functions, picnicking, promenading along the bay, and so forth. However, since the ratio of men to women was two or three to one or worse, there were few unmarried ladies to be courted or "gallanted"—no concern, as the overwhelming majority of the Charlestonians were already married. As for buying tickets to watch the unisex thespians, the exiles (like the locals) were far more interested in wagering and drinking.[39]

Soon the Continental Congress received word from the South Carolina delegates of the seizure and shipboard confinement of "a number of respectable citizens of the state, prisoners of war after the capitulation of Charlestown." Congress thereupon directed General Washington to query General Clinton regarding the accuracy of the intelligence. If the reports from South Carolina were true, what could possibly be the justification for such extreme measures? Accordingly Washington wrote to Clinton on October 6.[40]

Clinton replied to Washington three days later that yes, he had heard that persons in Charleston "had entered into a plot for the disruption of the place where they were protected and that the officer commanding there had found it necessary to interfere." He had this knowledge, he said, "from common fame" but had received no formal report on the subject.[41]

Clinton was either forgetful or he was being disingenuous—probably the latter. On September 3 Cornwallis had fully reported, in a dispatch to Clinton, the date of the arrests, the names of those arrested, and the ship to which they were sent. Washington himself did not believe in the veracity of the reports of the supposed plot to destroy Charleston, and he likely doubted Clinton's claimed vague awareness of the matter. He wrote another letter to Clinton on October 19 vigorously protesting that Cornwallis (and Rawdon, but without mention of Balfour) had breached the Charleston articles of capitulation and the laws of nations. Offering a thinly veiled threat of retaliation, Washington "flattered himself" that Clinton would interpose his authority and intervene to prevent a repetition "of measures, which cannot fail to aggravate the rigors of war, and to involve the most disagreeable consequences."[42]

When Cornwallis read Washington's protest, forwarded to him from Clinton, who may have requested more detail for the sake of clarity, he responded, "In regard to [Washington's] complaint . . . of the removal of some of the citizens from Charlestown to St. Augustine, I have only to say that the insolence of their behaviour, the threats with which they in the most daring manner endeavoured to intimidate our friends, the infamous falsehoods which they propagated through the town and country, and the correspondence which they constantly kept up with the enemy, rendered it indispensably necessary that they should either be closely confined or be sent out of the province. The milder measure was adopted, and they were sent, with every convenience which their situation would admit of, to a better climate than South Carolina."[43]

Before his receiving notification of the arrests from Congress, it is entirely possible that Washington knew of the Charleston exiles from another source. Maj. John André, adjutant general of the British army, wrote to Washington a day after his own capture in the aftermath of Benedict Arnold's defection to the British, and only a week before he would be hanged by the Continental Army for being a spy. André hoped to use the South Carolinians as leverage for good treatment: "I take the Liberty to mention the Condition of some Gentlemen at Charlestown who being either on parole or under protection were engaged in a Conspiracy against us. Tho' their Situation is not Similar, they are objects who may be Set in Exchange for me or are persons whom the Treatment I receive might affect." His plea was ignored but proves that the arrest of the patriots was at least common knowledge at Clinton's headquarters.[44]

Chapter 5

A Rather Dull Life of Restricted Routine

The prospect of ordinary conversation with the exiles was not rejected by one unusual segment of St. Augustine's heterogeneous population, namely those loosely referred to as the "Minorcans." As a group, and only recently arrived, they constituted the largest single infusion of permanent settlers in the East Florida capital. Their story is worth noting, especially as it places focus on one Dr. Andrew Turnbull, a very colorful figure who became particularly fond of the Charleston exiles as people, if not as supporters of independence. Turnbull was a Scotsman, properly trained as a medical doctor but full of energy and schemes for additional success in life. When the British gained possession of East Florida and found it virtually emptied of its former Hispanic population, they encouraged land speculation. Turnbull was among those who applied for and received land grants.[1]

Having lived several years in Mediterranean countries, Turnbull decided to seek cheap labor from that part of the world to work his own private colony that he would name New Smyrna, located some sixty miles south of St. Augustine on the ominously named Mosquito Inlet. In 1767, thirteen years before the Charlestonians came to St. Augustine, and with the financial backing of London capitalists, Turnbull organized the importing of some fifteen hundred workers, among them "a large company of starving Minorcans," from the island of Minorca in the western Mediterranean Sea, a property that England had acquired from Spain during the War of Spanish Succession.[2]

By 1776 Turnbull's New Smyrna scheme had failed, and upward of four hundred Minorcans trekked to St. Augustine, where they were received with open arms by Governor Tonyn, who had long been at odds with Turnbull over a variety of issues. Turnbull himself also settled in St. Augustine and took an interest in politics, eventually attaining a seat on the provincial governor's council. He was very much a presence in the small town and was fascinated by the Americans, who in turn profited from the more cooperative attitudes of the not-so-British Minorcans.[3]

By the time the exiles arrived in St. Augustine, most of the Minorcans had given up any agricultural pursuits beyond kitchen gardening. Some were enrolled in the militia despite Governor Tonyn's suspicion of their loyalty. Throughout the town they were principally present as petty shopkeepers, artisans, proprietors of little taverns, and fishermen, and they had no objection to the exiles. For instance the Carolinians gave business to one of these, a cobbler, who with his children lived in his father-in-law's house because his wife had died in the failed New Smyrna colony. The Charlestonians also befriended, but had no occasion to patronize, an eighteen-year-old Minorcan carpenter who had lost his mother, two sisters, and two brothers at New Smyrna before moving to St. Augustine in 1777 with his father, who died the next year. As would have been the case in any other town, the Charleston exiles were learning that the more they found out, the more interesting the place became. And as would have been true in any other population, they found that theirs were not the only troubles in the world—perhaps not even the worst.[4]

There was, however, a different sense of confusing newness in the old Florida town, as the struggles between Whigs and Tories had brought some eight thousand new refugees to East Florida in the two years before 1780. Many of these refugees brought their slaves with them, and in addition the British troops fighting their way northward from South Carolina would sometimes send their enslaved to Florida, so the black population soared along with the white. St. Augustine, therefore, was well stocked with people, many of whom had turbulent and intriguing stories to tell—but that did not mean there was much for the Charlestonians to do, especially when the townspeople were so specifically instructed not to hold discourse with them.[5]

Beyond the novel interruption of the first delivery of government rations on September 20, the Charlestonians faced a rather dull life of restricted routine. A sloop brought letters to nearly everyone on September 25, and another arrived from Charleston on September 29. Instead of mail this latter one brought tales from the crew, including exciting but discouraging stories of encounters with pirates at sea during which a fresh batch of letters intended for the exiles had been jettisoned into the brine. To the great delight of William Johnson and Edward McCrady, an unsolicited letter did make it through from the generous Charleston loyalist Capt. Thomas Buckel, enclosing an unlimited letter of credit on a St. Augustine merchant. Accompanying instructions extended its benefits to any other of the prisoners who might be in need. But fortunately for the generous donor, there was little in St. Augustine upon which to spend money.[6]

One of the Charleston exiles was a raucous fifty-five-year-old Whig named Peter Timothy, a Philadelphia immigrant from Holland with ties to Benjamin Franklin that had led him into the printing business in Charleston. From 1740 until May 1780, Timothy had edited and managed his family's paper, the *Gazette of the State of South-Carolina,* until it was seized by the British and renamed the *Royal South-Carolina Gazette.* His political opinions and his newspaper became intensely partisan as he progressed through the various patriot committees and subcommittees: the Sons of Liberty, the General Committee of Correspondence, the Committee of Observation, the Council of Safety, the Committee of Ninety-Nine, and the Provincial Congress.[7]

Of course since the British occupation, Charleston's official news was solely reported in the loyalist-owned newspapers the *Royal South-Carolina Gazette* and the *South-Carolina and American General Gazette* (later continued as the *Royal Gazette*). News items of primary interest to the rebels or their families were either absent or succinctly curtailed in the Charleston accounts. For example, on Wednesday, September 20, 1780, the *South-Carolina and American General Gazette* lightly noted, "The *Fidelity* transport, with the prisoners mentioned in our paper of the 6th instant, is arrived at St. Augustine." No further explanation or elaboration was offered.[8]

More unpalatable to those prisoners, had they seen it, would have been the published notice to those Charlestonians, including themselves and their families, who were affected by Cornwallis's announcement of property sequestration (government seizure). This was yet another strategically deployed hardship employed by the British to reward their friends and punish the opposition. The property of the revolutionaries included homes and acreage, crops, livestock, slaves, and personal possessions with only a fraction of the proceeds to be allotted for the subsistence of the families targeted by this deliberately cruel oppression. More than a hundred estates were seized, including more than five thousand enslaved persons.[9]

Falling into the hands of the British would not necessarily become a freedom windfall for the enslaved persons affected by sequestration. A few gained liberty by running away, but far more remained in submission to servitude. At war's end large numbers of them were evacuated to St. Augustine, Jamaica, St. Lucia, and other British sugar islands in the West Indies. Those sent to the Caribbean often wound up on sugar plantations, while those sent to East Florida labored at cultivating rice, indigo, and corn or perhaps the production of tar and turpentine from the pine forests.[10]

What the redcoats could not appropriate for their own use, they sold. Commissioner of sequestration John Cruden, a loyalist merchant from North Carolina, took his job seriously, as is evident in the notices of public sale ("estates real and personal") published in the newspapers. Such decrees indeed had their effect, and many men in the city were eventually forced to submit, accepting British protection in order to work gainfully and keep their own families from destitution or, in many cases, simply to preserve their own property rights.[11]

A number of South Carolinians, having reconsidered their loyalty, were desirous to show every mark of allegiance and attachment in their power to His Majesty's person and government—since such persons accordingly received certificates entitling them to exercise their trades and professions along with other loyal citizens of Charleston. Most of these were tradesmen who had to maintain their families, and a considerable number were foreigners; but a few represented families of influence who took the king's protection to save their estates. They included Col. Daniel Horry, who had fought the British but since given up hope of patriot victory, and prominent attorney and planter Col. Charles Pinckney. Conversely the list of sequestered properties by the end of the year is remarkable proof of how many indomitable landowners would not sign, a veritable roll call of gentry even two centuries later: Gibbes, Savage, Shubrick, Vanderhorst, Hutson, Parker, Drayton, Legaré, Cattell, Middleton, Goodwin, and Ziegler, among many others.[12]

Meanwhile in St. Augustine the gentlemen, so disgusted by having had to renew paroles and so haughty about being "treated with indignities unsuitable to their former rank and condition," were in fact having a distinctly better time than were their families and friends back home. Problems in East Florida were minor by comparison with the upheavals in Charleston. Along with ignorance of news, the exiles were plagued by disappointment, boredom, and resignation in what seemed an irrelevant and unentertaining place. It was becoming obvious to the enterprising patriots that their habits of socially and politically engaged living did not thrive in what was essentially a military-post town. The Minorcans seemed to enjoy making a living, but most everyone else—whether considering St. Augustine their primary address or just passing through on some temporary banishment (as from the Canary Islands, for instance)—appeared content to be idly dependent on Crown subsidies of one sort or another.[13]

It did not go unnoticed by the authorities that the Minorcans were a bit friendlier to the patriots than the St. Augustinians, who feared Governor Tonyn more than the Minorcans did. Tonyn himself was aware of the Minorcans' independent streak, particularly those in his militia. "There are several Minorcans," he wrote, "and I have my doubts as to their loyalty, being of Spanish and French extraction, and of the Roman Catholic religion." It was a singular twist that their being of Spanish and Roman Catholic extraction should have made them more sympathetic to the American revolutionaries, but in the contortion of loyalties, it was their dislike of the British governor that made them more lenient with the exiles.[14]

The town was not without a few individuals of energy and means. Mann and Penman have been mentioned already. Another case is the Rev. John Forbes, who as priest of the parish of St. Peter had at his disposal the rectory and garden on the main plaza, which he rented to the second largest of the three groups of exiles. The residence came with his ecclesiastical post (he was also deputy chaplain of the garrison), but he did not need it. He owned other properties in town, and he most preferred to live on his plantation west of town, "an elegant, beautiful and convenient location" that he called Mount Forbes. The Reverend Mr. Forbes, a Scot, had been sent to St. Augustine in 1764 at the age of twenty-four at the urging of his cousin, the new governor of East Florida, James Grant.[15]

Forbes must have been a great character, not ambitious in European terms (else why remain in such a remote and isolated situation?) but evidently pleased to be a big fish in this small Florida pond. Forbes was the principal and sometimes only cleric of the colony, and he remained in that position while holding other posts: judge of the vice-admiralty court, acting chief justice, assistant judge of the courts of general sessions and of common pleas, and member and treasurer of the governor's council. As his ecclesiastical salary was paid directly by the British parliament and was insufficient for the support of his family, his parishioners were not particularly critical of him for taking on these other employments.[16]

In fact, besides his tending to the priestly and secular offices, he was also a substantial planter who had managed to gain ownership of six thousand acres of farmland, some of which he efficiently worked with a force of only sixty slaves. He had large property holdings in the town, which during the Revolutionary years he rented both to loyalist refugees and to enemy prisoners on parole. An archconservative, he actually declared from the bench "that he is not bound by the Letter of the Law," for "in these Times, *that* is Law which is most for His Majesty's Service."[17]

Unsurprisingly Tonyn thought highly of the priest and personally declared to Lord Germain his own reliance on Forbes's "zeal and affection for his Majesty's service," recommending the clergyman "in a particular manner" and asserting that he was "warmly interested in his behalf." By contrast Turnbull, who was out of favor with Governor Tonyn but also a member of the council, serving as its secretary, described the priest as "a Man of a most Infamous Character in many Respects"—a bit vague, as criticism goes, but certainly not a compliment. Be that as it may, Forbes was not above renting St. Peter's rectory to the South Carolina exiles.[18]

The Charlestonians' reduced existence contrasted sharply with that of the local men of means in St. Augustine, who in another time and place would have been (or had been, in the case of John Moultrie) their equals and social cohorts. The exiles had to concern themselves with matters to which they had never before paid much attention. Milk being a rather difficult and expensive commodity to purchase in town, some of the Charleston gentlemen bought a cow and an eight-month-old calf, which they housed on the Forbes property. This guaranteed milk for breakfast and coffee in the evening, and though the price was dear, they figured that they could sell the animal at a profit upon departure, whenever that might be. Others undertook to entertain themselves with gardening, especially on the Mann property, where the yards were extensive.[19]

At first the exiles were not allowed access to newspapers for their idle review, as the authorities enjoyed tantalizing them with fictional accounts of the world. Moreover they were harassed by the predictably despotic treatment of persons in positions of little power as well as by indignities from the highest officers. For example they were officially and deliberately misinformed of several supposedly decisive battles represented as having destroyed all chance of success by the American armies and were told to prepare themselves for a fearsome and inevitable fate as vanquished rebels. But they had more faith in their patriotism and trusted that though they were kept confusedly in the dark, they were not forgotten in revolutionary circles.[20]

As mentioned above, the troubles of the British officer Maj. John André revealed that both Clinton and Washington were aware of the exiles' being in St. Augustine. In fact the André story would seriously perturb British inhabitants of St. Augustine and potentially could bring dire consequences to the Americans. On the second day of October, the Continental Army executed André for being complicit in the treachery of Maj. Gen. Benedict Arnold. André was caught behind American lines, court-martialed on charges of espionage, and sentenced to hang. Before the execution the British had indeed threatened that if André died they would retaliate by hanging a prominent American patriot. Lieutenant Colonel Glazier, who had been commandant of St. Augustine's castle for less than a year, was still enjoying his role as a petty tyrant and seized the opportunity to discomfit the exiles, telling them that the blood of the brave but unfortunate André would be required at their hands.[21]

According to Alexander Garden, Glazier spread the word that it was Gadsden who would probably be selected to pay for André's death. Yet even this threat did not break the old patriot's indomitable spirit. A heroic and rather fanciful version of this threat has Gadsden stoically announcing to the commandant that "to die for my country I am always prepared; and I would rather ascend the scaffold than purchase with my life her dishonor."[22]

Gadsden never had to make that ascent, as Glazier never made good on his threat, which was probably no more than a mean bluff. Whatever Gadsden actually said, he was evidently right in his assessment of the commandant's bravado. As he later told Washington, "My not being mentioned in the capitulation gave them an opportunity to affect treating me with rigour and contempt." What they really wanted was the pleasure of seeing him break down and sign the terms of the St. Augustine parole. What he wanted was to make the most effective show possible. "I thought it a duty I owed to the general cause to refuse to the last giving a second parole, that I might be as a standing protest against such outrageous, tyrannical conduct."[23]

The British in St. Augustine celebrated October 9 as the one-year anniversary of their important victory at Savannah over the combined Franco-American armies of Lt. Gen. Charles Henri Hector, comte d'Estaing, and Maj. Gen. Benjamin Lincoln, a battle that at the time seemed to assure English control of Savannah and southern Georgia. "The day was distinguished here, by the shew of Colours at Sun Rising, and Triumphant situation, on the Vessells in the harbour," described diarist Josiah Smith, "also by the firing of Cannon at noon, with a Royal Salute of 21 Guns from the Castle, a Dining together of Officers and Inhabitants, also a Ball at night for the Ladies." Not unexpectedly the Charlestonians were not invited to the festivities, and if invited they certainly would have declined.[24]

And they certainly were not impressed. "But to Crown all," Smith continued, "a truly ridiculous company, consisting mostly of Officers, headed by their Veteran Commandant, all of them seemingly much heated by liquor and attended by their Regimental Musick &c Paraded the Street on the following morning between 7 & 8 O'Clock, who in passing by our habitation, Insulted us with the tune of Yankey Doodle &c the which tune has also been often Struck up by the relief Guards in their Marching to & from the Castle, doubtless by way of Insult, and in derision to our Company of suffering Americans." In case the exiles failed to realize they were being affronted, another presentation of mystery pumpkins appeared, ten this time. Bemused by the obscure symbolism, the patriots accepted the fruits, which they thought inedible but found decorative for use at their own dinners—"a good garnish to our table."[25]

Perhaps aroused by disdain for the overripe pumpkins, this same day the group decided to apply to Charleston for a number of articles that they could not find in St. Augustine. They drew up a list for Messrs. Fisher and Blake, their home agents, and carefully calculated the probable costs and arrangements for payment. A few requests were so practical that it is surprising they could not be taken care of locally, such as having a decent quantity of soap and a dozen each of cotton and hemp fishing lines (the latter especially for catching bass), along with six dozen fishhooks.[26]

Clearly they could use a little more diversion and elegance in their idle living. They asked for two hundred-pound boxes of Carolina candles, six pounds of starch, butter, rice, corn, a hundred-pound bag of the best cocoa, a barrel of good onions, a ten-gallon keg of good vinegar, six dozen full-grown chickens with as many laying hens among them as possible, two gross of fresh eggs packed up in fine salt, a Cheshire cheese, six quarts of sweet oil, twelve bottles of mustard, and a supply of libations to mellow the candlelight: a hogshead of Old Jamaica rum, a quarter-pipe of port wine, a barrel of the best porter (dark beer), a five-gallon case of French brandy, with a gross of velvet corks. To accompany these items they requested twelve packs of playing cards. The earlier-expressed desire to retire to their apartments and improve themselves by reading is not reflected in this list.[27]

If the British authorities would not or could not provide vessels and shipping for such an order despite having previously agreed to do so, the Charleston agents were instructed to ship the desired goods on the first two vessels headed for Florida and to ask special permission to have those ships protected against British cruisers. Thinking to further their cause, Thomas Ferguson and Richard Hutson wrote on behalf of all of the captive gentlemen to Lieutenant Colonel Balfour in Charleston, complaining about the scarcity of provisions in St. Augustine and reminding him of his promise to pay for vessels to send "useful Articles." To crown the case of their deprivations, they submitted to Balfour that "since our arrival we have not been served with any [palatable] Rum." In conclusion they used the occasion to remind him that "as we have been sent to this place for reasons of Policy, and not for any violation of Parole, we flatter ourselves we shall not be thought Troublesome or unreasonable in requesting your attention to our situation."[28]

A few of the local inhabitants soon dared to go a step beyond merely being friendly and polite. Arredondo de Arrara, Francsico Sanchez, Jesse Fish, and Fishe's mysterious friend Luciano de Herrera occasionally sent fruit and other acceptable presents that were much appreciated. Andrew Turnbull and Edward Penman were among the most obliging, regularly saving the English newspapers they received by various ship arrivals and quietly passing them on to the American gentlemen for perusal.[29]

Even though such papers contained little solace for the rebels, they had to be read sub-rosa, as the military regime attempted to control all news allowed to their prisoners. Sometimes abandoned papers could be discreetly inspected in local taverns. There was no public library in St. Augustine. One could borrow a book now and then from a planter, lawyer, merchant, craftsman, or clergyman or purchase reading material in a single small shop, but St. Augustine possessed no literary society. There was no local newspaper printed in all of East Florida until after the exiles left.[30]

Turnbull's apparent affinity for the Charleston exiles counted as one more reason for Governor Tonyn to dislike and distrust him. Tonyn complained to Balfour and Cornwallis of Turnbull's behavior toward the rebels, telling Balfour that Turnbull, "under the colour of his profession, although two rebel physicians are prisoners and [there is] no sickness amongst them, passes daily some hours, and, frequently [appears] on the parade with them." From this he concludes, "I am convinced his behavior proceeds not only from principle but from other reasons."[31]

As a result of the relative dearth of information from home and abroad, it was all the more appreciated on October 10 when a schooner made it past the privateers and delivered a number of letters from Charleston. Josiah Smith received a half-dozen himself, from which he learned that his wife, Mary, had safely given birth to a daughter three weeks before. This was quite a relief in a time when maternal and infant mortality was high; hearty congratulations were undoubtedly received from his peers. But not all of the news was good. A young nephew had died after a languishing illness, and eight of those enslaved on the Austin plantation had contracted the dreaded smallpox (of which, fortunately, only one had died). Of course responses were penned immediately even though for the time being there was no ship to deliver them.[32]

Boredom continued among the gentlemen, who increasingly realized that the refinements of their previous lifestyles could not reasonably be demanded in this provincial outpost. The local Greek and Minorcan fishermen had discovered the Charlestonians' requirements of eating much and well and had dramatically inflated the price of their catch. This in turn caused "much murmurring among the Inhabitants," whose economy was threatened. The response of the Carolinians was to get the commissary's permission to allow their slaves to go out on their own to catch fish and harvest oysters, to which end they purchased a handsome cypress canoe (at five pounds) and sent off for the abovementioned hooks and lines.[33]

The rest of the week contained no excitement other than the bits of war news brought indirectly by one ship from Jamaica and another from England. By October 14 the wind had so long blown from the northeast that several ships bound for Charleston had been obliged to cancel their trips, preventing the return of any messages back to South Carolina. Smith was sure that lack of communication would cause uneasiness at home. However there would be many more boats than were at first apparent. As the year bore on, the exiles came to realize that Charleston was really the center of the East Florida trade. Of the sixty-odd vessels that entered or cleared the port while they were there, some thirty-five were sailing from or to Charleston—knowledge that served only to add to the frustration of the men's captivity.[34]

A wet October 15 was the fourth Sunday the captives had spent in St. Augustine, and being excluded by the limits of their paroles from the religious observances held on the military post, but wary of the parish services on the wrong side of their western limitations, they had not yet attended any formal service. There were two clergymen among the prisoners, who in order to offer up "prayer and adoration to the giver of all good gifts to man" arranged to use the house of the ever-accommodating Mann. James Hamden Thomson, the younger of the two clerics, was a sometime Presbyterian preacher, member of the Congregational Church in Charleston, and schoolmaster. It was Thomson who first officiated and "afforded the consolations of religion to his brethren in exile."[35]

The predominantly Anglican group appreciated that Thomson was liberal enough to conform to the prayers and liturgy of the *Book of Common Prayer* of the Church of England, "not altering any part, but omitting such as was opposed to the interests and feelings of his brother prisoners." They "met together in Solemn Assembly, and enjoyed the very great happiness of Religious Worship," which consisted of "selected Prayers from the Prayer book of the Church of England," a couple of psalms sung, and the reading from a printed Anglican collection of a "well pen'd Sermon of Doctor [Jonathan] Mayhews, no way tending towards Civil or Religious Sedition." This custom they decided to pursue for all subsequent Sundays as long as they were to remain in St. Augustine, "in the most peaceable and solemn manner that our circumstances will admit."[36]

Meantime the weather outside was neither peaceable nor solemn. For the next four days, the rains and consistent winds from the northeast afflicted the town. The Carolinians had already accustomed themselves to the harsher truths noted by the naturalist Bernard Romans five years before, who wrote to the Earl of Hillsborough that "dampness or discoloring of plaister and wainscot, the soon moulding of bread, moistness of spunge, dissolution of loaf sugar, rusting of metals and rotting of furniture, are certain marks of a bad air; now, every one of these marks . . . is more to be seen in St. Augustine than in any place I ever was at."[37]

Unbeknownst to St. Augustine's inhabitants, the bad weather system that was impeding shipping was part of the destructive and deadly 1780 Atlantic hurricane season. The rain worsened, and the winds reached gale force. A storm surge on October 19 raised the incoming tide several feet higher than usual, flooding the lanes as far as 150 feet from the bay. The group in the State House was above the flood level, high enough and dry, but unfortunately water surrounded the front of the large wooden house located on the northwest corner of Charlotte and Hypolita Streets, one street back from the bay—the house occupied by the largest group of patriots.[38]

The flood persisted for two days and damaged the fence, washed away a good deal of the yard, and broke into the garden they had just recently planted. It was very disappointing, said occupant Josiah Smith, because the garden "had given us a fair prespect of supplying our Table very soon with lettuce, Carrots, Raddish, Mustard, Scallions, Shelots, Cabbage and other Greens, so that, as 'twere in a moment our expectatons were cut off.—much damage has been done to others, and 'tis thought that the Crop of Oranges will be much hurt, as the Trees appear to be blasted, both fruit and leaves changing their colour and continually dropping to the Ground."[39]

Chapter 6

Robbery, Religious Differences, and New Arrivals

The damage to the town caused by the October storm was not sufficient to prevent a Friday-night ball for the British officers and their mercantile and political society. On such occasions, and at any other of the frequent balls and assemblies in this isolated post-town, the music was necessarily provided by the military. The dancing depended, repetitiously, on the few qualified ladies in town, who, as previously noted, had their ready choice of partners in the heavily male society. Like its predecessor, this event turned into another all-nighter, and once again the early morning of Saturday was greeted by a loose parade "well-warmed with Liquor" and attended by fife and drum and other instruments, singing their way through the streets of the town.[1]

The "company of Serenaders," who included the governor's nephew, once again "changed their merriment into Insult" when they neared the residences of the revolutionaries, striking up "Yankee Doodle," brandishing more pumpkins, and throwing a derisory orange or two at the South Carolinians' houses. It appears that overripe pumpkins in eighteenth-century East Florida carried the same connotation that rotten eggs and tomatoes did in twentieth-century vaudeville. At the roll call that evening, the Americans presumed to complain about the revelers, describing the "Drunken Frolick" to Commissary Brown. They did not yet realize that out-of-control revels were to be frequent, fueled by the brandy, rum, "shrub" (citrus juices with rum), cider, and the wine that the many public houses dispensed.[2]

They expected that Brown would obtain a proper apology, but in this they were sorely disappointed. All that the complainers got for satisfaction was a hollow disclaimer: that if the gentlemen found the behavior rude, they had been "unintendedly disobliged." The exiles took even greater offense at such lack of sympathy but had no recourse beyond observing to themselves "how much more like Gentlemen" the British would have been if only they had put "their Names to a few lines on Paper" and "declared their Repentance of such Indecent and unprovoked Conduct towards Strangers and Prisoners on Parole."[3]

Brown probably agreed at heart, but his post called for at least a modicum of severity—especially since the roll calls took place in full sight of the governor's adjacent residence. He was simply not in a position to appear too soft or openly sympathetic, and cases of this sort of trivial complaint actually gave him opportunity to emulate the meanness of the governor and commandant without really hurting anyone. It was good for his official reputation. Notwithstanding, the exiles came to acknowledge Brown as the one "whose kindness towards us, and Civilitys experienced in his family, . . . far exceeded [those of] any other Person in this place."[4]

The exiles also learned that St. Augustine's constables had a difficult and dangerous job and that they, the exiles themselves, were not immune to criminal activity. One night thieves made their way into the big residence. They had plenty of time for mischief—in the dark David Ramsay mistook them for other Charlestonians out to play some trick on their confederates. Finally realizing that the intruders' purposes were not friendly, Ramsay managed to chase them out and lock the door, only to find the next morning that the burglars had made off with a pair of his personal silk hose. They had also taken a pair of shoes and buckles belonging to Richard Hutson, a striped silk gown, two handkerchiefs, two penknives, a memo book, and a pair of shoes and buckles of James Thomson's, Anthony Toomer's shrimp net, and a forequarter of mutton with most of the knives and forks from the dining room. Especially irritating was that the robbers stole volume 2 of William Robertson's three-volume *History of Scotland,* a book which was on loan to its Charleston reader. The exiles never discovered the identities of the culprits.[5]

On October 25 the exiles had reason to believe they might soon be receiving mail. Lookouts at the fort fired two guns to announce the arrival of a sloop. The rains had cleared enough for the ship to be seen, but the roughness of the sea prevented any pilot from rowing out to lead her in, so there was no news from home. This frustration continued for weeks, worsened by the fact that requested supplies had not arrived from Charleston. It seemed that almost every day brought reports of foiled attempts at docking yet another ship.[6]

On October 28 the weather provided an exception by allowing a schooner to receive an initial load of goods from the Liverpool sloop that had been sighted just two days earlier. The next day happened to be a Sunday, and instead of encouraging the good fortune of supplies for the town, the proper Charlestonians were quick to scorn the British for disrespecting the divinely commanded Sabbath rest by going for a second load. Perhaps the Sabbath's Lord took the American view; the partly unloaded ship fell to leeward and had to wait for favorable winds to help set it straight. Three days later another schooner attempted to take a second load, but it also became grounded on the bar. Its starboard waist was so "beat in" that its contents suffered from much leaking.[7]

It was November 6 before the weather finally allowed a ship to set out for Charleston. All of the exiles took advantage of the opportunity and sent a great many letters home to family, friends, and business associates. Since the departure of the last ship carrying outgoing mail, Josiah Smith had written four more letters to his wife and three to his brother-in-law and attorney, Edward Darrell, all regarding family affairs and commercial matters. He could only hope the ship would be able "to reach Charles Town by at least Thursday next [three days at sea]," recorded Smith, "and thereby rejoice the hearts of our Friends, who must be very anxious to hear from us, after a silence of better than Six Weeks."[8]

The irregularity of shipped mail added to the dearth of information that was also felt at home and led not only to the spread of rumors but also, perhaps, in some instances the sowing of deliberate disinformation. In a December letter written from his camp in the northeastern part of the South Carolina backcountry, Gov. John Rutledge informed his state's delegates to the Continental Congress that he had been "told that Mr. Gadsden died, in the Castle at Augustine, (but I can't say how far that Intelligence may be depended on)." Of course, as governor in exile, Rutledge's own threads of communication were tenuous at best; therefore it is impossible to know when he learned that his lieutenant governor and erstwhile political opponent was actually still alive.[9]

When at last a large ship did manage to traverse the bar into St. Augustine's harbor proper, it was occasion for great rejoicing. After heaving about in the bay for a week and a half on account of the heavy seas and a strong lee current, the twenty-gun letter-of-marque sloop *Governour Tonyn* finally accomplished this feat on November 3. The event occasioned a "grand Parade" in the center of town. The ship fired a seventeen-gun salute that was returned by five guns from the Castle. Three-cheer ceremonies ruled the day, and decorative flags and pennants added to the festivities. After a week in port, the ship hosted a grand dinner for the officers and leading citizens of St. Augustine.[10]

As expected, the Charlestonians were excluded. Governor Tonyn boated out to begin the pleasures at about two o'clock, boosted by a seventeen-gun salute from the Castle and received by yet another from the ship. A sympathetic neighboring ship at bay added five more shots. Additional salutes were fired in the afternoon and evening. The party did not break up until about midnight, and the Charlestonians, for whom noting the occasion had been the principal interest of the day, commented in sour-grapes fashion that the British no doubt were going to bed with heavy heads and overcharged stomachs, perhaps even with some ringing in their ears.[11]

Sunday, November 12, was the exiles' fifth Sabbath of divine service in their own dwellings. Among them was a Church of England clergyman, the Reverend John Lewis, who was formerly rector of St. Paul's Parish in Colleton County, Charleston District. Balfour, the British commandant in Charleston, had officially deprived him of his priestly functions in that city, so he was reluctant to perform them in St. Augustine. After three Sundays of no services and four of lay leadership using pious selections from sermon books, Lewis was finally prevailed upon to resume his priestly function and officiate at Mann's house. At last the patriots were able to enjoy an original sermon, and the group expected to profit from his ministrations from then on. Though no spy was present to listen unsympathetically, Lewis was careful not to preach in any way that might offend the authorities. Or so he thought.[12]

Word got out that Lewis had preached on Genesis 43:14: "If I be bereaved of my children, I am bereaved," and Governor Tonyn was annoyed at Lewis for choosing this text. Meditation on how sad it was to be away from one's children struck the governor as a slippery slope toward sedition, implying by extension that such church services were "agreeable to their rebellious principles . . . highly injurious to his Majesty's government . . . of a seditious tendency, and an infringement of [the Charlestonians'] pledge of honor." A second rumor arose that Lewis had spoken (perhaps in the evening) on 1 Kings 21:3: "The Lord forbid it me that I should give the inheritance of my fathers unto thee." This was interpreted by the governor to imply that Britain, by God, was never going to get South Carolina back for itself. Much to the little congregation's surprise, on the following Friday Commissary Brown brought word that the governor officially disapproved of their private worship and that therefore such practice should be discontinued immediately.[13]

The righteous exiles, irate at the tyrannical verbal order and ever sure of themselves, replied that as gentlemen they were not obliged to honor oral dictates from subordinates and that they had every intention of continuing in their usage until such time as prohibition was served on them in writing from a proper authority. Poor Mr. Brown, the go-between, consulted the governor and returned the next day with the unhappy assignment of promulgating, apologetically, the text dictated by his superior, from whom the patriots' impertinence had triggered a quick response.[14]

"Having been informed that the Rebel Prisoners have very improperly held private meetings for the purpose of performing Divine Service agreeably to their rebellious principles," huffed Tonyn, "and as such proceedings are thought highly injurious to His Majesty's Government, and of seditious tendency, and an infringement of their pledge of honour: I desire you will acquaint them that such meetings will not be allowed, and that seats will be provided for their reception in the Parish Church [St. Peter's], where it is expected they will observe the utmost decency." Tonyn also ordered the Reverend Mr. Lewis to be confined in the Castle for the duration of the exile.[15]

The privately organized religious meetings therefore ceased, replaced by official allowance of decent seats in the Parish Church. Did the Charlestonians take as progress this new invitation to inclusion in the parish worship? No, they were rather insulted to be told like children to behave in church, and they were not about to join in any prayers for King George, especially those petitions that he might "vanquish and overcome all his enemies." Echoing the complaints of the Declaration of Independence, they replied that the invitation was "an Insult upon our understanding," since it would necessarily mean prayers for the "destruction or disappointment of our Brethren and friends or implore Success to a Man that has countinanced every kind of Oppression & Cruelty towards our connections, and all with the view of enslaving us & our Posterity, to whom we have sworn, that we will never be Subject, while we can have the power of remaining Free Citizens of the United States of America."[16]

Smith, a Presbyterian himself, was the only patriot whose contemporaneous notes and commentary about the exile experience survive. As one who himself occasionally preached, he picked up the emphatic style of his abandoned pulpit and wrote of this matter in his diary. If he and his fellows were to attend the British church, he felt sure, they would "be insulted with sermons calculated to affront us." It would be better to spend their Sabbaths worshiping silently as best they could by reading and meditation at their own dwellings. The governor's decision, he concluded, was "an Act neither Charitable in its nature nor pious in its intention, totally unworthy of the Christian Character, and even short of Heathen Tenderness."[17]

All they asked was to do their religious duty, "to spend some part of every Sabbath in holy adoration of that Divine Being who . . . in tender mercy supplies all our wants." The irreligious part of the inhabitants of St. Augustine, said Smith (whose words were prescient of modern times), spent too much time in neglect of church ordinances, "openly sporting away by Land and by Water those hours that ought to command their Serious devotions." Furthermore, he insisted, the proceedings of the South Carolina exiles had never been seditious, and in fact his fellow sufferers had carefully avoided in their readings, prayers, and sermons anything that could be misconstrued in that way. As for trying to convert the locals, they had never invited or even been visited by an inhabitant of St. Augustine during any of their Sabbath assemblies.[18]

Not long after they declined the invitation to attend services at St. Peter's, the American patriots received a surprise present of a thousand sweet oranges from the sympathetic Jesse Fish, whose plantation El Vergel (meaning *orchard* or *abundant garden*) on nearby Anastasia Island produced an abundant crop.

The hardworking and enthusiastic Fish's island escape had become Florida's first flourishing orange plantation. (A report from four years earlier indicates that in 1776 he shipped a total of sixty-five thousand oranges to markets as far away as London.) The gift was only a coincidence and had nothing to do with the exiles' refusal to hear Rev. Mr. Forbes's preaching, but it did come from one of those people Tonyn found to be dangerously modern in political ideas. The British authorities raised no objection to the fruit offering, even though the donor made it clear to the prisoners that the gift was sent "as a Testimony of his regard for, and kind inclination towards them."[19]

The limited patronage of Fish was certainly well received by the Charleston patriots, but history has treated him with ambivalence. Originally from New York, Fish lived for more than half a century in colonial St. Augustine under both Spanish and British rule. He had gained a reputation as "a sinister figure, an insidious [fellow] characteristically involved in contraband commerce, sedition, and illicit land transactions," who made money as an unscrupulous land speculator, slaver, smuggler, usurer, and cunning crook. His critics also accused him of performing espionage for England and Spain and claimed that he served as a double agent during the Seven Years' War.[20]

Suspicious activities aside, Fish was also known in some quarters as "the savior of St. Augustine" for having smuggled food and other provisions at great personal and financial risk in 1762–63 when the town was destitute and on the verge of starvation. It is entirely possible that both characterizations are correct. And along the way he became the leading exporter of Florida citrus—untold thousands of the sweetest oranges and hundreds of barrels of orange juice. During the colonial era, only the kings of Spain and England controlled more East Florida acreage than did Jesse Fish.[21]

For the Charleston patriots, another sympathizer in St. Augustine was Fish's friend Luciano de Herrera, who evidence reveals actually was a spy for Spain while the British held East Florida. Herrera was one of the few Spaniards remaining in St. Augustine after the exodus of 1763. He stayed on because of his strong friendship with Fish and also because, like Fish, he was involved in disposing of Spanish property. Both reasons led him to be a person of consequence during the British years. Governor Tonyn suspected him of espionage but was never able to catch him in the act, and in fact the governor's suspicions were correct; Herrera regularly sent reports to Havana. He became quite friendly with the Charlestonians during the fall of 1780 and was "discreetly obliging" when the situation allowed, but the exiles lost his amiable presence when Tonyn sent him away on an assignment to escort a dozen Spanish prisoners to Havana.[22]

Fish's oranges were greatly appreciated but eased the exiles' homesickness only a little. A note of despair entered their conversations as they began to suspect that the English were reluctant to negotiate any direct exchanges to have them sent homeward—this because by now the rebel prisoners were quite well acquainted with St. Augustine's topography, administration, and military disposition and could thus inform the Americans of the weaknesses of the isolated fort and town.[23]

On November 21 came unwelcome news in the form of a communiqué from Lieutenant Colonel Balfour in Charleston addressed specifically to Thomas Ferguson and Richard Hutson. Balfour notified them that contrary to the assertions made in their letter of October 9, he had never authorized a government vessel to convey supplies to them from Charleston in an ad hoc manner whenever they requested but that it was his intention to grant permits only when they were applied for, to carry such items only when ships happened to be leaving with provisions for St. Augustine's garrison.[24]

This letter was written by Balfour's executive officer, Lt. Charles Fraser of the Twenty-Third Regiment of Foot (the Royal Welsh Fusiliers), and carried none of Balfour's usual dismissive and vituperative tone. Fraser was also head of the military police, was in command of the jail and guards in Charleston, and was generally in charge of keeping good order. He later played a key role in a dramatic incident that involved Balfour, Lt. Col. Francis Rawdon, and Col. Isaac Hayne, a close friend and relative of several of the Charleston exiles. But now, whether Fraser softened the tenor of the message or not, Balfour threw the exiles a crumb by assuring them that he would order the commandant at St. Augustine to guarantee that they received their full rations, "and Rum if it can be done without hurting his Majesty's Service."[25]

Thus it appeared that the British in Charleston were confidently in control of the exiles' condition. London was satisfied that the banishment of patriots to St. Augustine had produced a salutary effect in keeping Charleston and South Carolina in line. Germain opined to Clinton that the example Cornwallis had made by removing "those taken in Charleston who had corresponded with the enemy" proved to the ungrateful rebels, who had enjoyed "that lenity which from principles of humanity has been too indiscriminately shown to them," that punishment would follow transgression.[26]

However Balfour in Charleston was not convinced that the desired outcome had been fully achieved, and he initiated another round of arrests and deportations. "I have . . . been obliged to take up some more of violent and principal men that were upon parole and to shipp them on board the *Sandwich* going as a convoy to St Augustine," he informed Cornwallis. "The necessity of this measure was evident to every person whom I consulted upon it and much pressed by Moncrieff and Simson [engineer Maj. James Moncrief and James Simpson]. The unweried assiduity with which they keep down every movement towards the success of our affairs, pains which they take to prevent every person over whom they have any influence to come in and become British subjects, is astonishing."[27]

Cornwallis fully agreed with Balfour that the earlier removal of identified revolutionary leaders from Charleston had not been enough to calm the city. Resistance in the South Carolina population was still tangible. By his orders more arrests were made on November 15, 1780, and a week later, on November 22, another vessel arrived off the bar from South Carolina. It was the same *Lord Sandwich* that, with its congenial crew and captain, had previously housed the original group of troublemakers.[28]

The closely censored *South-Carolina and American General Gazette* on the day of the arrests affected a hearsay attitude in announcing the occupational government's latest move: "We hear that the persons of several of the most dissatisfied of the inhabitants, prisoners on parole in Charleston, have this morning been secured. Experience has shown that many made the worst use of the indulgence granted them. Sound policy therefore forbids its being longer continued. Indeed, many are of opinion that had such a measure been adopted on a pretty extensive scale some time ago, the good consequences would be now generally felt."[29]

So once again the *Sandwich* carried some twenty-five more Charleston troublemakers to be housed in St. Augustine, and with them it brought new worries not only that so many heads of households had to be away from their families but also that this time the status of their property back home had become increasingly unclear. These insecurities were especially bleak during a fall season when a "very great Mortality among both Inhabitants and Soldiers" was reported in Charleston. The citizens so recently departed from that town were at least able to assure the first exiles that their families were well enough.[30]

The new shipload of revolutionaries included two North Carolina militiamen, Brig. Gen. Griffith Rutherford and Lt. Col. Elijah Isaacs, who were brought in on the schooner *Earl of Lincoln*. Rutherford had been captured at Camden on August 16, and Isaacs was taken by Tarleton at Fishing Creek two days later. They both were cast into the fort to suffer the same treatment as Gadsden, without the benefit of having his choice.[31]

This newly arrived group also included Arthur Middleton, a member of the Continental Congress whom Balfour considered "the most violent and traiterous of the rebell tribe." When Middleton joined Thomas Heyward Jr. and Edward Rutledge, all three of the South Carolina's living signers of the Declaration of Independence were now together in residence at St. Augustine (the fourth, Thomas Lynch, had died at sea the previous year).[32]

This stern action on the part of the British was manifestly worrisome to the families with absent fathers, and it was designed to enhance an atmosphere of conspiracy, treachery, and paranoia. From the time that the first cargo of patriots was shipped off from Charlestown, the prospect of St. Augustine was supposed to frighten Americans into finding British allegiance attractive. Citizens who delayed their submission were repeatedly threatened with banishment from their

Arthur Middleton. James B. Longacre's 1824 engraving from a drawing by Thomas Middleton after the 1771 painting by Benjamin West. From the Thomas Addis Emmet, Collection of Illustrations Relating to the American Revolution and Early United States History, The Miriam and Ira D. Wallach Division of Art, Prints and Photographs: Print Collection, The New York Public Library.

families and estates, and the plight of the St. Augustine exiles was proof that the threat was not an idle one.[33]

By contrast the righteous exiles already in St. Augustine were somewhat more relaxed because of their unavoidable ignorance. The friendship already existing between Edward McCrady and William Johnson had been well cemented during the first three months of their forced expedition together. One wonders if their fatherly reflections on the former's son (five years old at the time) and the latter's daughter (only two) contained any inkling of a marriage that would come about sixteen years later. At any rate, tired of residence as part of the State House twelve, they convinced two others to join them in renting a more private place, forming an additional "mess house."[34]

Hardly had this new household of four settled in when the arrival of the new gentlemen, their bondservants, and baggage from the *Sandwich* caused a small crisis in the town's prisoner-housing capacity. The number of "prisoners from Charleston on Parole" had now risen to sixty-three, and by November 25 they were all ashore. The generous response of the "Mess House of Johnson, McCrady & Co." was to take in four of the newly arrived. The resultant number of eight residents still seemed preferable to the more crowded State House arrangement.

A few days later, a separate group of eight took yet another mess house nearby, so the effect of a neighborhood environment was further enhanced.[35]

The gentlemen from Charleston were distressed to learn that the captain of the *Sandwich,* William Bett, had come under criticism in "some public Gazette" for being "a Person destitute of Humanity in the Treatment of those who were sent on board the *Sandwich*" the previous August. To refute the charges that impugned his reputation, they composed and signed a declaration complimenting the captain: "We think ourselves called upon as Men of honour to rescue from censure . . . a Character so undeserving of it as yours, and to declare that the whole of your Conduct and that of your Officers to every Gentleman on board, was regulated by the Rules of good manners and politeness."[36]

The declaration was signed by twenty-six of Bett's earlier passengers. The captain replied with thanks, stating that he appreciated the sincerity of the compliment, since he rested secure in his belief that no such publication could have occurred with their knowledge. "I claim no merit from it," Bett modestly said, "as I think it every Mans duty to Treat Gentlemen under his charge with Humanity."[37]

The captives observed from a distance another town celebration on November 30, the anniversary of the Feast of St. Andrew, patron saint of Scotland (St. Andrew's Day). A parade of the local St. Andrew's Society, their ranks swelled by the members of the Scottish Rite Masonic lodge, marched to a service at St. Peter's Church. Afterward the procession made its way to Brother Love's Coffee House, where the Scotsmen, according to Smith, sat down to "a good Fare, and to conclude the day with the Good Cheer [i.e., with libations] customary on such occasions." As usual the Charlestonians were not invited to the celebration, but any lingering disappointment was made up for by the arrival, two days later, of 172 gallons of "well Tasted West Indie rum"—given not as rations to be regularly expected in the future but as an allowance per direction of the commandant in Charleston, along with a promise of more to come in the future "if it can be spared from his Majesty of Great Britain's Troops in St. Augustine."[38]

Early on the morning of December 2, the North Carolina privateer brig *Bellona* of sixteen or eighteen guns and a crew of seventy ran aground while trying to escape a fast-sailing British man-of-war. One crewman drowned, but the rest came ashore on the beach of Anastasia Island (the orange-grove island that hid St. Augustine from the Atlantic). A detachment of the Sixtieth Regiment took them prisoner and brought them to town, where after a day they were dispersed: some of the crew signed on to British vessels, some joined the Sixtieth Regiment, and the rest, excepting the ship's master, Capt. Gilbert Harrison, were sent to confinement under guard back on Anastasia Island.[39]

Harrison, considered by the British to be a "notorious fellow" and a parole-breaker, was remanded to the Castle, where he shared arrangements similar to those of Christopher Gadsden. The exiles right away took up a collection of money for the relief of crewman sick in the hospital, and when they learned that the rest of the crew had been returned to Fish's island, they sent a collection of shirts, trousers, and shoes to their fellow sufferers.[40]

On the evening of December 5, the Americans received a second present in the form of a thousand sweet oranges from Jesse Fish of Anastasia Island. Again the British in St. Augustine did not openly object to the gift, though Fish's flouted generosity must have rankled Tonyn. He took no action. In contrast the British authority in Charleston, meaning Balfour, was simultaneously and angrily trying to restrict kindnesses to patriots. Balfour suspected that rebel Americans in the countryside were being supplied with materiel being carried out from the town he ruled. He acted on his suspicions by abruptly issuing a proclamation prohibiting local citizens from selling anything except within the limits of Charleston. The proclamation amounted to an admission of how tenuously the British controlled the realm of their occupation.[41]

It became increasingly evident to the prisoners in Florida that they had a dependable friend in William Brown, the commissary of prisoners who was their liaison with Governor Tonyn. Brown was a Scot by birth, an upright and honorable man, faithful to his king and country but consistently kind and even indulgent to the Charleston gentlemen—as far as he could be within the rules of his duty. Reported Johnson, "where entire satisfaction could not be afforded, he would soothe [our] feelings and console [us] in a friendly, gentlemanly manner." Brown was a tall, thin man with features so sharp that no one could fail to be impressed. John Berwick, one of the prisoners, was so struck with the commissary's looks that he carved with his penknife the likeness of Brown for the head of his walking stick. (Later the carved portrait was refashioned into a snuffbox, which then became an heirloom in Charleston's Legaré family.)[42]

Life dragged on in St. Augustine. Other ships came and went, some having earlier been reported lost, others bringing odd assortments of folk picked up at sea for one reason or another. Occasionally there were reports of masts snapped in storms and crewmembers tossed to their deaths overboard by the unmanageable violence of the open ocean. The gossip about these vessels, and the little bits of more personal news they occasionally brought (often outdated by many weeks or even months), were major factors in the outspoken conversations of the few dozen Charleston exiles who by their selection were men of strong opinions and a certain inclination to boldness. Perhaps they had begun to realize that the occupation of Charleston was not running smoothly. At any rate their revolutionary zeal was unabated, much to the consternation of Governor Tonyn, who referred to them in a letter to Lord Germain on December 9, 1780, as "Rebellious Prisoners who were troublesome in keeping alive the flame of Rebellious Principles amongst the Inhabitants in Charlestown."[43]

Chapter 7

A Charge of Haughty and Arrogant Behavior

The diarist Josiah Smith Jr. is one of the few St. Augustine exiles for whom contemporaneous correspondence exists. During the winter months of 1780–81, he availed himself of an opportunity to catch up on personal letter writing to acquaintances, his attorney, business associates, merchants, and clients in Charleston and in England. Although he often wrote to address financial and plantation management concerns, he was familiar enough with his recipients to reveal more intimate feelings about his banishment.

A letter to George Appleby in England, penned on December 2, 1780, provides a good example. Smith said to his correspondent, "Doubtless you will be surprised at my writing to you from this place, and possibly you may have before now read in some of the English Print that myself with a number of other Citizens of Charlestown, have been transported from thence to this Province as a [result?] of vile incendiaries but [concerning] all of this I hope you and my other Friends will suspend their Judgment 'till the truth shall break forth into light." Innocent people had been "cruelly treated in being suddenly torn away from [their] families and ignominiously conveyed on board Ship the 27th August last, for the purpose of banishment into this Tail of America."[1]

Smith pointed out to Appleby that his change in residence had occurred as a matter of policy and that he and his fellow exiles had "happily escaped the charge of being anyways guilty of breaking through our Paroles as prisoners of War." They patiently bore their affliction knowing that they suffered for conscience's sake. At least they were confined to a healthy spot and were "plentifully supplied with agreeable Provisions." He also had the happiness of knowing that his family had not yet suffered any loss at the hands of the many "Plundering Parties that scourged the Country."[2]

Three days later Smith wrote to his cousin and business partner, George Smith, who had taken British protection, asking him to take charge of his affairs in Charleston. Apparently cousin George's allegiance to the king was no obstacle to his trust. Josiah admitted that by this time he was reconciled to his captivity and that he was comforted in the knowledge that "the friends I had left behind me [such as his cousin], would not be lacking in administering to the necessities of my afflicted Wife in her then perilous situation," concerning her recent safe delivery of a daughter.[3]

To James Poyas in London, another business partner whose older brother John was among the exiles, Smith wrote, "Cou'd you think it probable, ever to have received a letter from me dated at this place? [We are] restricted to particular Streets of the Town beyond which we dare not pass without danger of being sent to the Castle so that our whole walk could not extend to the length of a Mile."[4]

Smith repeated concerns for the welfare of his wife and six children but also bemoaned what the war had brought to his country: "Carolina, since the arrival of British Troops and Gen'l Clinton, has indeed suffered great convulsions, and since the Capitulation of Charles Town much Blood has been spilt . . . —a scene of Devastation and distress has marked the soul of both Armies and their various detachments [such] that I may in truth say, the Sword, the Pestilence and fire hath ravaged our Land, many of the Inhabitants being laid in the dust, by Battle, the Small Pox and other diseases, a number of Houses burnt in Town and Country, and most of the Planters brought to a low ebb, by the desertion and death of their Slaves, with the destruction of their Crops and Cattle."[5]

The British continued to tighten their hold on Charleston's rebel populace. The very day that Governor Tonyn wrote his letter to Germain concerning his troublesome and rebellious prisoners, a new and unpopular policy was announced back home in South Carolina. Since preventing Charleston's patriots from supplying goods to their friends and relatives in the country had not kept them from sending aid in the form of money, the *South-Carolina and American General Gazette* of December 9 published yet another edict: from henceforth no gold or silver was to leave the province, under penalty of its being seized. As before, one half would be given to any informant and the other half kept by the government. All persons traveling in or out of town on business would be stopped and searched, and they would be required to produce legitimate invoices that justified their business dealings.[6]

There is no indication of just how many informants came forth, but the following week's paper did publish a list of estate seizures that included the real and personal properties of St. Augustine exiles Benjamin Cattell, John Edwards, William Gibbs, Richard Hutson, and Thomas Savage. The notices continued to appear, and at the end of the month a generous reward was offered "to all those who may make discoveries of the concealment of negroes, horses, cattle, plate, household furniture, books, bonds, deeds, etc., so that the property may be secured and the delinquents punished."[7]

The plight of the Charleston exiles was not forgotten; it continued to be argued at the upper levels of the American and British military. Maj. Gen. Nathanael Greene, commanding the Southern Department in the wake of Gates's debacle at Camden, also learned of the "respectable Citizens" who had been sent to St. Augustine. Samuel Huntington, the president of the Continental Congress, forwarded to Greene a copy of the resolution directing General Washington to query General Clinton concerning the matter. Greene then decided to register his own protest to his enemy's counterpart (the person who ordered the exile, Lord Cornwallis). Writing on December 17, 1780, from his camp in North Carolina, Greene condemned the arrests and banishments and stated his expectation that Cornwallis would redress the issue. He seemed unaware that there had been a second round of arrests and transports.[8]

Naturally his lordship was concerned more with repressing than with redressing the problems of the inhabitants of Charleston. The tightening rules made it increasingly difficult to send anything more than plain letters to St. Augustine, and the letters, of course, had to be carefully written. Only very irregularly did important information make it to St. Augustine, and even less regularly was there a chance to send meaningful word home. But on December 18 it became known that a departing schooner intended to take on a cargo at the little British settlement of Cowford (a narrow cattle-crossing point on the St. Johns River, predecessor to the future Jacksonville) from which it was to deliver to Charleston. By this means the gentlemen were able to send letters, some of them written weeks before, with their Christmas best wishes and a few barrels of oranges, to be delivered to their families.[9]

By Christmas Day there had still come no word from Charleston. The thoughtful Jesse Fish did his part by providing yet another batch of a thousand sweet oranges. These were dutifully distributed to the various houses of the now sixty-four Americans (Capt. Gilbert Harrison had been added to their number) as they busied themselves with plans for their Noel feasts. Smith reported that his mess enjoyed the pleasure of roasted turkey and pig, corned beef, ham, and plum pudding. Someone in the group had even managed to make tarts from the local pumpkins. That morning another schooner sailed for Charleston. More boxes of oranges accompanied more letters.[10]

Meanwhile the superficially effective British practices were actually working against their perpetrators on the larger scene. Cornwallis's repressive measures, his summary hanging of citizens without trial at Camden, his exile of popular figures from Charleston, his prohibition of pay to honest workers without proof of their loyalty, his sequestration of estates, and the ever more insolent and supercilious attitudes of certain occupying officers, all tended to determine the people to throw off the English presence rather than to join in with it. "There can be little doubt," said one historian, "that . . . Cornwallis's civil administration lost more of the friends of his Majesty's government than his victories had subdued of his enemies."[11]

And over time the balance of military power was slowly shifting in South Carolina. A band of nine hundred patriot militiamen, "overmountain frontiersmen" under Col. John Sevier and Col. Isaac Shelby, with Virginians under Col. William Campbell, decimated eleven hundred loyalist militia led by Scottish Maj. Patrick Ferguson at Kings Mountain on October 7, 1780, leaving the loyalist major dead on the field and capturing his loyalist survivors. On a lesser scale but very important to the rebel cause were the raids by American militia generals such as Francis Marion and Thomas Sumter who constantly picked at the British and loyalist forces.

The Charlestonians in St. Augustine were kept mostly ignorant of these American victories. Their attention was instead focused on more trivial events. Two days after Christmas, for instance (the Feast of St. John the Evangelist), the patriots watched while the local chapter of Ancient Free and Accepted Masons marched in procession, as was customary, to a special service in the parish church. Their Grand Master Forbes (the rector) was very much in evidence. The fraternity afterward processed to Brother Love's Coffee House and there "dined together &c in that harmony and chearfulness, peculiar to the Brotherhood."[12]

That more intellectual life did not dry out among the Charlestonians in exile is demonstrated by the activity of Dr. David Ramsay, who was determined not to let his idle time in St. Augustine go to waste. The Pennsylvania-born physician had graduated from both the College of New Jersey (now Princeton University) and the new medical school at the University of Pennsylvania in Philadelphia before he established what became a prosperous medical practice in Charleston in 1773. Soon Ramsay was known as an outspoken advocate for the patriot cause, and even though he was a newcomer to South Carolina, he served in the state legislature from 1776 to 1780. Along the way he forged solid friendships with radical patriots Christopher Gadsden, Arthur Middleton, and William Henry Drayton (who would likely have been exiled had he not died in 1779). Through Gadsden, whom he greatly admired, Ramsay garnered an appointment as surgeon to the Charleston Battalion of Artillery.[13]

Ramsay was a physician, a politician, a zealous patriot, and an exile, but in the end he would be best remembered as a historian—America's first leading historian. In the midst of the discomforts, deprivations, and uncertainties of exile, he began work on a future two-volume publication, *The History of the Revolution of South-Carolina: From a British Province to an Independent State,* which he published in 1785. This work was well written and readable, and while Ramsay wrote from the American viewpoint as one who had personally suffered British oppression, he was generally evenhanded and not at all vindictive, excepting perhaps in

David Ramsay, M.D. James Barton Longacre's engraving from a drawing by Charles Fraser after a painting by Charles Willson Peale, (New York: Herman Bancroft, 1836). From the collections of the Society of the Cincinnati, Washington, D.C. Reproduced with permission.

his treatment of Cornwallis, Tarleton, and Balfour. The work was well received by his contemporaries in America, but it is understandable that English booksellers "refused to advertise or sell [copies] for fear of legal reprisals from British officers described by Ramsay as barbaric and inhuman in their war conduct."[14]

It seems implausible that he should have begun such an undertaking under his St. Augustine circumstances. Within the preceding year, Ramsay had borne witness to and even participated in the Continental Army's worst defeat of the war—the disastrous fall of Charleston. It was widely believed that British armies dominated South Carolina and Georgia, and if American independence was attained in the north, there was ample concern that South Carolina might remain a British colony. Ramsay's biographer Arthur Shaffer called Ramsay's work an act of faith in the future.[15]

The accommodations of the largest mess, originally seventeen gentlemen occupying the house on the present corner of Hypolita and Charlotte, must have become too strained with the addition of five November exiles. On December 28 two of its members, Jacob Read (who had served as captain in the Charleston militia) and Richard Beresford (late aide-de-camp to General Moultrie) abruptly walked out without giving any notice, offending the feelings of those they deserted but realizing their own design for more gracious living. They had taken a house for themselves and had induced John Sansum to leave his mess at the State House to join them as their steward. Upon their departure the fair-minded referee Smith got Edward Blake to help him assess the quantity and value of the provisions to be reallotted and to insure that accounts were properly settled.[16]

The following day a small, sloop-rigged boat arrived from the struggling Cowford settlement and surprised everyone by delivering a number of travelers from South Carolina. They had originally set out from Charleston aboard the schooner *Endeavour*, which in addition to passengers carried letters, money, clothing, several cases of liquor, and other packages intended for some of the exiles.

While en route they were taken at sea by the ten-gun American privateer brigantine *Cutter*, captained by George Ashby out of Salem, Massachusetts. The "hard-hearted Captain Ashby" unceremoniously landed them on St. Catherine's Island, twenty-five miles below Savannah on the Georgia coast near the town of Sunbury, but not before searching through all of their belongings for money. Although informed of the ownership and identities of the goods and the identities of the persons to which they were consigned, Ashby nonetheless ignored all pleading and refused to let the passengers keep anything belonging to the exiles, even the letters directed to "his unfortunate suffering American Brethren" in St. Augustine. To passenger Thomas Johnson, Ashby explained "that he did not care for Country or Congress, that he came out to make money, and by God he would make it."[17]

Thomas Heyward reported the incident to General Moultrie in Charleston, sending a packet that included affidavits prepared by two gentlemen of St. Augustine who had sailed on the *Endeavour* and witnessed Ashby's behavior. Heyward requested that Moultrie forward the packet to the Continental Congress in Philadelphia, which Moultrie did, adding his own recommendation "that the person who so unfeelingly distressed our fellow prisoners may be called to some account and be obliged to recompense them for their loss, and if not [to be] divested of his commission, at least to receive a severe reprimand." Congress called for the papers to be transmitted to John Hancock, who was the governor of Massachusetts, so that he could conduct an inquiry into the matter. If the charges against Captain Ashby were substantiated, Congress wanted him to be punished in accordance with the law. From the lack of evidence of any response from Hancock concerning the matter, whether in the papers or in the journals of the Continental Congress, it is doubtful that Ashby suffered any consequences for his actions.[18]

At last, on New Year's Day, arrived the schooner *Recovery*, specifically flagged by the British commandant at Charleston for the purpose of conveying baggage, enslaved servants, provisions, and so forth for the use of the gentlemen prisoners on parole in St. Augustine. Since the contents were supposed to be entirely for the exiles, the intended recipients were irritated to discover that the ship contained three times as much merchandise for the local British subjects as it did for satisfying their own needs. Nonetheless they were pleased to learn of the health of their dear families and were happy to receive supplies even though it was almost three months since they had submitted their orders. Their cargo contained 42 gallons of quality rum, an equivalent value of madeira (in lieu of the port they had requested), a case of brandy, 146 pounds of cocoa nuts, vinegar, onions, eggs, salt, cheese, mustard, starch, 50 pounds of soap, a dozen packs of cards, a gross of corks, and two dozen cotton lines with hooks for fishing.[19]

The ship *Recovery* sat timidly in the Florida waters for a month before returning to Charleston. By contrast on January 5, the sloop *Governor Tonyn* ambitiously set out for Liverpool but was so leaky that Smith and many others believed that it would have to put in to Charleston for help. Several Americans risked sending messages via this unsure vessel.[20]

On the Feast of the Epiphany, representatives from Fish came bearing gifts as a testimony of his kind regard for and inclinations toward them, in the form of another thousand sweet oranges to be divided among the prisoners. Some of the oranges were sent to Charleston for families and friends. The complimented exiles felt they could no longer accept such generosity without giving something in return, so on the Monday after they sent slaves by canoe to deliver to their benefactor three bushels of new rice, a peck of onions, and a quarter hunk of their large Cheshire cheese.[21]

So far there seemed to have been no serious illness among the St. Augustine exiles, and in some ways the white Charlestonians were better off in the safe strictures of Florida than in the paranoid tyranny of South Carolina's occupied capital. The same could be said of the enslaved, who were trusted to go fishing and to take boats over to Jesse Fish's orange plantations on Anastasia Island. This bizarrely idyllic separation from the struggles of the world was brought suddenly back to earth: on January 18 the exile community in St. Augustine experienced the death and burial of one of the Charleston bondmen, Scipio, "a likely Young Negro Fellow" belonging to Anthony Toomer. It was thought among the exiles that a local black with whose wife Scipio had been too intimate had poisoned him—Scipio had been ill for about six days. But in the complexities of the city, there could be no appeal to justice.[22]

The next day brought a few letters from Charleston and intelligence that smallpox had once again broken out there. Smith's letter from home epitomizes what was most worrisome news for all of the exiles. Word from his wife was that her brother had died "under very Violent Symptoms of the Small Pox in the natural way." Of course the family was greatly distressed—Smith's deceased brother-in-law's wife and one daughter were recovering from the dreaded malady, and two other children were still lying ill with the disease. One child was yet to become sick. Edward McCrady and his wife, Elizabeth, had already lost two children in 1780, and now they had to worry about their son John (five years old) and his half-sister Catherine (aged six). William Moultrie described the smallpox in Charleston at the time as "a fever of the putrid type . . . a putrid dysentery." It is easy to imagine that a number of sad letters like the one from Smith's wife arrived in St. Augustine from time to time, especially during a smallpox outbreak, and that the Charleston gentlemen were doubly anguished by the suffering of their families and their own powerlessness to alleviate such misery. Florida isolation was not so idyllic after all.[23]

At that evening's State House roll call, Commissary Brown read aloud a most offensively condescending letter. The letter's authorship wasn't entirely clear—Brown stated that he was under orders not to let the paper out of his hands, and he did not identify the writer, but the tone and wording seemed to be more consistent with Governor Tonyn than with Lieutenant Colonel Glazier. It started with a hint of the carefree life the exiles had in part enjoyed: "The Parole I gave you was Simple, and not perplexed with any Law Phrases, the meaning of it was obvious, and it was my Intention to make your Confinement (if it cou'd be called such) as easy as possible."[24]

Then the tone of tyranny took over. The author was convinced that the exiles were abusing the privilege of maintaining correspondence with Charleston: "I pass over your haughty & arrogant behaviour, and shall only remark on the Improper use made of the Indulgence granted to correspond with your friends, letters have been sent from you, answers have been receiv'd from your friends in Carolina of a most dangerous Tendency, and inconsistent with the paroles you have given."[25]

The writer seemed to be trying to resurrect the original accusations that led to their exile in the first place and promised that "these letters will be laid before proper Judges, and due notice shall be taken of them." Was their correspondence being opened and read? That conclusion was unavoidable. "I caution you against a continuance of such practices," warned the author in closing, declaring that "if they are not discontinued they may draw upon you severe Vengeance." The letter's writer had been informed that the Continental Congress had received calls for retaliation for the arrest and transport of the gentlemen from Charleston and believed that the captives themselves had provided details about the state of affairs in St. Augustine in letters home—which according to their paroles they were bound not to do. The exiles were dismayed "that the whole Company shou'd be charged with a crime (if any such there was) on account of the [supposed] inadvertency of one or two."[26]

The mortified Charlestonians drew up a lengthy response, taking the concept of "indulgence granted" and running with it. What amazed them, they argued, was that the British claimed the virtue of indulgences and, even worse, expected "an Adequate return. . . . Was it an indulgence," they asked (launching an impressive rhetorical quartet), for them to be confined to the inner square of St. Augustine when they had formerly enjoyed the entire city of Charleston, including its outskirts? Was it an indulgence to have to attend roll call twice daily in St. Augustine when they had been entirely upon their honor in Charleston? Was it an indulgence that the British were reading their mail, whereas in Charleston they had been free to converse with and write to anyone they pleased? Was it an indulgence that the British had prejudiced the citizens of St. Augustine against the Americans and advised the locals not to have any communication with the visitors? The ordinary folk were so fearful of offending the military rulers that only three or four had been willing to engage in conversation.[27]

"And as to . . . Civilities towards us, We know of none," except possibly that the American black exiles had been allowed to go fishing (but only after permission had been requested). Could it be considered a civility that the authorities had in December finally provided some alcohol—a "Punche of West Indie Rum"—only because the commandant in Charleston had told them to do so almost a month before? With a distinct touch of indignation, they went on: "And as to the charge of haughty and arrogant behaviour, We are ignorant of such, unless it be that we refuse to pull off our hats or bow our bodies to the Commandant and his Officers, which we do not, as Strangers and Prisoners in a Strange land, think it our duty to do unless drawn thereto by compliments of that sort first offered on their part." Since, judging by the conduct of the commandant and officers so far, "we have no reason to expect from them Civilities of this sort, we shall be content to do without."[28]

Besides, huffed the exiles, how could the British talk of honor when the Americans saw with their own eyes the acts of open bribery and smuggling that went on in broad daylight at seaside: chests of sugar and the like left on the shore while Roman Catholic sailors from Spain—a nation openly at war with England—were freely permitted to walk all over the town. Smith wondered how such things could go on, "whilst us poor Americans, descendants from Worthy Parents of the Protestant People, and now Prisoners on Parole here per force, are restrained within Smaller limits and treated with too much contempt! How powerfully doth Self Interest and present Gain operate with all Ranks of Mankind, and even with those that should be foremost in putting into Execution the laws of their King!"[29]

It is not clear whether or not this profuse counterattack, anything but conciliatory, was actually delivered. It may have remained a private exercise in venting wrath, since actually delivering it could hardly have assuaged the British irritations. Incidentally nowhere did it say that the Americans were not, in fact, indulging in some underground mail. If they were not yet guilty of surreptitious correspondence, they began it shortly thereafter. Occasionally, for instance, a private boat from Georgia had aboard a slave who was willing to take an illegal letter back to someone who could then see that it got to Charleston. Messages were also slipped under false bottoms in the boxes containing oranges or orange juice that were sent to family and friends, and in at least one case an enslaved laundress agreed to smuggle a few letters folded into a bundle of shirts and other articles of clothing going on board. Actually this was all probably more for the thrill of operating covertly than for seditious revolutionary matters, as the prisoners were far too disconnected and uninformed to be effectively involved in serious plotting back home.[30]

Edward Rutledge later tangentially referred to the arrogant lecturing incident in a letter to George Washington when details of the captivity were being sought by the Continental Congress with a view toward retaliation. As Rutledge saw it, "one half of their Cruelty, and Injustice, is beyond the Reach of human Labor; however their most flagrant and atrocious Acts of violence and oppression will be pointed out, and if the Congress should retain their present Sentiments, they will soon possess Materials not only to justify, but to require an exact (if I may use a British officer's expression) 'Retaliation with a Vengeance.'"[31]

The attitude of certain British authorities notwithstanding, the exiles did not fail to grasp that their situation could have been worse. Smith informed his friend Charleston merchant John Dart (who back home had cautiously taken British protection) that the exiles were amply supplied with wholesome provisions and that thanks to their own thriving constitutions, they actually managed to enjoy a tolerable existence.[32]

As if to illustrate such tolerance, Jesse Fish continued his contributions. On January 31 he sent a seventh gift of sweet oranges, this time 1,280 in number, being thoughtfully calculated so that each of the sixty-four detainees should receive exactly 20, including the North Carolinian Captain Harrison in the Castle.[33]

A small vessel arrived on February 5, a sloop supposedly captained by a renegade Spaniard and crewed by Minorcans who had wives and families in St. Augustine. The sloop had taken twelve days to travel from Havana and brought interesting intelligence of impending Spanish attacks on Pensacola. More important were the rumors that a dozen Spanish galleys were preparing for an expedition against St. Augustine, bringing land forces with them.[34]

Perhaps the wildest story to fascinate the Americans came from a refugee Pensacola couple who had spent the last thirty-four days traveling overland to St. Augustine. The couple described what was surely the Battle of Mobile, fought on January 7, 1781. According to their tale, a party of British officers and soldiers had attacked a Spanish settlement, attaining what they thought was complete success by driving the Spaniards out of their entrenchments. The Spaniards, who in flight found their own boats aground and unusable, were then joined by reinforcements consisting of both whites and Choctaw Indians and returned en masse to recapture their post. This they accomplished, killing the British colonel and most of his officers, along with thirty men and several Indians. The British in St. Augustine were not much pleased with this news of Hispanic bravery and Indian revenge.[35]

The exiles were justly impressed with the seeming ease by which the Indians could take whatever side appealed to them. There was always something mysterious about the native presence in St. Augustine, and individual Indians were frequently seen, sometimes in tribal attire, though hardly any of them lived in the town. They had their own nearby settlements, and while they could easily emerge from or disappear into the woods, they regularly visited town to acquire rum.[36]

On one occasion during the exiles' confinement in St. Augustine, a Seminole chief's son became greatly intoxicated on rum and was consequently behaving in a confrontational manner. Guardsmen were called, and a soldier who mistook the order of his officer killed the Indian with a bayonet thrust to the groin. As an expression of regret, Governor Tonyn attended the Indian's solemn public funeral, held complete with military honors conferred. It fell to him to maintain diplomatic relations with the Seminoles, which he was able to accomplish satisfactorily by promising that the soldier would be tried by the laws of his country. At the same time, he had to consider the continual problem of how to staunch the flow of rum to the indigenous people.[37]

Ships came and went, riskily bringing their cargoes over the bar and into port laden with provisions for town, including gunpowder for the use of the garrison (useful at least for firing salutes), and carrying away naval stores and skins for the London and Bristol markets. Oftentimes these ships brought stories of other ships that were grounded or lost. Particularly disturbing to the exiles was news that the *Lord Sandwich,* having spent its month in St. Augustine and then set out on November 25 to return to Charleston, had foundered or been taken by the enemy. The patriots had become particularly fond of Captain Bett and were greatly relieved when another ship came in from the Caribbean and reported that the *Sandwich* was not lost at all but had merely been blown fifteen hundred miles off its Charleston course and wound up in Antigua.[38]

Chapter 8

The Winter and Spring of 1781

On the evening of February 16, Jacob Read was suddenly seized at the State House roll call, escorted by four armed soldiers to the Castle, and confined in a private cell separate from Christopher Gadsden's. The Charleston lawyer had served as captain in the Charleston militia, and his accomplishments as a young man would be eclipsed after the war by service in his state legislatures, the Continental Congress, and the U.S. Senate. But for now no explanation for his abrupt confinement was offered, and his confederates could only suppose that there had been something in his correspondence that the British considered inappropriate—an imprudent expression, perhaps. If such was the case, the warning issued on January 19 should have been taken more seriously. Read would spend long, dreary months in his solitary confinement.[1]

Sometime during those cheerless hours, he wrote on his prison wall a doggerel reflection on the vainglories of this world: "Life is a vapour, man needs repose; / He glories but a moment, down he goes." A British officer, showing his wit if not his sympathy or humanity, wrote underneath a response intended to intimidate the prisoner with thoughts of the gallows: "[Read] is a bubble, as his scribbling shows; / He cuts a caper, and then up he goes."[2]

On February 20 Jesse Fish finished the season's citrus crop by sending over a modest 365 sweet oranges. In case the recipients missed the symbolism by not counting, he reminded them that there was one fruit for each day of the year. That amounted to a little less than half a dozen for each patriot, and it was understood that there were not likely to be more until the new crop. The Charlestonians again thanked the "humane and kind Gentleman." That afternoon the schooner *Polly* came in from Charleston with letters, some a month old, as well as rum, gin, rice, and other provisions for sale. The smallpox scare had passed in Charleston, and it was reported that two families, the Smiths and Darrells, deprived financially as well as socially by the absence of their patriotic patriarchs,

Jacob Read (1752–1816).
Member of Congress from
South Carolina. Painted
1793. Miniature, oil on
wood by John Trumbull.
Courtesy of the Yale
University Art Gallery,
New Haven, Conn.

had merged into one household and thus been able to rent the other dwelling at a good wartime price.[3]

On March 1 a schooner arrived with an exciting account of there being fifty-three vessels in the area quite near to St. Augustine, yet that provocative statistic was not followed by any dramatic appearance or event. The unfazed patriots bided their time in enjoying the invigorating spring climate. Early January had brought the single freeze of that winter, and the whole season had been generally warm. The visitors were impressed with how quickly the vegetation flourished as they observed orange trees in bloom throughout the town for most of the month of February. Green fruit was already appearing on the trees, and even a few ripened oranges.[4]

Patriot exile Richard Lushington, another Charleston merchant and militia captain, had been dangerously ill with the "flux" or dysentery but was recovering nicely. He had an idea that the healthier clime of Fish's Anastasia Island would greatly contribute to a reestablishment of his health. No doubt the trip would have made a pleasant break in the confined routine of exile, so he applied to the generally friendly Commissary Brown. Unfortunately the commandant gave "an absolute denial of so small an Indulgence, saying the Air in Town was as good as that on the Island." It was reputed that the commandant had always enjoyed exceptionally good health and therefore had little sympathy with those who did not. But in all fairness to British precautionary decisions, one never knew what Fish might be up to.[5]

At the same time Lushington was seeking his holiday from town, flag signals from the lookout station warned of an approaching fleet from the south. The town was much alarmed, imagining the threat of some Spanish armada preparing to attack East Florida. By the next morning, it was evident that the only ships interested in St. Augustine were those bringing provisions and ordnance stores for the fort and those eager to sell rice, corn, rum, and other articles. Some recent newspapers and even a few timely letters from Charleston arrived, written a mere two weeks before. Over the next ten days, ships arrived or departed nearly every other day, traffic having picked up during the good weather.[6]

This increased traffic enabled Robert Cochran to get an important letter through to his wife in Charleston. He avoided including prohibited details but advised her to leave town and make her way to Philadelphia if she could. Several of the exiles had received letters from home intimating that prisoner exchanges had actually taken place. This news added to their hope of being released sometime in the near future—"should this really be the case," wrote Josiah Smith, "I can hardly expect our Masters will permit our return to Charleston but rather [they may well] order us away directly to Philadelphia from here." Smith was remarkably prescient.[7]

Cochran (1735–1824) was a former Massachusetts seaman. As second mate of a large transport ship of the Royal Navy during the Seven Years' War, he was present at the Siege of Louisbourg in 1758 and the Siege of Quebec in 1759, where he commanded a landing barge. Afterward he continued in the merchant service and settled in Charleston, where he established a shipyard on the Cooper River in 1763. In 1775 and 1776, Cochran served as ordnance storekeeper for the Council of Safety.[8]

According to a biographical sketch written by his son, Cochran was a member of the raiding party led by Capt. Clement Lemprière of the sloop *Commerce* that had run down and boarded the armed brigantine *Betsey* off the St. Augustine bar on August 7, 1775. The raiders removed 111 barrels of His Majesty's gunpowder and other military stores for patriot use, powder that was likely employed during the successful defense of Sullivan's Island on June 28, 1776. Participation in this raid would make him the only Charleston exile to have visited the British port of St. Augustine prior to being sent there involuntarily.[9]

Cochran had been dispatched to New England in 1776 to recruit five hundred seamen for the defense of his adopted colony, a plan fully sanctioned by the Continental Congress (though only half-heartedly endorsed by General Washington). While in the northern colonies, Cochran learned of the intended British expedition against Charleston, and aware of the relative defenselessness at home, he immediately set off on a twenty-one-day journey southward on horseback to give first warning of the impending surprise to his countrymen. For his work on Charleston's defensive works, Maj. Gen. Charles Lee lauded him as "a very active man" and tasked him with constructing a bridge of planks as an escape route from Sullivan's Island to the mainland.[10]

In 1777 Cochran became captain of the eighteen-gun South Carolina brig *Notre Dame* that he sailed to France, making the ship the first American vessel to dock at a French port. He accomplished this feat under the guise of being a Dutch trader because France had not yet formally recognized the United States.[11]

Besides Cochran, several other exiles had connections to the South Carolina navy. Josiah Smith, John Edwards, Thomas Savage, George Abbot Hall, and Edward Blake had all served as commissioners appointed to superintend and direct the naval affairs of South Carolina. And Captain Cochran was not the only former commanding officer of the *Notre Dame* among them. William Hall (1757–1814) was the ship's third captain—*Notre Dame* sailed under his command from 1778 until the surrender of Charleston in May 1780. Hall enjoyed great success aboard the *Notre Dame* protecting the commerce of Charleston, transporting and landing troops for the disastrous siege at Savannah during the fall of 1779, and capturing valuable prizes.[12]

The most noteworthy engagement in which Hall was involved was the *Notre Dame*'s support of the thirty-two-gun Continental frigate *Randolph* against the British sixty-four-gun, double-decked frigate *Yarmouth,* on March 7, 1778. The American ship, commanded by the promising young Capt. Nicholas Biddle, seemed to be winning the fight when she suddenly disintegrated in a great ball of fire that annihilated all but four crewmembers and showered her adversary with flaming debris. Hall and the *Notre Dame* were badly outgunned and were forced to flee the scene, narrowly escaping the Royal Navy after hours of pursuit. Coincidentally Dr. Thomas Budd, younger brother of exile Dr. John Budd, was one of those who perished aboard the *Randolph*.[13]

Where Cochran, Smith, and the others got rumors of exchange (and particularly exchange to Philadelphia) is unknown. Both sides had been discussing prisoner exchange since September 1780, and a limited number of informal exchanges had occurred, but negotiations did not really begin in earnest until February 1781. The articles of exchange for the Southern Department would not be finalized until May of that year.[14]

During exchange negotiations General Washington politely responded to a query from South Carolina Continental Congress delegate John Mathews regarding the exchange of prisoners, particularly those at St. Augustine, but had little to reveal. "Nothing particular has therefore been done respecting the Gentlemen who are confined at St. Augustine as it could not be supposed that the enemy would consent to a partial exchange of persons of the most considerable influence in the southern States and who besides are pretended to have rendered themselves obnoxious." Besides, said Washington, observing that many of the exiles had held high positions in the civil government, the Americans had captured nobody of equivalent rank or influence to be offered in exchange.[15]

Arguing for his friends' speedy exchange, Mathews countered that the St. Augustine exiles were acting as officers or private soldiers at the time they were taken prisoner at Charleston and that they should not be considered in any other way. The fact that many of them had been prominent men and some had held important governmental posts was incidental—they were captured as soldiers, and that was what they were (except that Christopher Gadsden was lieutenant governor and just that). Captured British officers who were members of Parliament had been exchanged at their British army rank, not as members of the House of Commons or the House of Lords. John Burgoyne had been a governor but was never considered in any other light than that of a general officer.[16]

In his return Washington replied, "I meant only to express my apprehensions that the British Commander in Chief would make some difficulty in the exchange of those Citizens of eminence who were not clearly invested with military Commissions. You may rest assured as I before mentioned that whenever it shall be expedient to make an offer of a general exchange of southern prisoners that the cases of the Gentlemen in Captivity at Augustine will be particularly attended to and every advantage which they ought to derive from the capitulation of Charlestown will be insisted upon should the enemy attempt to deprive them of them."[17]

For the time being, Cochran and his involuntarily exiled friends had to settle for the status quo. Most of them were not really uncomfortable. But not everyone could afford to live as well as did most of the exiles. In mid-March two gentlemen, William Hasell Gibbes and Isaac Holmes, both of whom in particular had received little help from home, were obliged to reduce their expenses by renting a local room at a dollar a week and confining their diet to the prisoner rations provided by the king. Thus they separated from the largest mess, the one that occupied the large, wooden two-story house one street back from the bay, and the same one vacated by Jacob Read and Richard Beresford at the end of December. It is clear that the departure of the two gentlemen had nothing to do with personal animosities resulting from "cabin fever" and was merely a realistic financial consequence. The relocation of two members reduced the size of the mess to nineteen persons and necessitated another revaluation of funds and provisions so that a cash settlement, a sort of buyout, could be paid to Gibbes and Holmes. Smith was good at the pedantries of such bookkeeping.[18]

Weak or nonexistent provincial assemblies partly explain why Floridians had not opposed British policies in the years preceding the Revolutionary War. In fact there were no popularly elected assemblies in either of the Floridas—the assembly in Pensacola had been prorogued (discontinued without being dissolved) by West Florida's governor in 1772 and never reconstituted, and no assembly had ever been elected in St. Augustine. East Florida was the only other British American colony besides Quebec without an elected representative assembly as part of its government. All power was vested completely in the beleaguered governor and his council, who met in the State House (where a continuing group of the exiles still resided). The council had originally been intended to constitute only the upper chamber of a bicameral system, but after nearly two decades no lower house had been elected.[19]

Governor Tonyn long maintained that the colony did not have sufficient population to warrant a body of representative voices, an excuse that served as a means of keeping his political opponents out of power. And the presence of the Charleston exiles gave the governor yet another excuse to delay summoning his projected assembly, as it was apparent to him that many of the inhabitants were friendly toward them and might be developing unsavory democratic ideas.[20]

In February 1781 the governor finally issued a proclamation requiring all Protestant male inhabitants of the province qualified by the ownership of at least fifty acres to congregate in town for a polling at the courthouse. This development meant that the idle Charlestonians had all the gossip of local politics to entertain them during the month of March. The long-delayed election of a house of representatives for East Florida was finally held over a three-day period ending on March 16, as duly noted by Smith in his diary. A total of forty-six ballots were cast, and the nineteen newly elected and sworn representatives chose as speaker of the house the kindhearted commissary of prisoners, William Brown.[21]

The choice of Brown undoubtedly pleased the governor, and it certainly did not displease the exiles, who had already noted him as a "dependable friend." However though the exiles could congratulate him on his new honor, they had little expectation of the new assembly's being anything more than sycophantic, especially given that a number of the members had incomes that were dependent on either the governor or his council's decisions. Nor did Governor Tonyn think this unjust; he had held off elections as long as possible until he was sure that his major enemies were broken or gone. And now he had his own legislature well packed with friends. The South Carolina newspaper reports of the governor's speeches to the new assembly and its replies to him seemed to bear out a suspiciously happy harmony and left the Charlestonians quite smug in their republican convictions.[22]

Occasionally exile in St. Augustine could be more humorous than the sober and tight-lipped submission to the status quo called for in Charleston. Over the seven months already passed in their proud exile, the patriots had become increasingly sure that the amiable Brown, who dropped by on official business

St. Augustine and its Environs, 1782, pen and ink. Geography and Map Division, Library of Congress, Washington, D.C.

at least once daily to deliver the carefully scrutinized mail, was friendly enough to assist them in carrying out a prank on one of their own. This unnamed individual, it seems, regularly exaggerated his self-importance by claiming to have received valuable news from important contacts at home. The boastful attitude was harmless but was apparently irritating to the more egalitarian brotherhood of fellow sufferers.[23]

To call their compatriot's suspected bluff, they devised a ruse that necessitated the cooperation of Brown. The wags composed a mysterious letter addressed to the suspected embellisher that contained only the cryptic message, "Yahoo———, Yahoo———, Yahoo———!" and convinced Brown to insert it into the contents of a roll-call delivery of mail from Charleston. When the recipient opened it, true to form, he swelled with "an exclamation of rapturous delight . . . kissed it with ardour," and handed it off to the nearest fellow Charlestonian, exclaiming authoritatively, "Read this and rejoice, the day is our own, victory crowns our efforts, and freedom and independence are at hand."[24]

The gentleman who was supposed to be impressed looked at the piece of paper and objected, "I see nothing but an uncouth name thrice repeated and followed by three scratches preceding a point of admiration." That is "the very cause of my joy," replied the bearer of privileged news, explaining, "You have seen the secret cypher agreed upon between my friend and myself, to communicate intelligence. 'Yahoo' stands for Cornwallis, and the three scratches give positive assurance that he is taken." The patriots were tremendously amused by the apparent emptiness of the claim but did not reveal their secret.[25]

What the exiles did not know, and could not know because it was not being honestly reported in the British-controlled newspapers, was that the tide of war in the southern theater had taken a decided turn in their favor. A British detachment led by Lieutenant Colonel Tarleton (whose earlier captives included the North Carolina exile, Elijah Isaacs, now imprisoned in the Castle) had stumbled into a trap and was decisively beaten by Brig. Gen. Daniel Morgan's force of Continentals and militia at Cowpens on January 17. This brilliant American victory was reported in the Philadelphia newspapers on February 9, but the Charleston press was notably silent.[26]

In addition to its boosting American morale, Cowpens had the strategic effect of causing Cornwallis to march into North Carolina in pursuit of Nathanael Greene, who drew him all the way to the Virginia border before escaping to temporary safety across the flooded Dan River on February 14. Cornwallis fell back to Hillsborough, North Carolina, to recruit and resupply, and while in Virginia the Americans did the same. It would be a month later at the small North Carolina hamlet of Guilford Courthouse that the two opposing generals and their armies would face off in the largest and most hotly contested battle in the southern theater. On March 15, 1781, Cornwallis's veteran soldiers attacked an American army that outnumbered them more than two to one, forcing Greene to withdraw.

The British held the field at the end of the battle and thus claimed a victory, albeit a sanguinary one on account of the large number of irreplaceable casualties. For the British subjects in St. Augustine, word of the battle finally arrived and seemed cause for rejoicing. Commissary Brown advised the Charlestonians to keep within their enclosures during the celebration of the splendid victory being claimed for His Majesty's arms. Ever facetiously impertinent, the exiles asked the Scottish commissary if he was sure it was not one of those victories described in the old ballad from his homeland, "They baith did fight, and baith did beat, and baith did rin awaw." Brown, recognizing the words of the old Jacobite ballad, smiled but said no, that the official statement really had been received of a decided victory for the British.[27]

The Americans accepted Brown's report with equanimity and agreed to his advice to keep indoors, since he was always sincerely concerned for their safety. To prevent the prisoners from being endangered by the drunken British revelers celebrating the supposed victory, he posted sentinels outside their gates. "One of these sentinels was a German, probably an old Swiss soldier. A party of low characters assailed him and attempted to break in at the gate. The German warned them off, but when they persisted, he bayonetted the ringleader and killed him." Brown was called for and was genuinely shocked at how a simple bayonet wound could so speedily cause death. The German replied, "Ach, but I gafe my gun a tvesh [twist]," and that seemed to satisfy any complaints in the midst of the celebrating.[28]

Hardly had Brown left the scene when a second and more accurate version of the Guilford battle made the rounds, so that the Americans found they had more cause for celebration than did the British. The tactical British victory had proven pyrrhic for them, entailing such a high casualty rate—more than 25 percent—that the event emerged as a strategic victory for the revolutionary forces. When Brown dropped by the next day, the prisoners joked with him about the "splendid victory" and asked him to join them in their rejoicing at the real results of the battle. Their joy was pleasantly flavored with the ironic fact that the "Yahoo" explanation had turned out to have a correct interpretation—even though it was a total fiction. Cornwallis subsequently withdrew southeast to Wilmington before moving his army further north, taking the first steps along the path that ultimately led to Yorktown. By vacating North Carolina, he left Greene free to deal with the British forces in South Carolina, leading slowly to the recapture of the territory for the United States.[29]

On March 28 a sloop arrived in St. Augustine bringing news of England's occupation of the small Dutch West Indies island of Sint [St.] Eustatius. As a Dutch property, the island had illicitly channeled a significant amount of arms and ammunition to the United States. Taken by the British, that supply channel would be closed to the American revolutionaries. The island had also (in 1776) earned the distinction of being the first to recognize ceremonially the sovereignty of the new republic, accomplished by firing an official gun salute in positive response to an American ship's thirteen-gun salute of independence (one shot for each colony). Now the island could no longer traffic weapons to the patriots, nor could it offer protection to the several American vessels that were trapped in its conquered port.[30]

It was also reported that the British had dispatched ships to seize the island of Curaçao, another Dutch territory. The exiles viewed this possibility in a positive light: "twill be a very heavy stroke upon the Dutch, and must of necessity bring on a Dutch War," Smith postulated, "and with them perhaps the whole Armed Neutrals confederation may fall upon Devoted Old England . . . which will prevent the happy expectation of Peace in America this Year." (Note that in those days "prevent" still meant "come before.") But the British excursion against Curaçao (and also against the Dutch colony of Surinam) on the northeastern coast of South America never actually materialized. The exiles could not know that the Dutch Republic, which never formally aligned with the United States, was already at war with Britain (the Fourth Anglo-Dutch War) and had been since December 20, 1780.[31]

On April 4 arrived a schooner transporting a cargo of corn, lumber, and sundry supplies for some of the exiles. Aboard was an unexpected cargo from Charleston in the form of Catherine Cudworth, wife of Benjamin Cudworth. Neither her reason for being in St. Augustine nor from whom she received permission to travel is known, but she remained in town with her husband for five weeks before returning to Charleston. Her husband was a native of Massachusetts who had come to Charleston in 1775 and rapidly assimilated himself; he served in the Charleston militia in Col. Alexander Moultrie's regiment and saw action at Savannah in October 1779. Doubtless Mrs. Cudworth was very popular, as the exiles queried her for information regarding the wellbeing of their families and conditions at home.[32]

Notwithstanding Catherine Cudworth's welcome firsthand accounts, news from home remained exasperatingly sporadic. Smith's diary provides a careful accounting of the movements of ships in and out of St. Augustine, often with notes of their cargos and the persons they carried. Perhaps he did this out of boredom to occupy the time, but it is easy to suspect that in minding the docks he was anxiously awaiting word from home.

And word did come eventually. On April 14 Smith received letters from his son Samuel and daughter Polly informing him that all were well, the household having recovered from smallpox. It was almost a month before more news came (on May 12) in the form a two-week-old letter from his wife, one from his daughter Betsy, and two from Samuel. He also received his wig box containing two new shirts, two spotted-jean waistcoats, and a calico morning gown. And on May 28 accompanying foodstuffs and another bundle of clothing were two letters from Samuel, one from Betsy, two from Polly, one each from a friend and a cousin, and "also four lines as a first letter from my Young Son William."[33]

Early April brought a petty drama of more proximate concern to the exiled rebel society. One of their members was suddenly arrested by Capt. Patrick Murray of the Sixtieth Regiment and forced into the guardhouse "for a supposed trifling Libel 'tis said against the Commandant." He was detained there for three days, but as the authorities could not construct a serious case against him, he was just as suddenly discharged by the officer of the day and made to renew his vow to abide by the terms of his parole. Predictably his fellow exiles used their ready hyperbole to declare this unjust confinement, though brief, a case of "scandalous treatment." The identity of the alleged perpetrator is impossible to determine, as Smith provides only his first name, William, and that was the given name of fully eight of the gentlemen from Charleston.[34]

On April 23 the schooner *Maria* set out on the return trip to Charleston carrying Philip Smith of Ashepoo, a member of the second group of exiles (transported in November 1780). Smith was one of only two of the South Carolina prisoners to be allowed to return directly to Charleston. He had petitioned the occupying commandant before leaving that city and had at last received his answer, being granted permission to come home. Josiah Smith was fairly certain that Philip Smith was permitted to take leave of St. Augustine "doubtless to be Sworn in as an additional Subject to George the Third, King of Great Britain."[35]

Philip Smith's departure raises several unanswerable questions. If he was not a stalwart patriot, then how was he received or perceived by his fellow exiles? As an exile-insider could he have provided intelligence to the St. Augustine authorities? Perhaps he was just one of the lukewarm patriots who doubted the Revolution and sought to align with the winning side for the sake of his family and his estate. In any event his despair of American independence was clearly not brought about by the St. Augustine experience in itself. It is hard to imagine that his fellows bid him a fond farewell and smooth sailing.

On the other hand, the growing discouragement of most of the exiles could have evoked sympathy for this Ashepoo renegade. There is no way to ascertain the situation of his family; it is entirely possible that he was willing to take protection out of a sense of sheer necessity. William Moultrie considered it not an unpardonable sin: "The taking protection, and remaining quiet was no great offence; it was unavoidable with many. I advised several of my friends, after the fall of Charleston (who were not in the Continental Army) to take that step, and to stay with their families."[36]

Reinforcements of 150 men, including some Hessians, arrived in that last week of April to strengthen the Castle's garrison of 450 against the threat of invasion from the Spaniards at Havana. At the head of these troops was British Lt. Col. Alured Clarke. The increased size of the garrison strained distribution of rations, and the Charleston exiles—not about to be deprived—lost no time in claiming their rights. Bearing a memorial dated April 27, a committee of three, consisting of Thomas Ferguson, Edward Blake, and Thomas Savage, brought the group's grievances to Clarke in hopes that he would grant some relief.[37]

The opening of their memorial was the now familiar litany, but Clarke had not heard it before, so the committee explained about their being transported to St. Augustine for reasons of policy rather than any breach of parole. They reasoned that if they had all simply been left at home they could and would have housed and fed themselves—"all of us possessed the means of Subsistence, and most of us Habitations." The British occupation of Charleston and broader areas, with the subsequent sequestration of estates, had deprived them of any means of supporting themselves in Florida, and there they had been reduced to the "necessity of providing Lodgings . . . at the enormous expence of more than £140 Sterling."[38]

Even before their arrival in St. Augustine, they had been led to believe that full rations would be supplied them, and yet the exiles had consistently found such rations insufficient for their comfortable support. They were all men of integrity who could be expected to continue faithful on their parole, stated the memorial. Could they not enjoy at least an extension of their limits around town without the formality of the daily roll call? They were honorable gentlemen, and as such thought that their parole—their word of honor—should suffice.[39]

An immediate answer from Lieutenant Colonel Clarke was not forthcoming, but on May 16 the exiles heard from their sympathetic commissary that Clarke had decided to grant them a single leniency, namely that on any given day, up to ten of the Americans could go fishing in the bay in front of the town. Prior to this time this privilege had been allowed only to the bondservants. The fishing zone was no longer limited to the area just around the fort and the barracks and under the immediate eyes of the soldiers but now extended all along the "river" shoreline up to the fort and down to the barracks, a distance of about one mile, to which were added the mouths of the creeks that ran into Anastasia Island. The fishermen were not allowed to make landfall on Anastasia Island, nor could they board any other vessels except to return to town. These fishing excursions were limited to the hours from "Gun Fire in the Morning until four of the Clock, afternoon." Relatively speaking, that was a welcome adjustment.[40]

In Charleston conditions for the patriots were becoming increasingly difficult. The city had capitulated a full year ago, on May 12, 1780, and the soldiers of the entire Continental Army were, from a British point of view, technically prisoners. Until recently the British had controlled virtually all of the state, and confident of victory, their "insult and arrogance became the order of the day, and adversity was aggravated by every variety of insolence that malice could invent, and tyranny inflict." Apart from the most distinguished patriots, all sent to Florida, many others had been arrested on frivolous pretexts, and a growing number of young men, as subjects of retaliation, had been crowded onto prison ships to await exchange. More than ever there were women who, absent their husbands' protection, were left to their own devices under the protection of friends and relatives or in each other's care while living in an occupied city.[41]

The above comes from Alexander Garden, who was twenty-three when the British captured and occupied his city. He later compiled his *Anecdotes of the American Revolution* (1822), taking particular pleasure in "exhibiting instances of that magnanimity and intrepid firmness, that so preeminently distinguished the fair daughters of Carolina." According to Garden it was no idle compliment to credit the patriotism of the ladies of South Carolina as being, to a great degree, responsible for the freedom of their country. He could personally remember the magnanimity and intrepidity of many patriotic women, and he chose a few of them for inclusion in his narrative.[42]

One of Garden's examples was Elizabeth Mathews Heyward, wife of exile Thomas Heyward Jr. and sister of John Mathews, the aforementioned delegate to the Continental Congress who showed such concern for "the Gentlemen confined at St. Augustine." Garden described her as graceful and majestic in person, beautiful in countenance, angelic in disposition. In the third week of March 1781, she let her anger toward the British show.[43]

"An order having been issued for a general illumination, to celebrate the supposed victory at Guilford, the front of the house occupied by Mrs. Heyward and her sister Lois [pregnant wife of Charleston merchant and St. Augustine exile George Abbot Hall], remained in darkness. Indignant at so decided a mark of disrespect, an officer . . . forced his way into her presence, and sternly demanded of Mrs. Heyward, 'how dare you disobey the order which has been issued; why, Madam, is not your house illuminated?'"[44]

Elizabeth replied that it was impossible for her to feel a spark of joy or celebrate a British victory while her husband was a prisoner at St. Augustine. "'That,' rejoined the officer, 'is a matter of little consequence; the last hopes of rebellion are crushed by the defeat of Greene: You *shall* illuminate.'" Again Elizabeth refused, and the British soldier promised to return before midnight and burn her house to the ground. "'You have power to destroy, Sir, and seem well disposed to use it, but over my opinions you possess no control. I disregard your menaces, and resolutely declare, *I will not illuminate.*'" Lois Hall was late in her twelfth pregnancy, and the stress of the incident precipitated her decline.[45]

Two months later, on the first anniversary of the surrender of Charleston, another illumination was again demanded. Lois Hall, who was in a more precarious condition than before, was in an upstairs bedroom of the Heyward house laboring to give birth. Again Elizabeth Heyward adamantly refused to obey an order to illuminate. According to Garden, "violent anger was excited, and the house was assailed by a mob with brickbats, and every species of nauseating trash that could offend or annoy. Her resolution remained unshaken, and while the tumult continued, and shouts and clamour increased indignity, Mrs. Hall expired." The extent to which the mob scene contributed to Lois Hall's demise in childbirth cannot be ascertained, but the British authorities were humiliated. Their apology and offer to repair the damage to the house was curtly and peremptorily refused—Elizabeth Heyward preferred that the damage remain as a testimony to the British failure to protect the weak and innocent. The horror of such a tale must have been unimaginably tragic to the widowed Mr. Hall, helpless in his Florida exile.[46]

Col. William Lee, miniature attributed to Jeremiah Theus. Courtesy of Lee Young-blood Greene, Jr., Hartselle, Alabama. Reproduced with permission.

Garden gave Rebecca Edwards as another of his examples of women's patriotism. Rebecca was the third wife of exile John Edwards, a wealthy dealer in commodities, slaves, and indentured servants, who had come from England in 1750. Little else is known about her, as is unfortunately true of many women of the era. But her husband served in the Commons House of Assembly, and his devotion to the patriot cause was unquestionable—as a member of the Privy Council a year before the capitulation, he sided with future exiles Christopher Gadsden and Thomas Ferguson in vehemently opposing negotiation with the British during the 1779 siege of Charleston.[47]

After the 1780 surrender of Charleston, Vice Admiral Mariot Arbuthnot of the Royal Navy was quartered temporarily in the Edwardses' house. Rebecca was alone after her husband's transport to St. Augustine, forced to put up with the enemy admiral in her home, and further forced to cope with the arrest of her two sons and one stepson, who were taken aboard harbor prison ships in May 1781. She "stifled the tender feelings of the mother, and heroically bade them despise the threats of their enemies" and encouraged them to support steadfastly their glorious cause: if the "threatened sacrifice should follow, they would carry a parent's blessing, and the good opinion of every virtuous citizen along with them to the grave." But if they were to waver, give in to the British, "and exchange their liberty for safety, they must forget her as a mother, nor subject her to the misery of ever beholding them again."[48]

And there was Eliza Yonge Wilkinson, the beautiful, young, widowed sister-in-law of exile Morton Wilkinson, who had experienced firsthand the frightening depredations committed by British regulars, provincials, and loyalist marauders who preyed on defenseless civilians living on the plantations. Eliza came to town and spent time visiting and tending to the unfortunate American soldiers aboard the infamous British prison ships—and was much relieved to find the inmates in high spirits at the prospect of being exchanged. She rudely rebuffed every red-coated officer's attempts to befriend or assist her, never disguising her sentiments and assuring them at every opportunity that she was a recalcitrant rebel. When one officer asked her how long she would continue to be melancholy, she replied, "Until my countrymen return, Sir." Return, he asked, "as prisoners or subjects?" She haughtily replied, "As conquerors! Sir," abruptly ending the conversation.[49]

Chapter 9

All Fortunes Reverse

The erratic delivery of mail to the exiles kept them mostly in the dark about their revolution; it was not at all apparent that through the winter and into the spring of 1781 British primacy was waning. Already mentioned were the stunning American victories at Kings Mountain in October 1780 and at Cowpens the next January. And though Cornwallis retained the field and claimed victory at Guilford Courthouse on March 15, 1781, he sustained casualties he could ill afford to lose. Lieutenant Colonel Rawdon defeated Nathanael Greene at Hobkirk's Hill on April 25 but eventually relinquished Camden. Maj. John Cruger's loyalist militiamen at Ninety Six resisted a besieging force of Greene's Continentals in May and June but finally abandoned their star-shaped fort in July.[1]

With Cornwallis in North Carolina, Greene gained control of most of South Carolina as the British sphere of influence contracted ever closer to Charleston. Patriot militias under generals Francis Marion, Andrew Pickens, and Thomas Sumter enjoyed a resurgence and varying degrees of success, taking Orangeburg and other British-held outposts and severing communications between Charleston and Savannah. The notorious loyalist Maj. Thomas Brown, who commanded the King's Carolina Rangers, surrendered Augusta, Georgia, on June 6, 1781. Brown's capture would have potential ramifications for the exiles in faraway St. Augustine.[2]

Further afield, Britain and Spain had been at war since 1779, with Spain systematically going after the entire Gulf Coast. By May 1781 all of West Florida was in Spanish hands, which for the rest of the period of the Charlestonians' exile gave St. Augustine every reason to fear invasion by the Spaniards.[3]

Though British domination was still strong in Charleston and St. Augustine, at the diplomatic level a virtually independent United States was being taken more seriously. After months of negotiations, commissioners representing both sides finally agreed upon an exchange cartel for the Southern Department (the so-called Pee Dee Cartel, signed on May 3, 1781), and in Charleston, Balfour was obliged to take heed.[4]

As the Charleston commandant, Balfour was not particularly pleased to honor the terms of the cartel when it was first signed. To Greene he wrote that he would happily join in measures that would "mitigate the general horrors of War, or soften the distresses of individuals," a seemingly noble sentiment. But he betrayed a less generous attitude by his remarks to Cornwallis, complaining that under the cartel he would have to "give up all the Augustine gentry . . . to go home upon their Paroles as Militia." He most certainly did not want them returning to his jurisdiction in Charleston and was determined that he would "try to keep them off . . . as much as possible."[5]

Almost immediately after the signing of the cartel, Balfour began showing his mounting unease, sensing well that his situation was deteriorating. In a letter to General Clinton written on May 6, 1781, he said of South Carolina, "Indeed I should betray the duty I owe your Excellency, did I not represent the defection of this province so universal, that I know of no mode short of depopulation, to retain it. This spirit of revolt is in a great measure kept up by the many officers prisoners of war here; and I should therefore think it advisable to remove them." Cartel or not, he removed a number of captives to prison ships in Charleston Harbor.[6]

The reputation of this mode of incarceration was cause for considerable consternation—Continental and militia prisoners had been sent to similar ships since the beginning of hostilities, and it was well known that an alarming prevalence of sickness and mortality resulted from the close quarters. The ships made dangerously miserable prisons.

These prisoners were by Balfour's own assertions officially being held hostage in retaliation for alleged mistreatment of loyalist militia by Gen. Francis Marion's men, "in many cases extending unto Death." But Balfour had ulterior motives that suggested panic: he desperately needed to quell the irrepressible spirit of revolt and was resorting to alleged parole violations as an excuse for getting local impertinents out of circulation. His reasoning was hardly in accord with Charleston's earlier established capitulation agreements, but it was rationale enough for Balfour to set the prisoners afloat. In his words, his actions "may militate with the Capitulation of Charlestown," but at this point it was not feasible to relocate them as he had earlier with the troublemakers he sent to St. Augustine. Besides, he had long used prison ships to confine various miscreants in the harbor.[7]

Josiah Smith was convinced that the exchange cartel was to some extent known in Charleston even before the militiamen were herded aboard the prison ships, a conviction that justified outrage. He and his cohorts believed the hostage-taking to be "a wicked contrivance of the Commandant, to inflict his last punishment on those Obstinate friends to their Country, or at least to terrify them into a Submission to British Government."[8]

But the duplicitous Balfour was not yet finished with imposing his authority on the patriots of Charleston. On May 11 he issued orders that after sunset the next day, those persons who had not taken protection and become loyal British subjects were to remain as prisoners in their respective houses and "on no account, be found out of them." And they were to be largely ignored. All of His Majesty's loyal subjects were "required to take notice hereof, and abstain from any connection with Persons under such predicament." The prisoners were also required to register a return of their names and places of abode with the town major to enable the guards and patrols to enforce these orders.[9]

Back in St. Augustine, letters from home apprised the exiles of the shocking new British policies, especially those by which militiamen officially on parole were being incarcerated in the notorious harbor ships. Many of the exiles were affected by what appeared to be (and was, pure and simple) yet one more breach of the town's original articles of capitulation. Smith was disheartened but not surprised to learn that his son Samuel was one of the more than 130 taken aboard the prison ship *Torbay* and the schooner *Pack Horse* on May 17, 1781. John Edwards had one son and two stepsons now floating in the harbor, along with sons of other exiles, Bee, DeSaussure, Gadsden, Neufville, Poyas, and Prioleau, and brothers of Blake, Cochran, and Heyward.[10]

In St. Augustine a particularly poignant example of vicarious suffering for what was happening in Charleston was found in Samuel Prioleau, whose father and son were taken aboard the *Torbay.* Comparing his own exile of relative freedom in Florida with that ignominious confinement in his home harbor, Prioleau stewed on the irony. To his wife, Katy, he wrote that nothing had given him "greater pleasure than to hear of his Friends behaving in a Noble and Spirited a Manner when they were put on Board the prison ships. . . . We that are here, I find by Balfour's Letter, are also Hostage."[11]

Prioleau must have seen a copy of the Charleston commandant's letter to the militia prisoners aboard the prison ships explaining his rationale for depriving them of their liberty. They were to be hostages, "and those persons [the exiles], who some time since were sent from thence to St. Augustine, should, in this respect, be considered in the same point of view as yourselves." It was a title to which they were not accustomed, but the term *hostage* did contain an allusion to possible exchange.[12]

As a merchant Prioleau had done much business with England, but the war, his exile, and the oppression of his family had ruined any hope of reconciliation with the British: "If anything in that way shou'd happen to me," he admonished Katy, "my sons will revenge it when they are able and never to be at peace with Great Britain." Samuel and his fellows had also heard over and over that their families were being insulted. He intended to remember and repay the offenders:

"I beg as a particular favour if any has insulted you or any of my family you will let me know who it was, and what was the insult, as I think I stand a chance of being relieved and may meet them in some part of the world."[13]

Florida exile Daniel DeSaussure was another good example of someone justified in resenting the prison ships back in Charleston. He was a Charleston and Beaufort merchant who had served in the Provincial Congress and as paymaster general of the South Carolina militia. Exile aside, he had a number of other reasons to be bitter against the British. He had lost his brother Louis the year before, killed in the 1779 siege of Savannah. Another brother, Henry, died while fighting in the 1780 siege of Charleston. (A third brother, Thomas, would be killed at Yorktown later this same year of 1781.) Daniel had fought against the British in the defensive lines of Charleston alongside his sixteen-year-old son, Henry, and they both were taken prisoner at the capitulation. Daniel was considered sufficiently dangerous that he was soon sent to St. Augustine with the others. And now young Henry was one of those just recently confined aboard the *Pack Horse* in Charleston Harbor.[14]

As Smith pointed out, the threat of the prison ships was supposed to terrify patriots into a submission to British government. However if terrifying them into submission was indeed the intent, then the patriots could proclaim the move an utter failure. According to Smith, only about twenty men were driven to switch sides, and then only because of infirmity of age or distress of family. And despite all the very real complaints of misery aboard the prison ships in Charleston Harbor, the shipboard detainment of these particular captives was ultimately shortened by the application of the exchange cartel.[15]

Looking back from a postwar perspective, Maj. Alexander Garden (a Continental officer) wrote of "a happy trait in the human character, that proportioned to the pressure of adverse fortune, men's energies are frequently increased, and constancy sustained with a courage invincible." Young Henry DeSaussure amply exemplified this when he later recalled the unhappy floating prison experience with his sense of good humor. "Every species of insult was offered to us, when we were marched down from the main-guard to the place of our confinement. We were hooted at, hissed, reviled, and ultimately pelted with every offensive kind of trash," and the treatment by the British was no better once the prisoners were quartered on the ship. Henry insisted that he and the other captives had remained undaunted and refused to show fear of their captors. After all, wives and sisters were allowed to visit, which was very good for their spirits.[16]

"We were even sportive in our amusements, and by a variety of contrivances dispelled that *ennui* which must otherwise have proved oppressively irksome. . . . Cheerfulness was our sauce and our stimulant to appetite. Our spirits were exalted without liquor. The cup of cherished hope was passed from lip to lip, and the glow of becoming mirth and hilarity never knew abatement." The single item that would cause "any sensation of sorrow," Henry claimed, was news of a dereliction of duty on the part of any friend or person they wished to think well of but who, "cajoled by the delusive promises of the enemy, or natural imbecility of their minds and temperament," had decided to cooperate with the British occupiers.[17]

The determinedly happy prisoners even provided themselves with ongoing amusement by forming an Ugly Club, to which they elected officers and by which they kept track of "ugly points" awarded to fellow prisoners who became fretful or peevish or who lost their tempers or became argumentative. But even with that exemplary attitude the prison-boat fellows were not immune to physical sickness from the unsanitary conditions, and seventeen-year-old Henry De-Saussure in fact suffered such ill health on the ship that he was mercifully released to his mother's custody in town.[18]

In faraway Philadelphia the Continental Congress acted to display its outrage over British violations of the articles of capitulation agreed upon by generals Lincoln and Clinton at the surrender of Charleston. The delegates protested, among other things, the confinement of prisoners aboard ships in Charleston Harbor and (looking back a few months) the transportation of citizens to St. Augustine. Consistent with the etiquette of their time, they protested against the manners by which the exiles had been "seized in their beds" and that the British "Major Benson, who executed the business of seizing these Gentlemen, was guilty of the Greatest indecency, not suffering the wives of the persons who were in bed to retire, and compelling them to listen to the abusive and Scurrilous ribaldry of both himself and the Soldiers who were with him."[19]

With righteous indignation the Congress therefore resolved that the Board of War issue immediate orders for retaliatory action, revoking the paroles of British and German officers captured three years before at Saratoga and other places and removing them to the dank and dreary abandoned copper mines of Newgate Prison in Simsbury, Connecticut (less populous than St. Augustine). There they would be treated "in such a manner as will be most conformable to the usage which the American soldiers in captivity receive from the enemy." Furthermore the delegates resolved that the Board of War be directed to order a sufficient number of British to be confined as hostages for the citizens of South Carolina and Georgia who had been sent to St Augustine, "and for such as are confined on board prison ships in the Harbour of Charlestown or in the provost of that Town." The delegates' intent notwithstanding, these orders do not seem to have been carried out.[20]

The exiles themselves, always a little out of touch with the larger scene, of necessity occupied their minds with local trivia. On June 4 they were distracted and annoyed by the noise from a celebration of the birthday of King George III. Twenty-one guns ceremoniously fired in salute from the Castle, and another twenty-one answered from a galley in the bay. Then followed three volleys of musketry and twenty rounds from field pieces on the parade grounds. The governor gave a dinner and a ball that night for the entertainment of the ladies, but their festivities were dampened by a report late in the evening of an armed American galley that had entered the St. Johns River area to discomfit the loyalist settlers at Cowford.[21]

A week passed before a small British pilot boat arrived from Savannah with a wild tale of having been taken by two North Carolina whaling boats. The pilot crew had thrown all of the English mail overboard, but for the sake of two women passengers, the marauders allowed the little vessel to continue on to St. Augustine. It turned out that those same two whalers had also taken the pilot boat from the St. Johns River and captured several other sea vessels, one of which was described as "a fine large Armed Ship" called the *Britannia,* seized in a surprise raid under the cover of darkness. Four days later another small poultry and tobacco boat made port. Its crew reported that the cruising Americans had stopped them at sea and taken all their chickens but allowed them to continue on with the tobacco they were delivering to St. Augustine citizens. In each case the vessels had been released only after making their crews take parole as prisoners of the United States.[22]

The outlook of the active military war in the southern theater increasingly favored the American side. Lord Cornwallis was stuck in Virginia, Greene gained control of most of South Carolina, and the British sphere of influence contracted ever closer to Charleston. Revolutionary militias enjoyed resurgence with varying degrees of success. Savannah still remained British, but the patriots had managed to sever the Georgia town's communications with Charleston.[23]

News of another event reached St. Augustine, more dramatic than stories of pirated chickens and tobacco deliveries. Augusta, Georgia, fell to patriot militia led by Brig. Gen. Andrew Pickens and assisted by the Continental Legion of Lt. Col. Henry "Light Horse Harry" Lee on June 5, 1781. The notorious loyalist Lt. Col. Thomas Brown (no relation to Commissary William Brown) commanded the King's Carolina Rangers in defense of Augusta, and his surrender of the town and resultant capture posed a serious problem for the exiles in faraway St. Augustine.[24]

The fall of Augusta and capture of Brown was especially maddening to St. Augustine's British commandant, the short-tempered and vengeful Lieutenant Colonel Glazier. Glazier happened to be a good friend of Brown the defeated loyalist. So despised was Brown by the Americans that when he was captured at Augusta, were it not for special protection provided by Lieutenant Colonel Lee, he might well have been murdered in captivity.[25]

Glazier's ire was stoked at the news of Brown's apprehension—just as burning as it had been the previous October when he had threatened to hang Christopher

Gadsden to avenge John André. But this time he announced his intention to hang not one but six of the exiled patriots in St. Augustine if Brown was killed. Fortunately the magnanimous General Greene approved Brown's parole and transport under guard to safety in Savannah. Glazier's hanging bluff would not be called. Unlike Brown, however, the exiles could not so easily be whisked away from danger. Nevertheless they were unfazed—not once did they flinch from these indignities and dangers. Never was there an application for British protection from a single one of them.[26]

When Glazier made another such retaliatory threat of capital punishment, they reacted not with fear but with humor. One of them, John Budd (a medical doctor who had enjoyed a rather risqué reputation for his youthful extravagances before becoming one of Charleston's "most respectable" citizens), was immediately seized not by dread but by a pun, which he thought worth a special trip over to the house where fellow Charlestonian George Flagg was staying. Happily, when he entered, someone set him up perfectly by asking if he had heard any interesting news. "Ah," he replied, "the British have resolved to hoist Flagg and nip the rebellion in its Budd!" The pun may have taken a moment for comprehension, but it did get a laugh. And not at all does it sound like the voice of a cowering victim.[27]

It was Lieutenant Colonel Clarke who bent the rules in favor of kindness by allowing George Abbot Hall to be the second St. Augustine exile to return home. Hall's wife had died six weeks before, and Clarke granted him passage to Charleston to care for his numerous children. This was a most unusual exception, so with both joy and sorrow, Hall boarded the sloop *Swift* and sailed for Charleston on June 22. His wife, Lois Mathews Hall, had spent her last days under the care of her sister Elizabeth Heyward and had expired while giving birth during or very soon after the mobbing of the Heyward house on May 12, the anniversary of the surrender of Charleston. The bereaved Hall was more than willing to carry a parcel of letters home to the families of his compatriots.[28]

For the rest of the exiles, rumors of the cartel continued to swirl. Details concerning the "immediate" exchange clause were repressed, and it was not until June 22, fifty days after its signing, that it appeared in the newspapers. (That was the very day that George Abbot Hall set sail to return to Charleston.) Instead of rumor, actual text now informed the Charlestonians that "all the Militia prisoners of War, Citizens of America taken by the British Arms in the Southern department, from the first commencement of this present War, to the 15th day of this present Month of June, shall be immediately exchanged for all the Militia Prisoners of War Subjects of Great Britain, taken by the American Arms in the said department, within the above mentioned term." Not just equally matched allotments, but all such British and American prisoners wherever they were held (and so including the exiles in St. Augustine) were "hereby declared to be fully, absolutely and reciprocally Exchanged, and such of them as are on parole within the lines of their respective parties, are hereby declared to be released therefrom . . . [and] shall be immediately liberated and permitted to pass without restriction to the party to whom they belong."[29]

Some of the merchants in St. Augustine may have regretted the prospect of losing the Charlestonians' business, but for the St. Augustine governmental and military authorities, it was welcome news. The exiles had presented logistical problems from the start, as well as being a challenge both from the ethical and the social point of view; they were an annoyance, and their departure would be nothing but good riddance.

Nonetheless arrangements for the liberation mandated by the exchange had yet to be made, and Governor Tonyn's authorities seemed to be in no hurry to make them. The exiles were thus left in the dark about any essential details of the exchange; but they nonetheless had been able to piece together an encouraging collage of secondhand war news. This and an unexpected concession on the part of Glazier sufficed to stimulate the spirits of the Charlestonians in time for the Fourth of July.

Perhaps out of ignorance of the anniversary, or maybe because the British knew the Americans were not to remain in St. Augustine much longer, or perchance the commandant was just weary of dealing with them, he gave a rather generous permission for an assembly of all of the messes together for a grand banquet in the State House. Behind the closed doors of St. Augustine's most elegant building, patriotic enthusiasm made up for the plain but ample fare. The only luxury on the menu was a gigantic English plum pudding, brought in surreptitiously and defiantly sporting on its top a tiny flag waving thirteen stars and stripes.[30]

A British soldier on guard outside, peeking in at the windows when he heard a surprisingly familiar air, wondered at what sounded like a sudden return of loyalty to King George: a robust performance of the stately and rousing anthem "God Save the King" was being sung by all the revolutionary Americans present. What the guard could not quite hear was the new lyrics, a clever text composed under Forbes's orange trees that very morning by Thomas Heyward—"God save the thirteen States, thirteen United States, God save them all." Handwritten copies were passed out at the dinner, and the words were sung with great animation and exultation. The next day the American version leaked to the British soldiers, who observed with some amusement that the rebels had not changed their tune—just the text.[31]

On July 5 the British authorities in St. Augustine made a wholly unexpected announcement that the prisoners, knowing so little of the exchange cartel, could only see as another unnecessary and cruel design on the part of their commandant. Glazier gave three days' notice for all of the Americans to be ready to pack up and march some forty miles north through the wild terrain to Cowford on the St. Johns River. There they would be put into a collection of small, open boats and conveyed—not by open sea but by the inland waterway behind the long series of coastal islands—to Savannah, where they presumably would begin a new period of exile. No explanation was given for such a miserable midsummer's venture.[32]

Within twenty-four hours of the extraordinary order, the alarmed prisoners had drawn up and signed a memorial to commandant Glazier. They once again restated rather politely the familiar and wearisome arguments that their original paroles and liberties in Charleston had been changed to St. Augustine not because of any unworthiness or misbehavior on their part—they claimed to have adhered strictly to their paroles—but simply for reasons of policy, and that part of the understanding was that they should not be subjected to any unnecessary difficulties or sufferings. They could only suppose that once again some unexplained reasons of policy had triggered the proposed change of residence. After a few hypocritical compliments to the commandant's long experience, humanity, and presumed desire to mitigate the horrors of war, they pointed out to him the difficulties and sufferings that his order would produce.[33]

"There are many among us Aged and Infirm, and all of us since our Captivity [are] more or less enervated by an inactive and sedentary life," they wrote, giving their reasons for protesting the order to move. First, a fatiguing march during such a hot, dry, and sultry season, "through a Wilderness destitute of every accommodation . . . even of the necessary refreshment of Water," was entirely untenable. Second, "to be confined for near a fortnight on board Small Boats, exposed to every inclemency of the weather, will probably to many of us be attended with fatal consequences." Third, they also recalled the known presence of hostile Indians along the proposed route.[34]

Finally they urged him to consider the rumor that a cartel of exchange might be in the offing and pointed out that there were two ships currently in the harbor that might well take at least the greater part of them if not to British occupied Charleston then to some port in American hands. Or, as an easier suggestion, if he would merely let them stay where they already were, their honorable good behavior would continue and in no way be a problem for the local garrison. All of the prisoners from Charleston remaining in St. Augustine signed this document, excepting Christopher Gadsden and Jacob Read, who were still confined in the Castle. More privately they considered the means by which their expulsion might, if necessary, be forcibly resisted.[35]

No written answer came from the commandant, but Commissary Brown confided to the exiles that a British man-of-war was waiting outside the bar and might well be bringing news that could affect their case. For that reason alone, he expected the commandant to defer the transfer, at least temporarily. The reprieve sent Smith into the throes of religious adulation: "Oh! how plain hath the finger of Providence in our favour, appear'd in this matter; may we therefore adore that Mercy, which hath Saved us from the dangers & distresses that must have attended us in a voyage hence to Georgia."[36]

At last on July 7, the very day originally slated for the dreaded overland trek, the Anastasia tower hung out signals that indicated several vessels in sight. The winds being contrary, the ships could not enter the town harbor until the next evening, but along with new recruits, cannons, and provisions came welcome news that almost a month earlier General Cornwallis had agreed to the long-awaited exchange: all prisoners, whether civilian or military, taken by the British in the Southern Department from the beginning of the war through June 15, 1781, were to be released back to American control in return for British prisoners released to His Majesty's authorities. Lieutenant Colonel Glazier withheld this information for a day before allowing Brown to inform the exiles, who were ecstatic.[37]

According to the *Royal Gazette,* all "such as are within the Towns, Garrisons, Camps, Ports, or Lines of the powers who captured them, shall be immediately liberated and permitted to pass without restriction to the party to whom they belong." It was stipulated that the exiles would be released to American control, but Charleston was not under American control. So none of them would be allowed to return to their homes and the welcoming arms of their dear families in Carolina—no, instead they were to go to Virginia or Philadelphia. They were happy nonetheless, for it was certain that they had escaped Glazier's "cruel design" to send them to Savannah. The patriots' great joy was tempered by news in the next issue of the *Gazette* from which they learned of Balfour's expulsion of their families from Charleston. This was especially distressing considering that nothing in the paper indicated where the families were to go.[38]

On the evening of July 9, the commissary informed the exiles that Glazier had received orders from Balfour in Charleston to permit them all, including Christopher Gadsden and Jacob Read, "to depart from St. Augustine as Prisoners exchanged either for Virginia or Philadelphia as we shou'd chuse." Unfortunately by no means were they to be allowed to call on their beloved city along the way. One of the victualers, a small schooner that happened to be already in the bay, would be furnished for their transport. The gentlemen realized immediately and protested to Glazier via Brown that the vessel was not half large enough. It was too small to carry their baggage alone, much less the human cargo, which included not only the exiles but also the enslaved people that they brought with them.[39]

An annoyed Glazier responded the next day. The schooner *East Florida* with a draught of sixty tons was available and large enough to convey them and their baggage if they would only consent to pay one hundred pounds sterling for its hire. As to chartering an additional schooner at their own expense, he would allow it and grant the ship a flag of truce. They did not have the funds, they said, and proceeded tiresomely to remind him once again of the hot and sultry midsummer season, that their rights had been violated under the capitulation, that they had undergone considerable expenses in consequence of that violation, and that they were not in a position to earn anything further for themselves while exiled—in a word that they could not afford to pay for their own expulsion and that hence the proposal was neither satisfactory nor even practicable.[40]

This was the last straw for the Glazier, who was distinctly weary of the exiles' irritating presence. Already impatient and now rankled by really ominous developments in the war, he answered with a final ultimatum: he offered the *East Florida* at British expense, that ship and that alone for the whole group, slaves, baggage, and all. He included four weeks' provisions for the trip but insisted that all of the South Carolina rebels be out of St. Augustine within a week. Evidently he had never in their nearly ten-month presence gained a whit of sympathy for the imperious patriots from Charleston, of whose "haughty and arrogant behaviour" he had already complained the previous January. They had been nothing but a thorn in his side.[41]

The commandant's final and nonnegotiable proposal could only cover a half of the party—at least, in conditions acceptable to them—and thus reduced the patriots to the necessity of hiring some additional and appropriate vessel entirely at their own expense. There was in fact a private ship available for charter, the brigantine *Nancy*, but it took a good bit of haggling on the part of Edward Blake and Edward Darrell to settle the price with the agent of the *Nancy*'s owner, who was prone to equivocation.[42]

At last they agreed that two hundred guineas would suffice; the money was to be held in escrow with the son of Andrew Turnbull in St. Augustine, who would then pay that sum to the shipowner's account only after he received a certificate verifying that the brigantine had arrived safely in Philadelphia, which they agreed was now their destination.[43]

The dickering over the cost of transportation was grating. Over the ten months they had endured away from home, many of them had expended all of their money, and the rest were so hard up for cash that it seemed well-nigh impossible to raise the two hundred guineas needed to engage the *Nancy*. To raise money Smith's mess organized a "vendue sale" (what would be called in modern times a yard sale or garage sale). They were thus able to rid themselves of utensils and provisions acquired over their months of idle Florida life and deemed unnecessary for use in Philadelphia. The other messes contributed articles for the event and shared the profits accordingly. The sale was a great success that far exceeded their expectations.[44]

In Charleston the results of the cartel were more problematic. The decree "liberated and permitted" its beneficiaries to pass without restriction "to the

party to whom they belong," and since Balfour's Charleston was still unquestionably in British control, the St. Augustine exiles did not "belong" there and would
therefore not be liberated and permitted to return. Within a week of the public
announcement of the prisoner exchange cartel, Balfour further complicated the
lives of the exiles and their families when he issued a proclamation ordering the
departure from his town and province of all the wives and children of those men
who were now exchanged as prisoners of war. They were directed to relocate
themselves to some place under American control.[45]

The cartel said "immediately," but Balfour allowed the families forty days to
pack, requiring them to take their leave by August 1. Balfour based their ejec-
tion on the cartel clause pertaining to all former prisoners on parole; it read that
"such as are within the towns . . . of the powers who captured them, shall be . . .
liberated and permitted to pass, without restriction, to the party to whom they
belong." He interpreted "such" to include their families, and he decided that
"permitted to pass" meant forced to leave.[46]

Balfour's presumed logic was that since the husbands and fathers were not
going to be allowed to come home, it would be impolitic for their wives and
families to remain without them. He also realized that the economic burden
of supporting the families thereby left fatherless in Charleston rested on the
resources of the occupying British government. Whatever his reasoning, his decision had the effect of throwing many families into utmost turmoil. It was up to
the ladies to make all of the arrangements for their abrupt departure within the
month of July, even though Balfour's May 11 decree said they had to remain as
prisoners in their respective houses "and on no account, be found out of them."[47]

To make arrangements even more difficult, all of His Majesty's loyal subjects
had been "required to take notice hereof, and abstain from any connection with
Persons under such predicament." The patriot families were in a quandary. Who
would be able to help them, where and how would they get the money for a
voyage, and how would they support themselves when they reached their destination?[48]

It seems as though the Charleston commandant, mentally rearranging the
deck chairs on his perceptibly sinking ship, took pleasure in the thought that
the departure of the patriot families might provide him and Charleston's loyalists
with real estate, to be used at his discretion. He let it be known that no rebels
"shall have liberty or grant powers to others for so doing to let or lease any house
within this town without a special license for so doing, as it is intended to take
all such houses as may be wanted for the publick service, paying to the owners
of those secured by the capitulation a reasonable rent for the same; as by this
means government will be enabled to reinstate its firm friends in possession of
their own houses within a short space of time." The word *reasonable* raised some

eyebrows in the insecurity and confusion of the moment, but conceivably the forcibly abandoned real estate might give a little income to a family in absentia.[49]

To complicate matters even further, it was obviously impossible for the exiled patriarchs of these now-to-be-exiled families to assist them. The fathers themselves were largely ignorant of the problems for want of communication with home and in any event were in no position to finance the departures. Many mothers were obliged to sacrifice furniture, ornaments, and other properties to pay for the move—none knowing where, when, or even if they might again see their husbands.[50]

The reality of this crisis and the humiliation of having to beg to suffer shows in a letter written to Balfour by Mary DeSaussure, dated July 3, 1781. She informed him that she was "unable, in her present circumstances, to provide for the expense that must necessarily attend the removal of herself and family from this Province; therefore," she apologized, she was forced to pray that his honor would "be pleased to grant her the indulgence of making sale of the furniture belonging to her dwelling house and kitchen, also a riding chaise."[51]

The commandant did not bother to acknowledge the request personally but had the letter endorsed by a clerk of the Board of Police, who notified her of permission granted to sell the requested articles after letting her stew for a week. Mary DeSaussure was right to ask permission to dispose of her household goods. Loyalists quickly realized that some rebel families might depart without having settled their debts, and for that reason explicit official permission and oversight was required of any exchanged prisoner of war or their wives and families before liquidating any species of property.[52]

Smith later lamented the universal distress caused by Balfour's "Cruel Edict" —"a large number of helpless Women & Children, and even Aged Persons, to be turned out of their Habitations . . . to be exposed to the danger of the Seas at a very Tempestious Season of the Year; and to Transport themselves at their own expence in a land of Strangers, with money insufficient to subsist on, even after Selling off their household furniture at half its value, of which the greater part [would then have] to be paid down for their passages at an extravagant rate." They would be crowded, he supposed, "in some Vessels not unlike to Guinea Ships" (i.e., slave ships) and "provided with water of such a quality as cou'd not be drank by Persons of their delicate frame." Smith was afraid the ladies would arrive at their destination as complete strangers and helpless without friends to assist them—"and all this occasion'd through the persecuting Spirit of a Truce-breaking British Commandant."[53]

Ultimately banished from Charleston were the wives and families of every man who refused the oath-bought protection of the loyalists, which compelled the departure of a large number besides the original exiles and their families. In all some 570 men, women, and children were ousted from their homes, virtually all headed for Philadelphia. Mary Cochran was a typical example, still worried about how to pay her son's school bills and get him out of France and now concerned with taking her other children to a strange city without assurance that her husband could ever join them there.[54]

Added to that number were seventy-one enslaved servants, all of whom were exiles in their own right, doubly so, forced from their homes and lives in order to accompany and attend to the needs of their owners. They too had to navigate an unfamiliar environment, although their exile was not due to their own political allegiances, which may or may not have aligned with those of the white refugees. Instead they were banished as a matter of fate, due simply to the households in which they found themselves enslaved.[55]

Chapter 10

Freedom Bound

Among the Florida citizens to whom the patriots owed a debt of gratitude, they appreciated several in particular. The most obvious, of course, was Jesse Fish, who had provided literally thousands of fresh oranges during the citrus harvest season. Hearing of the celebration of final departure, Fish sent over from his island a chicken turtle and a supply of lemons and limes. The exiles immediately composed a formal letter expressing their thanks for his kindnesses throughout their stay.[1]

At long last the great move from St. Augustine was about to take place. During the negotiations for the schooner *East Florida* and the brigantine *Nancy*, the enslaved laborers brought from Charleston were already busily helping prepare the two ships; among other tasks this involved hauling on board enough fresh water for a trip estimated to take two weeks. And then there was food. Fortunately the exiles' friendship with another local citizen paid off unexpectedly; Francisco Sanchez, the meat merchant to whom the gourmand Charlestonians had given considerable and regular patronage, had profited from ten months of their special orders. When the time came for such transactions to cease, he sent each boat of departing Americans the gift of a good yearling heifer, half a large hog, some fowls and ducks, and some hundred pumpkins. At last the presentation of that maligned fruit, which made such good pies, could be taken as a friendly compliment.[2]

Even some of the local Tory society, self-imposed exiles from South Carolina, sent gifts for the voyage (fowls, eggs, cakes and bottles of wine), though their politics had not permitted them to be more sociable during the forced residency of their revolutionary connections. Lt. Gov. and Mrs. Moultrie contributed a dozen young fowls, six dozen eggs, four bottles of "burnt wine" (brandy), and a parcel of sweet cakes. Josiah Smith noted in his diary that he esteemed this outpouring from John Moultrie as even more extraordinary considering that despite having worked hard as the trustee for his father-in-law's estate in Carolina, he "never saw the Colour of his Wine, or soiled a plate at his Table" the whole while in St. Augustine.[3]

As it was readily apparent that the two vessels were not equally swift or comfortable, the gentlemen democratically selected a committee of five to make assignments, stipulating only that the congenial mess groups into which they had divided in St. Augustine should remain together as nearly as possible. The group lists were announced, one of thirty-one and the other of thirty, each of which appointed a representative for the drawing of lots. Enslaved people who had made the forced journey to St. Augustine were also among the passengers. It subsequently fell to the thirty-one to take the brigantine, and this was satisfactory to the whole of them. By the luck of the draw the schooner (which though lighter in weight was the slower ship) would carry many names still familiar to modern ears, including the only family unit of the entire exodus—that of Alexander Moultrie, whose wife and daughter had come with him aboard a privately chartered schooner to St. Augustine.[4]

At the same time, anxious negotiations were ongoing in Charleston, where last-minute arrangements were being made to fulfill Balfour's order banishing to Philadelphia the wives, children, and others considered household dependents, including enslaved. During the five years that preceded the fall of Charleston, William Johnson had carried on an extensive and profitable business. He had not only purchased houses and lands but also had bought stocks and indents of South Carolina and of the United States. However at the moment Sarah Johnson was ordered away from her home, she had little actual cash on hand with which to defray expenses.[5]

Sarah's backup solution was to remember that her enslaved property was legally movable capital. A painful possibility but a calculation that was not uncommon in a slave society. Once in Philadelphia, the enslaved might be hired out or sold, according to necessity. She also carried with her the indents and certificates of stock that were of little or no value in British Charleston but might be sold for good money in Philadelphia. Finally she assembled a wagonload of basic furnishings from her East Bay Street house and arranged to get that, herself, her selected slaves, and her five children sufficiently organized to set out for the Federal capital. The wagon was sent on ahead; she and her entourage would go by sea.[6]

The Charlestonians in St. Augustine were somewhat perplexed as to whether or not they should attempt to correspond further with their families with instructions for the disposition of papers and other details. For all they knew, their wives and children might already have been sent to Philadelphia. Smith gave a letter to a pilot from Charleston who was sailing from St. Augustine to Georgia on July 18, hoping that it would reach Mary's hands before she departed. At least the exiles could take consolation in the hope of a reunion in the not-too-distant future. And certainly their families shared these hopes. Mary Cochran, who had already arrived in the Pennsylvania capital by July 16, wrote to her son in France,

"I flatter myself your Papa will shortly be here. . . . I suppose you had heard he was one of the Gentlemen sent to St. Augustine. It is almost eleven months since he was taken from me, which you may be sure caused me a great deal of trouble and distress."[7]

Remarkably the St. Augustine commandant's ultimatum of departure within seven days was actually achieved, if just barely, and probably more out of the natural desire of the Charlestonians to leave than from any anxiety to respect or please the military authority. The week sufficed to clear out the accommodations in town, settle the local accounts, say the appropriate goodbyes—the exiles were surprised at how many and how warm—and get everything loaded onto the two ships. Breakfast on July 17 was the exiles' last meal on Florida soil. They had received official passport and flag-of-truce documents to get them past any difficulties of war. On this day of actual departure, the ever-thoughtful Jesse Fish came through one last time, sending a boatload of watermelons and freshly caught fish. Amid general rejoicing, it remained only to board the two ships. Thirty-one exiles and their twenty-three slaves boarded the brigantine *Nancy*, and thirty-two exiles (the two Moultrie ladies included) with their twenty-eight slaves boarded the schooner *East Florida*—the slightly more elegant group on the slightly less elegant ship.[8]

The two ships first dropped down to a point about two miles from the Castle, where they spent the night preparing to exit the harbor and begin their voyage in earnest on the open sea. The next morning, however, the wind and tide were unfavorable and would not allow the delicate maneuvering necessary for getting over the bar and out of St. Augustine's treacherous port. The two ships were obliged again to drop anchor and spend yet another night in the basin. With their arms on the rails, the exiles looked out over the waters where they had been allowed to fish and contemplated the low skyline of the little town that had become so familiar.[9]

St. Augustine's harbor was notoriously difficult to clear and certainly lived up to its reputation on this occasion. On the morning of July 19, both vessels made an early attempt to warp over the bar. This maneuver was the method of moving a ship against an unfavorable wind, tide, or in this case an obstacle by hauling on a line (called a warp) attached to a kedge anchor that had been carried ahead and dropped from a small boat. But the *Nancy*'s pilot had not properly calculated the changing tide, and the water depth was only ten feet—not deep enough to allay fears of striking the bottom.[10]

Impatience mounted, and by midafternoon the passengers aboard the brigantine insisted that the pilot give it another try, even against his own better judgment. An hour and a half of struggling and tugging, with the labor of the enslaved added to those of the crew, and finally the brigantine was able to get over the bar and through the north channel, where they found only twelve feet of water, just barely enough draft to float the ship. For his daring and dedication, they tipped the pilot "half a Joe," or about thirty-eight shillings.[11]

The *East Florida* was of course emboldened to follow suit, but because her warping anchor proved to be too light, the sloop was nearly driven onto the breakers in a mere eight feet of water. The brigantine sent over its pilot and a small boat with a larger anchor. A similarly dramatic struggle took place, and finally the schooner also made it across—but by that time the sun had set and the air grown still. Meanwhile the brigantine, awaiting the return of its boat and anchor, had drifted so far north that the small boat was unable to reach her before nine o'clock in the evening. The schooner had to employ its own boat in returning the two pilots to town, by which time it was so hopelessly late that anchor was dropped for yet another night.[12]

Winds on the morning of July 20 were much more favorable. By noontime calculations the *Nancy* was off the coast of Georgia just south of Savannah, and by the end of the day, it was estimated that she had sailed some eighty miles in fifteen hours. That was not accomplished without drama, for at one point an unknown brigantine appeared and seemed to want to make contact. When the traveling exiles decided they dared not risk an encounter, the stranger ship fired a warning shot. The Americans hastily ran up the appropriate flags to show their neutrality, and the captain raised the mainsail to the top of the mast. To their relief the Americans found that they were lighter and faster than the challenger and were thus soon enough able to sail out of sight. The ship was indeed fast, but being a shallow vessel, it rolled quite a bit, keeping the deck wet and slippery.[13]

The next day was very favorable for sailing, and the *Nancy*'s estimated position at noontime put her passengers almost due east of home—the still-forbidden city of Charleston. The afternoon ended in a dark sky ominously active with lightning. No storm came upon them during the night, but on the next morning, which was the Sabbath, the water was so calm that there was hardly any movement, and the sky so overcast that it was impossible to take readings to calculate their latitude. Nonetheless the day turned out to be innocent and even memorable by the visit of a great school of dolphins—not the mammal but the fish now called mahi-mahi—so numerous that they provided great diversion and a hearty dinner as well.[14]

And thus the days passed, the ships sometimes tacking with their clumsy sails against uncooperative winds and sometimes being forced to use only "small Sail" for nervous threading through coastal waters. One night while under high winds and heavy seas, the *Nancy* operated under a reefed mainsail, which required much attention from the crew—so much attention that at about three o'clock in the morning, the man assigned to watch the helm failed to notice a small fire breaking out in the binnacle, the enclosed compartment used to store navigational instruments and compasses and an oil lamp for using them. Smoke nearly suffocated some of the Americans sleeping in the cabin immediately beneath, and only by the exertions of those working above and below was the blaze extinguished without further harm.[15]

There were days of fair sailing weather. On July 24 another school of dolphins came alongside the *Nancy* to contribute to the passengers' sustenance. And once there was an impressive display of five "Grampusses [probably *Grampus griseus*] which came close under our Stern, Spouting like unto Porpoisses." Six days after embarking from St. Augustine, the *Nancy* reached the Outer Banks of North Carolina. Passing Ocracoke Inlet and Cape Hatteras, the brig successfully avoided the dangerous shoals that had wrecked many a ship and claimed the lives of numerous unfortunate sailors. On July 26 there was light rain, but the sky eventually cleared so that they were able to calculate their position opposite the Maryland shore. They would have had time to find the waterway inland to Philadelphia had not the weather prevented sighting of the lighthouse markers.[16]

All of July 27 was wasted waiting for conditions that would enable navigation along the coastal waters. Then on July 28 two rather unfriendly-looking ships accosted the *Nancy*. From a distance the marauders looked like British cruisers, but they turned out to be loyalist privateer sloops: the eighteen-gun *Triumph* and the twelve-gun *Hibernia,* both out of New York. Their captains demanded that the *Nancy*'s master, Captain Watson, bring his ship's legal papers aboard each of them for inspection. While they were stopped, the exiles sought information from the privateers regarding the war but learned nothing significant. Finally they were released and on their way, relieved of the inevitable concern that having endured so much for so long, they might be stopped short of their goals of refuge in Philadelphia and reunion with their families.[17]

The *Nancy* eased her way along the coast and finally entered the Delaware River, the last leg of the route to Philadelphia. A boat was sent to the lighthouse on Cape Henlopen on the Maryland side of the river's mouth to fetch a pilot to direct them the rest of the way upriver. While they nervously waited, they were approached by yet another vessel, only this time it was one friendly to their cause. A barge pulled alongside, and an officer from the thirty-two-gun Continental frigate *Trumbull* came aboard. (The *Trumbull* was part of an outbound flotilla anchored just upstream that consisted of eleven merchantmen, another frigate, and a privateer.) Eventually their pilot arrived and, being in a good humor, kept them going all night until seven o'clock the next morning, when the wind grew too calm for further progress. All they could do at this point was to anchor opposite Reedy Island to wait for the next flood tide. Patience was paramount, for they were now only about thirty-five miles shy of their destination.[18]

The exiles spent a good part of July 29 bobbing in the Delaware River while they watched downstream traffic pass. They warned those whom they could of the danger of being captured by a British cruiser that was patrolling in the vicinity—the twenty-eight-gun frigate *Medea*. Their admonitions were largely unheeded, and at least one vessel was taken. About two hours later, an American privateer, the *Royal Louis,* carrying twenty nine-pounders and commanded by Capt. Stephen Decatur Sr., came downriver accompanied by another privateer. On the word of the exiles aboard the *Nancy,* the American cruisers took off in pursuit of the *Medea.* The flood tide came in at about two o'clock in the afternoon and fair wind blew from the southeast, so, no longer a passive spectator to downriver traffic, the *Nancy* made sail and began its slow progress up the Delaware River. For nine hours the exiles leisurely glided past picturesque farms and small towns before stopping for the night sixteen miles below Philadelphia.[19]

Early on July 30, after a quiet and comfortable night's sleep, they took advantage of a flood tide and a southwesterly breeze to proceed further upriver, but not before first having to maneuver around the obstacle of a sunken ship. There was to be yet one more delay: at Fort Billingsport on the New Jersey side of the river, they were hailed and ordered to anchor until the health officer at Philadelphia came to approve their entry to the city. The exiles fully understood and even anticipated the cause for this delay, as Smith recorded in his diary that "all Flaggs [truce ships] with Prisoners on board, [were] subject to this necessary regulation, to prevent the spreading of infection." Notwithstanding, the erstwhile Charleston gentlemen were understandably anxious to get where they were going. Just before the *Nancy* was stopped, Isaac Holmes, Edward Blake, and Robert Cochran preemptively took passage on a small shallop over to the fort so that they could explain who they were and from whence they had come, hoping to expedite their passage.[20]

Instead of the delay being a cause for exasperation, it became a celebration. Charleston friends and fellow refugees already in Philadelphia were so pleased to hear of the ship's safe arrival that during the morning a number of them came out in small boats to shout their greetings to the temporarily off-limits newcomers. Ignoring the risk of quarantine, some accepted an invitation to come aboard the *Nancy,* where they remained for a hearty repast from the ship's abundant provisions. Since the long trip had actually taken a little less than the time estimated and fishing along the way had enhanced the menu, all was well.[21]

Permission to land came from the commissary for prisoners about noon, and the water was just right at 5:00 P.M. The actual landing and debarking process took about two hours. At the Chestnut Street wharf, there was a crowd of evening spectators and a great show of loyalty and relief. Some of the families, it turned out, had not yet arrived from Charleston, but many of the newly arrived exiles already had friends and connections in Philadelphia. That meant that there was little trouble in finding at least temporary accommodations.[22]

The schooner *East Florida* lagged somewhat behind the *Nancy* and had at least one remarkable experience of its own, almost at the expense of Thomas

Heyward's life. One night, the weather being extremely hot and the hold of the vessel very much crowded, Heyward came on deck for fresh air. He sat himself on a hen coop near the railing, where, in spite of the discomfort, he fell asleep. Another passenger, John Sansum, also came on deck some time afterward. Just as he stepped out into the warm night air, Sansum heard a sudden plunge into the water alongside. He was totally unacquainted with seafaring matters, but surmising that some person or thing must have fallen overboard, he instinctively grabbed a coil of rope and threw its loose end over the same side.[23]

For a time he could neither hear nor see any results of this procedure, performed impromptu and without practiced skill, but at last a voice called from the water in gratitude. Sansum had become "the agent of Providence in preserving the life of Heyward, one of the most valuable men in the State," a privileged signer of the Declaration of Independence. Seizing the rope, Heyward was able to reach the rudder of the vessel, to which he clung until taken up by his friends.[24]

The *East Florida* had early in the voyage lost sight of the faster brigantine, but those aboard the schooner toward the end were able to find themselves another brig to follow—another flag-of-truce ship. They tagged along behind this substitute lead for the entire day of August 2, which turned out to be their day of arrival, two days behind their friends aboard the *Nancy*. As the *East Florida* anchored in the evening, they found themselves alongside their mystery guides, already at anchor. The other ship was so close that William Johnson, being on deck, hailed them without the use of the normal "trumpet" (megaphone), and a man's familiar voice called back, identifying his ship as having just arrived from Charleston. "Is that you, Downham Newton?" yelled Johnson. "Aye, and is that you, William Johnson?—we have your family on board!"[25]

The *East Florida* docked in Philadelphia on August 10, and a joyful reunion between William, his wife, and their five children soon followed. Edward Mc-Crady found that his wife, Elizabeth, and son John were already waiting for him in town. "The pious effusions of their gratitude were offered up to Him who had so unexpectedly effected the meeting of families, relatives, and friends, without preconcert or provision on their part."[26]

There are only a few anecdotes regarding the passage of patriot families from Charleston to Philadelphia. Of course Lieutenant Colonel Balfour's order to evacuate gave many of them precious little time to prepare. Mary Sansum's journey began rather poorly. She pooled her resources with other families and hired a vessel to convey them northward. Their baggage was all aboard and they were ready to set sail on August 10, when they were lashed so hard by a sudden, violent shift in the weather that the storm "stove the Vessel, then lying at the Wharf, in such a manner, as demolished most of [her] baggage." As a consequence Balfour allowed the families to remain another two weeks, after which her journey seems to have been mercifully uneventful. Brig. Gen. William Moultrie and his family had boarded the small British cartel brig *Burton* to sail for Philadelphia. There was room for others, so upward of ninety persons, Continental officers and militia with their families accompanied the Moultries for what was reportedly a pleasant trip.[27]

How long they were to stay in Philadelphia was unknown, and many of the displaced South Carolinians were eager to hurry home to help liberate Charleston. Even before all of the relatives had been reunited, Christopher Gadsden wrote to George Washington that "Mr. [Thomas] Ferguson and I are waiting for our families, expected in a few days. As soon as we see them a little fixed, we shall set off for our state, as will most of the Carolina gentlemen here. We hope to be gone by the middle of next month, as at farthest."[28]

On August 3 a brigantine loaded with twelve families, 130 souls in total, completed their ten-day trip from Charleston. On board were Josiah Smith's wife, Mary, his 5 children, his aged father, and 4 of their enslaved people. His daughter Betsy was taken ashore "in a dangerous situation," sick with a fever. The strain of taking care of a sick child and the fatigue of the journey had nearly broken Mary, but through the ministrations of two physicians who kindly offered their services and the generous hospitality of Philadelphians who graciously took the Smiths into their homes, Betsy was eventually nourished back to her previous state of perfect health. Like many of the families from Charleston, the Smiths were nearly destitute. Without means to "gain a penny," they were obliged to live in Philadelphia "very savingly."[29]

By August 14 all of the St. Augustine exiles and families from Charleston had arrived safe and sound. David Ramsay remarked that he encountered more South Carolina friends on the streets of Philadelphia than he did in post-capitulation Charleston. Fortunately the Continental Congress was not caught completely unprepared for the influx from Charleston of 641 refugees, a number that included 71 enslaved people. On July 13 South Carolinians John Mathews and Isaac Motte had proposed that the Board of War furnish rations to recently exchanged prisoners and their families who had arrived or would soon arrive from Charleston, Savannah, or St. Augustine. Careful accounting of the number of these refugees who drew rations (excepting displaced Continental officers and their families) would be necessary to manage the distributions.[30]

The financial considerations were real. "The distresses of the unhappy sufferers from the Southern States call forth my Compassion and inspire the strongest desire to afford them relief," wrote superintendent of finance Robert Morris to Thomas McKean (then the president of Congress), asserting that there was "no private Man in the United States who would more readily, cheerfully or liberally exert himself for this benevolent purpose." Morris concluded regretfully that as a public officer he could not permit his feelings and sympathy to dictate his conduct. Government subsistence would require contracts that had not been made and funding he did not have and would be complicated to administer and possibly subject to abuse. If money was raised for the relief of those in need, he would be happy to assist in the procurement and disbursement of rations, but he wanted Congress and the Board of War to understand that in the future he could not be answerable to claims of this sort.[31]

Congress responded to Morris's suggestion of fundraising by authorizing the appointment of five commissioners to open a subscription for a loan of thirty thousand dollars for the support of South Carolina and Georgia refugees. The delegates from these two states guaranteed reimbursement with interest as soon as their state legislatures reconvened and were able to repay. The five commissioners were also authorized to accept "voluntary and free" donations to be applied to the relief of the sufferers. The idea was to make the refugees' "situations comfortable, tho' not affluent."[32]

Interestingly enough, the only state to respond legislatively to this appeal was Massachusetts, where (in those pre-Constitution days) an executive order called for a collection to be taken in all churches. That alone brought in some $6,296, including Governor Hancock's own contribution of $400, and most admirably, all but $100 of it was given outright (i.e., not as loans to be repaid). There were also two independent donations of $100 each from Massachusetts.[33]

Perhaps such admirable largesse reflects the basic sympathies often recognized between old Boston and old Charleston. The wealthier state of Pennsylvania responded with promises of $15,132 in 86 personal loans to be repaid and $3,312 in outright donation by 236 six individuals. But after three months (by mid-November), all that had actually been collected was some $7,568. Distribution of the money began in late September, at first in doles of $100 that were soon reduced to $30 with the realization that funds would have to be limited. Even after reduction, however, the distributed monies were of great service to the exiles. Smith commented that without such charity several of his contemporaries would have been impoverished almost to the point of starvation.[34]

Not that the sensitively honorable South Carolinians did not find something to ruffle their touchy feathers. In the first place, citizens fleeing all three southern states, people simply taking refuge in the middle states from the dangers and troubles harassing them at home, had preceded them in Philadelphia. The "kind-hearted Philadelphians, though apparently formal and cold in their deportment, generously afforded every possible aid to the wants of these new residents." But unfortunately the local citizens rather naturally referred to the temporary visitors as "refugees," a term that they meant to be of compassion and good will, not of slight or reproach.[35]

When the Charlestonians heard themselves referred to as refugees, they immediately took offense, presumably because they felt that the designation implied some sort of desperate and impoverished lower class. Moreover the term was now commonly applied to loyalists who had sought safety within British lines. They were neither desperate nor seriously impoverished, and above all they preferred to think of themselves as exiled martyrs of patriotism. The more elegant term *émigré* would have been acceptable, but it was not yet current, its vogue having to await the French Revolution eight years later.[36]

In the second place, the Charlestonians had scruples about accepting any charitable gestures or social condensations that might suggest they were products of a lesser way of life. But in spite of Charleston sensibilities, in Philadelphia contributions were raised and distributed, habitations were sought for the use of the South Carolinians, and even entire houses were offered free of expense. Philadelphians received many refugees under their own roofs and into the bosoms of their families. The Pennsylvanians also relaxed their laws in order to allow the southerners to hire out their enslaved people or, in some cases, even to sell them in order to generate ready capital. This step was notable, especially considering that Philadelphia was home to America's first antislavery society, the Pennsylvania Society for Promoting the Abolition of Slavery, founded by a small group of Quakers in the city in 1775.[37]

Still, in the midst of this hospitable republican spirit, there remained a tenacious degree of exclusiveness and aristocratic feelings. General Greene, like William Johnson, had in the past been employed at a foundry, and neither of them was ashamed on occasion to wield the tools of blacksmithery in person. "A fastidious lady of Philadelphia," recounted Johnson's son, "was making observations on the dress and address of other ladies in a ball-room when Mrs. Greene appeared before the group who were thus amusing themselves. A gentleman asked the Philadelphia lady if she did not admire Mrs. Greene. 'Oh yes,' said she, 'but I think I hear the clink of the iron on the anvil at every step she takes.'" The remark was perceived as scandalously crass and offensive.[38]

On another occasion Sarah Bee and Alice Izard, whom young Johnson called two of the finest women in South Carolina, were at an elegant Philadelphia social assembly in the company of their husbands. The polished manners of these two Carolinians were highly commended in a nearby conversation. "Oh yes," said one Philadelphia lady to another, grasping the chance to pun on the names of Bee and Izard, "but they are all a proud set, from B to Z." Instead of appreciating the rather contrived humor, the Charlestonians sniffed at the perceived snobbery and took the imagined affront to heart.[39]

The children of Edward McCrady and William Johnson later recalled more pleasant experiences from the child's-eye viewpoint, such as the times when Pennsylvania farmers, recognizing them as dislocated southerners, gave them apples to eat and to take home. Joseph Johnson, who was then only five, never forgot watching a whole division of the American and French soldiers on their march across an impressive floating bridge, hauling their baggage wagons and heavy artillery. Grown-ups explained to him that the bridge "settled a little, but that the water did not rise above the soldiers' shoes"—a scene and commentary that remained vivid in his mind seventy years later.[40]

The adults were less easily amused and found news from Charleston to be mixed. In some cases homes forcibly abandoned by these exiled families had been occupied by the British for their own uses. And though His Majesty's forces were willing to pay a reasonable rent for spaces thus commandeered, this turn of events did not bode well for the temporary Philadelphians, who at some point in the present unforeseeable future had every intention of returning home.[41]

Smith's Charleston house on Meeting Street was a prime example. A number of his enslaved people had been left behind to keep up the house, including Nellie, a washerwoman, and her elderly mother, Peggy. Also remaining in Charleston were Frank, Smith's body servant, and his wife, Dolly, who was the family cook, along with their son Cesar. Frank, Dolly, and Cesar were not exactly left behind; they had expressly chosen not to go to Philadelphia with the family, preferring the responsibility of staying in Charleston and maintaining the residence.[42]

One imagines that others of the enslaved who were forced to leave Charleston might have preferred a similar arrangement. Perhaps Frank was able to leverage his position within the household, and his personal relationship with Smith, in order to negotiate for himself and his family to be left behind, gaining some measure of autonomy in the wartime city while keeping watch over the Smith home. In any event all of them were turned out of the house when Balfour ordered its use as a hospital for British soldiers. Smith feared that if he was ever able to return to Charleston, he would find his home in ruins.[43]

One item of dreadful news soon came to everyone's attention. While the exiles in St. Augustine and patriot families in Charleston were making their way to Philadelphia, Col. Isaac Hayne of the Colleton County Militia was held captive in the Royal Exchange. He had been taken prisoner on July 7, 1781, by British dragoons after leading a daring raid behind British lines to apprehend Brig. Gen. Andrew Williamson, a former American militia leader who was suspected of treason. Hayne was a handsome, articulate, and educated member of the South Carolina lowcountry aristocracy who was well thought of by Charlestonians in general. His closest friends were St. Augustine exiles Dr. David Ramsay and Richard Hutson, who was also his brother-in-law. More poignantly Hayne was a recent widower with four young children.[44]

The previous year, after the capitulation of Charleston and while under threat of imprisonment, Hayne had reluctantly and half-heartedly given his oath of allegiance to King George III. According to Ramsay, James Simpson, the intendant of the British civil police who had been so involved in identifying the citizens to be exiled, was present and encouraged the desperate Hayne to take British protection, to which Hayne agreed. Afterward Hayne remained at home

Richard Hutson, Member of the Continental Congress. Etching by Max Rosenthal (n.d.). From the Thomas Addis Emmet, Collection of Illustrations Relating to the American Revolution and Early United States History, The Miriam and Ira D. Wallach Division of Art, Prints and Photographs: Print Collection, The New York Public Library.

peaceably until American forces regained control of most of South Carolina. He and others believed this circumstance cancelled their obligation to the British.[45]

Hayne returned to American service but was unfortunate in being captured at a time when lieutenant colonels Balfour and Rawdon were seeking to make an example of some American officer who had violated his allegiance. Hayne was condemned to death "for being found in arms, and levying a Regiment to oppose the British Government, notwithstanding he had become a subject, and had accepted the protection under that government, after the reduction of Charles Town."[46]

Balfour and Rawdon were frustrated by British reverses and could not be swayed by appeals for mercy on Hayne's behalf. Evidence suggests that they acted in part to exact vengeance for the October 1780 execution of their friend Maj. John André as a spy (after Maj. Gen. Benedict Arnold's infamous defection to the British). Without due process, despite the attempted intervention of Charleston patriots and loyalists, and notwithstanding the pleas of the Hayne children on their knees tearfully begging Balfour to spare their father's life, Hayne was hanged by the British on August 4.[47]

General Greene learned of Hayne's execution on or about August 10. Not knowing exactly where the St. Augustine exiles were in the process of exchange and not wanting to cause any untoward effects for them, he delayed retaliatory action. He did, however, inform the Continental Congress, who also heard of Hayne's death from the eyewitness account of fourteen-year-old Isaac Neufville, son of St. Augustine exile John Neufville. Copies of the correspondence between Hayne and his captors reached Philadelphia, purportedly conveyed in some way by Rebecca Edwards, and were published in the newspapers, spreading word of the dreadful incident across the United States and abroad. British officers faced the threat of reprisal, the exchange cartel was halted for a time, and untold numbers of lukewarm patriots eventually returned to the fight—all for an act from which the British derived no lasting benefit. Balfour and Rawdon were later criticized at home in England. South Carolinians in Philadelphia were immediately outraged—they considered the unfortunate Hayne to be one of them.[48]

Christopher Gadsden proposed that "ample and instantaneous retaliation" would put a stop to this "newly adopted system of British policy" and that Rawdon, who had since been captured by the French, should be among the first to suffer. After Cornwallis surrendered at Yorktown on October 19, the South Carolinians in Congress, well stocked with personal enmity, maintained that the British officers generally and Cornwallis in particular were being treated too gently. Former St. Augustine captive Arthur Middleton made a motion "that General Washington be directed to detain Earl Cornwallis, and the officers captured in the garrisons of York and Gloucester, till the further order of Congress." Fortunately this motion, which would have violated the Yorktown articles of capitulation, failed.[49]

According to the journal of New Jersey delegate Elias Boudinot, the South Carolina delegates wanted Cornwallis specially charged with the murder of Isaac Hayne as an atrocity committed under pretext of martial law. The situation "enraged the Gentlemen from the Southward, & particularly a Mr. Middleton and soon after Lord Cornwallis' Capture, a Motion was made in Congress, that General Washington should cause his Lordship to be executed in retaliation of Col Haines and other cruelties committed by him." The prospect of the motion's success greatly alarmed many moderate members of Congress. According to Boudinot (but not the congressional record), the debate continued back and forth for several days, and it was only with great difficulty that the moderates "succeeded in putting a negative on it, by a small Majority."[50]

Chapter 11

Homecoming

The reunited exiles and their families exercised patience for at least the autumn months, if not longer. Pennsylvania was their temporary home, and that in itself represented progress. The intoxicating atmosphere of a freely American Philadelphia was definitely more comfortable than the repressed air of St. Augustine or occupied Charleston, and individuals were now distinctly better informed and more at ease about talking. The exiled families closely followed the operations of the Continental Army and took pleasure in reports of the spirited endeavors of the South Carolina militia.

Particularly exciting was the news of what would be the last major engagement of the war in the south. Approximately sixty miles northwest of Charleston, at Eutaw Springs on September 8, 1781, Nathanael Greene's army of two thousand Continentals and patriot militia collided with fourteen hundred British regulars and loyalist militia led by Lt. Col. Alexander Stewart. Both sides suffered heavy losses in this bloody and obstinate battle, and though Stewart, who had replaced Rawdon as the British field commander, could arguably be granted a pyrrhic tactical victory for retaining the field at day's end, Greene again had rightful claim to the strategic victory. Stewart abandoned the South Carolina interior and withdrew to Charleston, his rearguard harassed by Greene for most of the way.[1]

In the aftermath of the earlier battle of Guilford Courthouse (March 15, 1781), Lord Cornwallis had retreated to Wilmington, North Carolina. While Greene was regaining control of South Carolina and Georgia, Cornwallis marched his army northward to Virginia, first to Petersburg for reinforcement and eventually to a coastal position at Yorktown, where he acted on Clinton's orders to establish a fortified deepwater port on the Chesapeake Bay. The exiles had been in Philadelphia scarcely three weeks when, on August 30, the appearance of a French fleet along the Virginia coast cut off Cornwallis's escape by water. Only days later the arrival of Washington's combined sixteen-thousand-man Franco-American army at the outskirts of Yorktown trapped Cornwallis's seven thousand redcoats, Hessians, and provincial troops in the town.[2]

Continental and French engineers waited three weeks before commencing formal siege operations, and on October 9 French and American artillerists began shelling the town. A joint attack on October 14 resulted in the capture of two British redoubts, allowing the allies to tighten their lines and bombard the British from a closer range. The fate of the surrounded, outnumbered, starving, and exhausted British army was sealed; Cornwallis had little choice but to surrender, which he did on October 19, 1781. Washington's dramatic victory at Yorktown effectively brought about the end the Revolutionary War, though it took more than a year before Charleston was free.[3]

In Philadelphia the children were delighted by the illumination of the city upon its receiving the glad tidings of Lord Cornwallis's surrender at Yorktown. They were awed to hear the dramatic report brought by a messenger who had run a great distance and "had scarcely entered the hall of Congress when he fell dead with apoplexy" (though it was actually the aged doorkeeper who died). They would long remember the Dutch accents of the night watchmen who, after midnight, made the rounds calling out (as Joseph Johnson recorded), "Bast twelfe o'glock, and Cornwallis is dagen." Thomas Legaré, unsure of the word *dagen,* yelled from his window, "Are you saying that Cornwallis has been 'taken'?," to which the answer of "Yaw!" was mirthfully and forever stamped in his children's memories.[4]

But the British were slow to admit defeat and give up Charleston, so it was not yet time for the exiled patriots to go home. As the winter of 1781–82 bore on, the Philadelphia-exiled William Johnson family added several relatives to their number—William's mother had been living as a widow on New York property that had been in the Johnson family since the 1600s. During the Revolution her houses near Wall Street in lower Manhattan were destroyed by fire, so she had moved to the country to live with her widowed daughter. Not long after Cornwallis's defeat, William's elder brother Capt. John Johnson learned that William and his family were not far away. He resigned his military commission and visited his relatives in Philadelphia, where he proposed that all the Johnsons should return to South Carolina in the spring—at least to William's country properties, if the British would still not let them into Charleston proper. To that end he had fetched his aged mother, his widowed sister and her children, and his own family and brought them all to Philadelphia.[5]

In Philadelphia the swollen Johnson household began to take money matters into their own hands. While other exiles waited for official government decisions as to how they might eventually get home, the Johnsons were reasonably certain that their number had been too much increased by their in-laws to qualify for any of the expected financial assistance. They therefore chose to set out privately on an overland route, joined by the displaced families of Thomas Cochran,

Thomas Legaré, and Thomas Harris (none of whom had suffered through the St. Augustine exile).[6]

William Johnson had been able to liquidate the stock Sarah had wisely brought from home, its value having appreciated after the young nation became allied with France. This money enabled him to buy a wagon and team and a stage wagon with two horses. Thus mobilized, they set out, hauling with them the load of Charleston furniture that had accompanied them through their Philadelphia exile. The stage wagon, which William himself drove, carried the aged grandmother, the ladies and children, and anyone else who from time to time could not walk fast enough to keep up with the pace set by the furniture wagon.[7]

By day the families traveled in a caravan, and at night they camped along the roadside or in the woods, staying together for mutual protection. The ladies and children slept in the wagons, while the men took turns standing guard duty. Traveling together in such a large group was intended to assure safety in numbers, but this proved to be a mixed blessing as the party was too large for residents along the way to accommodate or supply. They were frequently obliged to separate in order to obtain food for themselves and forage for their horses.[8]

Their way southward was lengthened by the perceived necessity of keeping as far as possible from any remnant armies battling in these last months of the war. They went through York, Pennsylvania, toward Lancaster, crossed the famous Natural Bridge in Virginia, and circuitously crept south until they arrived at Charlotte, North Carolina, close to the South Carolina border. There they learned they were traveling too rapidly, as the British who still retained possession of Charleston could yet make trouble in the upstate countryside. The triple household of Johnsons rented a log cabin and put the horses in good pastures while they awaited a better opportunity to proceed farther south.[9]

For a while the Johnson family played pioneer in their Charlotte log cabin, but William Johnson eventually found it impossible to remain idle on the border of South Carolina and so close to home. Leaving his patient family to await his return, he took one horse for himself and another for his old St. Augustine bondman Stephen and set out to offer his services to General Greene. The two men, reminiscent of a latter-day Don Quixote and Sancho Panza, had a number of colorful adventures and close encounters but were always too late or too distant to involve themselves in any actual fighting. Feeling surer of the odds, they finally returned to Charlotte and collected the other Johnsons to make a long trek by way of Hanging Rock and Flat Rock to Camden.[10]

The children later recalled eerie areas of destruction and deserted habitations, and the important-feeling assignment of the boys to find drinkable water at each campsite. Joseph Johnson described the process: "Our little troop would traverse round and round the settlement or its ruins, gradually enlarging the circle until we discovered a foot path, which would lead us almost always to the desired branch or spring." Passing through battlefields of the previous year, they picked up from scattered survivors many anecdotes of the fighting, of the dead, and even of their ghosts.[11]

When early winter added a chill to the nights, the want of decent shelter became a distinct concern. The children were duly impressed with the privations of their parents. "Our wants were comparatively light," recalled Johnson, "and yet I remember perfectly to have seen my mother wade into a stream of running water to assist in washing out the family clothes." The feminine assignment of perpetual needlework continued throughout the adventure. At one point during the long journey, little Joseph received his first pocket handkerchief, "made from the skirt of an old calico frock worn by my sister, [Jane, who later became] Mrs. McCrady. . . . It is probable that this [handkerchief] was afforded by my mother cutting up her old gown to make my sister two new frocks."[12]

The procession arrived at a plantation called Thorogood, the property of John Deas, about twenty-two miles from Charleston on the Moncks Corner road. There they were entertained for several days while William scouted down to Goose Creek Neck, about twelve miles distant, to inquire after his farmlands and chattel. At Deas's the children were kept amused by a number of interesting folk. Deas himself was something of a character and loved to tell people that he had nine sons and that each of them had a sister. (The total, of course, was ten children.)[13]

Less amusing but more joyful was the news that William Johnson had reached his property without difficulty, the White House plantation on the Red Bank of the Cooper River, about thirteen miles by water from Charleston. Though he could safely go no nearer to the still-occupied city, at White House he was immensely grateful to find that the enslaved people had remained during his two-and-a-half-year absence. They had also made a good crop of provisions that they concealed in the woods to prevent British plunder.[14]

Johnson sent back to John Deas's place for the wagon of furniture, which was taken to the plantation and its contents arranged in the house—the items deliberately placed more or less as they had been in the Charleston house, in order to help the children feel more at home. Though the farmhouse was a humble dwelling compared with the house in Charleston, it afforded peace and rest after the family's truly remarkable adventures. The atmosphere was joyful beyond expectation, so reassuring it was to find everyone alive and well. Here they could comfortably await the final leg of the trip to take them to their city home.[15]

While the Johnsons carried out their long journey homeward, back in Philadelphia other friends and families of the exiles reconstructed their lives and caught up on long-awaited news. Good tidings, for instance, finally came from Paris to mollify the more personal anxieties of the Cochran family. Robert Cochran had shipped indigo to France for his son Charles to convert into cash to pay his bills. A letter arrived for Robert, not from Charles but from his friend Louis-Casimir, Baron de Holtzendorff, a Franco-German army officer who had served as a lieutenant colonel in the Continental Army during 1777 and 1778. "At length my dear friend," wrote Holtzendorff, "you will have your beloved Charles with you. . . . It is high time that he joins you, having learnt all what he could in the school he was in, so that it would have been fruitless to him to spend there a longer time. The pouer child was almost despaired about the believed loss [of funds that his parents had attempted to send in the form of indigo]." Without money Charles could not fund passage home.[16]

In France, Benjamin Franklin had taken an earlier interest in Charles, writing to his father in 1779 his opinion that Charles was "truely a fine Boy, ingenious, active, industrious, and capable of any Improvement you may think fit to bestow upon him in his Education." Right after she arrived in Philadelphia, Mary Cochran wrote to Franklin explaining that her husband was a prisoner of the British in St. Augustine and asking him to reassure Charles's schoolmaster that payment for the boy's education would be remitted as soon as circumstances allowed. In the meantime, now that she was restored to a place of liberty, Mary would "endeavour to be as contended as possible, till one of the best of Husbands is again restored to me," which she believed would be soon. And it was.[17]

Franklin, it turned out, was too busy tending to the affairs of his country to be of any help when Robert Cochran requested the old diplomat's assistance. It began to look as though the British had taken the indigo intended for France. Fortunately Holtzendorff had advised Charles to apply to the Marquis de Lafayette for aid, and Lafayette had immediately granted his requests. When the indigo made port unexpectedly, the marquis needed only to add a small sum out of pocket for Charles to settle his debts and pay his tuition in full.[18]

The Johnsons' fall trek home lasted much of the remarkably long time it took for the British to finally withdraw from Charleston. Most of the other St. Augustine survivors passed their time more prosaically among the exile community in Philadelphia while the calendar slipped deeper into 1782. There was no reason to rush impatiently while the British occupiers dragged their feet, and there were other things to do. Former ship captain William Hall, for instance, lingered long enough to make the acquaintance of Philadelphian Ann Wilson in early 1782. It was a happy love match, and they married on April 23, 1782. The couple finally headed south aboard a cartel ship captained by Hall in the fall of that year and arrived in Savannah by November to await the British evacuation. Only when that blessed event occurred, in mid-December, would they be able to return to home in Charleston and start their family.[19]

As the Johnsons' adventures in 1782 had borne witness, South Carolina was still dangerous in spite of Cornwallis's Yorktown defeat. Even though General Greene and Gov. John Rutledge urgently desired the reestablishment of civil government in South Carolina without waiting for the expected British withdrawal, it would take time.

The South Carolina legislature had last met in Charleston in February 1780. As early as August 1781, even with Charleston still occupied, Rutledge informed the South Carolina delegates to Congress in Philadelphia that he wanted to convene an assembly. But, he said, he felt "it would be injurious to exclude our worthy friends lately prisoners in St. Augustine and Charles Town, from a share in the Legislature (which might probably be the case if one was immediately called) and injurious to the publick to deprive it of their abilities and service." He would postpone issuing writs of election until most of them had returned home, and he encouraged them to do so as soon as they could—"any expense on that score shall be speedily reimbursed by means of Indigo, which I hope to be able to send soon."[20]

And expensive it was. Aedanus Burke (not himself one of the exiles), after departing from Philadelphia for South Carolina in early October 1781, warned Arthur Middleton from Baltimore to "request our Carolina friends bound Southerly, not to come this road unless they are well stocked with Cash. Their charges are most unreasonable. Since I left Philadelphia it has cost me between five & Six Dollars each day, and in a few days more at this rate I shall not have a Shilling in my pocket. Warn them against this rout for God's Sake." He also advised them to avoid visiting the army at Yorktown. Orders had been issued to discourage the curious, "to prevent the Provisions & forage being eat up by a Set of idle Spectators, who had before flocked from all parts in thousands to see the Shew."[21]

Some patriots had managed to set out for South Carolina even before the Yorktown siege and surrender. Christopher Gadsden was still the nominal lieutenant governor of South Carolina. He and members of the Privy Council Thomas Ferguson, Richard Hutson, and David Ramsay (all, like Gadsden, among the St. Augustine exiles), along with Benjamin Cattell, had been eager to return home from the moment they arrived in Philadelphia. Together these five constituted the greater part of independent South Carolina's executive branch. Being financially destitute, Gadsden and the others applied to the Philadelphia Congress for traveling assistance, which they received in the form of wagons, horses, and to each a one-hundred-pound loan to be repaid to Greene once they arrived home.[22]

The five South Carolinians left Philadelphia in late September and were on the road when Cornwallis surrendered at Yorktown on October 19. Their circuitous overland route finally brought them to the High Hills of the Santee in South Carolina, where Greene's army camped. Seeing these exhausted and careworn returning Carolinians touched Greene, who told Robert Morris that he thought it "little less than cruelty to push a demand [for loan repayment] in their present situation."[23]

Sadly, privy counselor John Edwards was not among this group—after all of the travails of war, surrender, occupation, transport to St. Augustine, and liberation to Philadelphia, he had died of "a Fit of Apoplexy" on August 18, 1781. Smith reported that his "appetite began to fail him, often pukeing up the little food he was able to eat, which weakened him so much, that on Sunday the 30th September he was obliged to take to his Bed." Though bedridden and suffering miserably, he "was happy in the exercise of much patience and resignation, often expressing his desire (and even longing for) to depart this miserable World, and to be with Christ, which he said was far better." During his last week, Edwards became increasingly helpless, taking only liquids by a spoon, and for the two or three days preceding his death, "seem'd to be afflicted with much pain in the lower part of his body, owing I believe, to his not being able to discharge in the Urinary way." Edwards died prior to the arrival in Philadelphia of his wife and ten children.[24]

South Carolina attorney general Alexander Moultrie found another way home. Governor Rutledge had sent nineteen wagonloads of indigo to Philadelphia to be sold to supply the needs of the state's congressional delegation and of the citizens sent to Philadelphia from Charleston. From the proceeds a sum of two hundred dollars was allotted for each South Carolinian who then could return immediately. Moultrie sought and received permission to obtain conveyance on this wagon train when it headed south, transporting much-needed supplies, medicine, and arms obtained for the use of the state militia.[25]

Rutledge and his council intended to convene their general assembly in Camden on January 8, 1782, but General Greene convinced them otherwise. Jacksonboro, on the Edisto River thirty miles west of Charleston, was more advantageous militarily and was closer to the coast. The town of about sixty houses could be more easily defended by Greene's Continental Army and available South Carolina militia. Moreover it was important to convene the legislature in the lowcountry as a projection of the state's American recovery. Greene posted his army to the east, between Jacksonboro and Charleston, to deny the British any opportunity of interrupting the assembly's deliberations.[26]

On January 8, 1782, the legislature convened for the first time since May 1780, and it met until February 26, 1782. By South Carolina's constitution of 1778, its full membership consisted of 28 senators and 174 representatives. A quorum was met on January 17 with 13 senators and 75 representatives. Of these, 25 representatives were former St. Augustine exiles, as were 3 of the senators. Thomas Heyward Jr. had been elected to the House from both St. Helena's parish (he declined) and from St. Philip's and St. Michael's parishes (accepted). Hugh Rutledge was elected speaker of the house, and John Berwick volunteered his services as the house clerk. The restored government of South Carolina was at last officially back at work.[27]

Thomas Heyward Jr. was clearly pleased to be back and in service to South Carolina, though the duty meant another separation from his wife, Elizabeth. They loved each other dearly and had endured separation before—while Thomas was in Philadelphia serving in the Continental Congress, while he was soldiering, and during his sojourn in St. Augustine. The couple's attempts to have children had met with mostly tragic results—six pregnancies produced only one child who would survive to adulthood: Daniel, who was born in 1774. Thomas's happy August 1781 reunion with Elizabeth in Philadelphia led to another pregnancy, but while he traveled southward for the legislature, she remained behind out of caution for her health. It is not known whether or not they saw each other ever again. Elizabeth died of complications of childbirth on August 16, 1782, and was buried in St. Peter's churchyard in Philadelphia.[28]

The constitutional terms of office of Governor Rutledge and Lieutenant Governor Gadsden had expired a year earlier, in January 1781, during the British occupation and Gadsden's exile. So, properly enough, on January 29, 1782, Gadsden officially tendered his resignation as lieutenant governor. He then was admitted as a duly elected member of the house from Prince George Parish. Later in that day's session, the assembly elected him governor, but he declined, pleading as his excuse "the increasing infirmities of old age." John Mathews, who also had returned to South Carolina from the Continental Congress, was elected in his stead. Richard Hutson was elected lieutenant governor. Gadsden, Edward Rutledge, Peter Bocquet, Morton Wilkinson, and Richard Beresford were subsequently chosen to serve on the Privy Council, and Arthur Middleton and David Ramsay were sent back to Philadelphia to represent South Carolina in the Continental Congress. Of these men only Mathews and Bocquet had not been among the St. Augustine exiles.[29]

Writing of Gadsden's declination of the governorship to his friend in Philadelphia, Dr. Benjamin Rush, David Ramsay observed, "The Divine Old Man never appeared greater than on this occasion. . . . Figure to your self an old man declining the highest honor his country could confer on him & at the same time declaring that he declined for their sakes, not his own, being sensible that his age & infirmities make him incapable of the duties of such an active office."[30]

Over the course of seven weeks, the members of the Jacksonboro Assembly enacted measures necessary for the reestablishment of law and order and all of the governmental functions that had been suspended for two years. They dealt with defense and other matters of military importance, establishing rules for elections, regulation of the courts, collection of taxes, and settling of debts. On the last day of the session, the legislature empowered former exiles Thomas Ferguson and Morton Wilkinson (along with John Ward) to purchase an estate to be held in trust for General Greene "as suitable testimony of approbation and gratitude for the eminent services which he has rendered to this State."[31]

But what the Jacksonboro Assembly is best remembered for are the acts passed to punish South Carolina loyalists. The preamble of the first bill, passed on February 26, 1782, lists a litany of perceived offenses and depredations perpetrated on the patriot citizens of South Carolina during the war in general and during the occupation specifically. While the British held South Carolina, "the inhabitants were to expect the utmost severities, and to hold their lives, liberties, and properties, solely at the will of his Britannic Majesty's officers." Now, that majesty having lost its power, "it is therefore inconsistent with public justice and policy, to afford protection any longer to the property of British subjects, and just and reasonable to apply the same toward alleviating and lessening the burdens and expenses of the war, which must otherwise fall very heavy on the distressed inhabitants of the State."[32]

Two hundred thirty-nine loyalists who were named by the legislators forfeited their property and were banished from South Carolina. Sequestration of property had been initially considered for loyalists "whose conduct [was] not considered Sufficiently criminal to merit Confiscation," but this was changed to amercement (i.e., a fine), and consequently an additional law required forty-seven individuals who had accepted British protection to pay an amercement equal to 12 percent of the value of their estates. They could retain their property and could remain at home, but they had to pay.[33]

Notably absent from the confiscation and amercement lists was former South Carolina attorney general James Simpson. As will be recalled, Simpson was the one who had organized and headed Charleston's Board of Police during the British occupation and had been instrumental in identifying the Charleston patriots who were exiled to St. Augustine. He also had a hand in Col. Isaac Hayne's reluctant submission to British protection in 1780. In February 1781 Simpson relocated to New York at the behest of General Clinton to become secretary to Clinton and Vice Admiral Mariot Arbuthnot in their ineffectual roles as the king's commissioners for restoring peace to the colonies and plantations in North America. Notwithstanding his absence from the lists, Simpson found that whatever remained of his estate after his banishment from South Carolina in 1777 had been confiscated for his having returned contrary to state law. His brother John Simpson of Georgia, who also had property in South Carolina that he had inherited from their father, was listed.[34]

On the surface the assembly's motivation in these sequestrations was vengeance and justice in retribution for oppression endured by South Carolina patriots during the British occupation. But the preamble was clear that the proceeds garnered from the sale of loyalist estates would be useful in "alleviating and lessening the burdens and expenses of the war, which must otherwise fall very heavy on the distressed inhabitants of this State." Arguably, generation of revenues superseded retribution in importance. Former exile Edward Rutledge, who wrote the initial draft of the law, certainly saw it as a painful necessity, since at this point taxation was impossible. And Rutledge believed that justice was being meted out with moderation, reminding Arthur Middleton that for the representatives voting, "their Provocations have been excessive, their losses immense, & I did expect their Resentments would have been in proportion to their sufferings."[35]

If justifiable in principle, the confiscation and amercement acts had serious problems in application. The penalties were imposed rather arbitrarily and without due process or evidentiary hearings, and the legislators indulged in a great deal of partiality. Middleton objected to the harsh effects on the families of loyalist offenders: "I cannot approve of the inhuman Sentence of visiting the Sins of the Fathers upon the guiltless women [and] Children. . . . It is a Doctrine suited only to the Climates of Despotism, & abhorrent to the dignified Spirit of pure & genuine republicanism. . . . Banishment of the Individual, & a deprivation of the Benefits of Citizenship & property for life are surely sufficient both as a punishment & a prevention of Crimes, without reducing a whole family for the Sin of one to misery & destruction."[36]

William Moultrie summarized the attitude of many concerning those persons who took British protection, pointing out that the cases were not all parallel. "A great many exchanged their paroles for protections . . . many at first refused, some were persuaded, and others threatened that if they did not sign, they would be informed against." In Moultrie's view "the taking protection . . . was unavoidable with many. I advised several of my friends, after the fall of Charleston (who were not in the Continental Army) to take that step, and to stay with their families, till we could come in force to release them." In other words Moultrie asserted that taking British protection was sometimes (if not necessarily always) a pardonable sin. In time many of those persons listed in the Confiscation Act later had their property restored under the terms of subsequent acts and were subjected instead to amercement. Likewise quite a number had their banishment rescinded. By the time the legislature finished amending the Jacksonboro legislation in 1783 and 1784, only 144 estates were actually confiscated and 58 amerced.[37]

Gadsden had as much right to be vindictive as anyone else, or more, considering his nearly year-long confinement in the Castle St. Mark in St. Augustine and his immense loss of property during the war. Yet he was somewhat ambivalent about revenge, telling Morton Wilkinson, "Revenge is below a brave man; vengeance belongeth to the Almighty; He has claimed it expressly as His right, wisely foreseeing the shocking havoc man would make with such a weapon left to his discretion." But at the same time, he was willing to hang a few British officers as an example and was sorry that Cornwallis would not be made to suffer for his "numberless cruelties, in cold blood."[38]

At any rate, in spite of the treatment he had received at the hands of the British, Gadsden remained prominently on the side of the few who spoke out against confiscation and amercement. With admiration Alexander Garden, who had been present in person, said of Gadsden that "no individual advocated with greater ardour and humanity the cause of the unfortunates who had incurred the public displeasure [i.e., the Americans who had cooperated with the British], nor more strenuously endeavoured to mollify the punishments denounced against them."[39]

Self-preservation, after all, is a basic human instinct and forgiveness a virtue. Gadsden was willing to forgive and forget when possible, even to the point of subjecting himself to the disapprobation of his peers. He told Francis Marion that even before he was released from his cell in Fort St. Mark, he had already met with "rebukes from my friends, and not a few gross affronts for doing everything in my power to mitigate their rage and impetuosity; even before I left St. Augustine I was sneeringly told [that] the confinement in Augustine Castle, had wonderously turn'd me."[40]

As for confiscating property owned by people who had been sincere loyalists but now wished to remain as American citizens, Gadsden was steady in his ability to acknowledge wrong while advocating charity: "I fought [such confiscation] through, inch by inch, as unjust, impolitic, cruel, premature, oppressing numbers of innocent [loyalist families] for one man supposed to be guilty, formerly signing a paper, when visibly under the power and restraint of a known cruel, oppressive and tyrannical enemy." It is significant that in spite of intimidation on this subject from the majority of the assembly, admiration for his worthiness won him the gubernatorial election (although he gallantly declined the honor).[41]

And Gadsden's appeals did have some effect. If he actually did as he told Marion he had done—holding up his two hands and announcing to the House that he would cut them both off before voting in favor of confiscation—once he saw the act was inevitably going to pass, he joined in editing certain clauses in order, as much as possible, to lessen the consequences. He also tried to exert a mitigating influence in the drawing up of the confiscation lists. And his, Marion's, and Aedanus Burke's constant criticisms of the acts passed to punish loyalists were factors in the legislatures' softening of them over the next few years.[42]

Among other matters the legislature considered the distress of the families still in Philadelphia. In anticipation of the approaching liberation of Charleston, on February 14, 1782, the South Carolina House of Representatives instructed their delegates in the Philadelphia Congress to make what might seem to be an unlikely motion—asking the British commander in chief at New York to provide ships at British expense for sending back to the Carolinas those refugees, particularly women and children, who very much wanted to be closer to home. Congress in turn referred the matter to General Washington, who opened correspondence on the matter with Maj. Gen. Sir Guy Carleton, Henry Clinton's successor as the British commander in North America in the aftermath of Yorktown. "As these unfortunate persons have been removed by Orders of the British Commanders," wrote Washington, "I am directed to further propose, that the Expense of their Transportation shall be borne by the King of G[reat] Britain."[43]

Remarkably Carleton gave written consent right away, something that Washington (even more remarkably) found disagreeable. He was not feeling disposed "to seek favors of, or Submit to an Idea of being under Obligation to Sir Guy, at this moment of *conciliatory War.*" Carleton was of a mind to cooperate. The peace negotiations had begun in Paris in April, and American independence was virtually assured, so there was no point in continuing hostilities. Washington was uncertain of the circumstances under which the South Carolinians had been forced to leave their state, since the British had never made that case very clear. He supposed that it would be alleged that the exiles had been "sent off as persons factious, disaffected and dangerous to the British Government." Surely the British "would think the request of a very extraordinary Nature, and would consider their Compliance in the Light of conferring a high Obligation, especially by bearing the Expence of their Transportation." On these grounds it seemed to Washington that such a request was tantamount to asking a favor.[44]

Former St. Augustine exile David Ramsay, now in the Congress and serving on a committee to consider Washington's concerns, remarked to Nathanael Greene that he was not sure that it was quite yet fully in the interest of the United States to be completely at peace, adding, "Sir Guy Carleton is all good natu[re]. He has granted us flags to send back the inhabitants of South Carolina at the expence of the King of G.B., & adds 'that is in perfect conformity to the Kings benevolent intentions,' & talks very largely about 'forgetting the severities that have imbittered our unhappy divisions.' . . . We are puzzled what to do— to refuse them would argue inconstancy & would be unkind to our people, to accept them in this moment of conciliation would perhaps be injurious to the [U]nited [S]tates." Congress enjoined Washington to proceed in cooperation with Carleton, which he did by sending Carleton a list of the displaced South Carolinians and the ports to which they chose to be conveyed (Georgetown, South Carolina, or Edenton, North Carolina). Charleston, still stubbornly occupied, could not be considered.[45]

Events moved much faster than expected. Expressly intending to treat the Carolinians with kindness and accommodation, the British dispatched posthaste from New York three ships: a schooner, a brigantine, and a sloop. They docked at Philadelphia by mid-July and took only weeks to be provisioned (at British expense) and boarded. From Philadelphia the schooner set out for Edenton on August 3, 1782, with a mere 25 people on board—all who were able to get ready on such surprisingly short notice. With five additional days of preparation, on

August 8, six times that number (about 150, including wives, children, and slaves) boarded the other two vessels and were soon bound for Georgetown.[46]

The lists of those taking their departure in the second group on August 8 show Edward, Eliza, and seven-year-old John McCrady aboard the sloop *Exchange,* the first of the two ships bound for Georgetown. In Georgetown the McCradys would have to wait another four months before a liberated Charleston was ready to receive them.[47]

According to Joseph Johnson, "many of our countrymen had suffered great privations, and were unable to move homeward for want of means." Approximately 430 exiles stayed behind in Philadelphia: Georgians and Charlestonians, whites and blacks, young and old, some of whom remained there for many months afterward. The motive behind the promptness with which Carleton was able to honor Washington's request for additional transportation in September is unclear, but it was all a great help to the South Carolinians who were able to take full advantage.[48]

At long last from the southwest part of his land across the Cooper River, Johnson could see the British burning their stores and blowing up their forts preparatory to a definitive departure. For him the rising plumes of smoke signaled a prospect of returning peace and prosperity. In a few days, news arrived that the last of the British had sailed away on December 14, 1782. Greene's Continentals moved in to take possession as the redcoats boarded their transports at Gadsden's Wharf. General Greene, Governor Mathews, Privy Counsellors Gadsden, Rutledge, Bocquet, Wilkinson, and Beresford, and other citizens who undoubtedly included other former St. Augustine exiles, marched into town behind an advance contingent of Continental dragoons.[49]

According to William Moultrie, "The great joy that was felt on this day, by the citizens and soldiers, was inexpressible: the widows, the orphans, the aged men and others, who, from their particular situations, were obliged to remain in Charlestown, many of whom had been cooped up in one room of their own elegant houses for upwards of two years, whilst the other parts were occupied by the British officers, many of whom where a rude uncivil set of gentlemen. . . . I felt myself much elated, at seeing the balconies, the doors, and windows crowded with the patriotic fair, the aged citizens and others, congratulating us on our return home, saying, 'God bless you, gentlemen! you are welcome home, gentlemen!' Both citizens and soldiers shed mutual tears of joy."[50]

From White Hall plantation, Johnson took some of his own boatmen and proceeded to Charleston, where he was inexpressibly delighted to find his East Bay house still in the care of his own slaves. The fences had been torn down and burned, but the house was inhabitable. What was more, the blacksmith shop, with its tools and two of his best men, were there and ready to get back to work. The household servants had all maintained themselves comfortably during the eighteen months of Mrs. Johnson's exile. She was so well pleased to see them again and to be at home that she decided to ask no questions about what money they had brought in during her absence (in those days all money earned by enslaved persons was, by law, to be turned over to the slaves' owner).[51]

Johnson returned to the plantation with a few necessaries (shoes, etc.). By late December the entire family was finally able to return to Charleston. Johnson was thankful to have reached this point with just enough money in his pocket to pay for a few coals and a small supply of iron, therewith to resume his smithy business. Though Mrs. Johnson "was debarred of her tea for a week or two," a renewed prosperity soon set in. At Christmas the family managed to have a plum pudding for the festal meal.[52]

Long years later Joseph Johnson poignantly recalled the general sentiments of the day, writing in his 1851 *Traditions and Reminiscences* that "few can appreciate our feelings on this occasion. They were not merely heightened by contrast with our late long and fatiguing journey, by sufferings and privations; they were excited by our recent return from exile, after expulsion from home by a ruthless enemy, while victorious, but now vanquished and driven out of the country. It was at the moment of our first assurance of this joyful change from war to peace—of peace in the arms of victory—of our having once more a home, in the enjoyment of health, peace and competence, at that season of joy and congratulation in every part of our beloved country. It was a joyful re-union with bosom friends and affectionate faithful domestics in our own home, at our own fireside."[53]

Epilogue

The Charleston-to–St. Augustine exiles were finally home.

They had been well acquainted prior to the surrender of Charleston in 1780 and were certainly much more so by the end of their shared banishment and captivity. Before the war they had socialized, worshiped together, transacted business, and engaged with each other in politics. Many had enjoyed wealth before the war, but all had since endured some degree of privation. During the war some of them had fought side by side against the British, while others had taken important supportive roles. All together they had individually and mutually sacrificed their personal fortunes on the altar of independence, and in so doing they had participated in the birth of a new nation. It would require additional volumes to detail their postwar accomplishments and the achievements of their progeny. Instead the ancestors of one of this book's authors will provide a brief illustrative example in closing.

William Johnson and Edward McCrady had both migrated to Charleston from New York as young men. They were both entrepreneurs, fellow Anglicans who attended St. Philip's, and ardent patriots. They were arrested together, transported to St. Augustine together, messed together, and sailed together to Philadelphia on the schooner *East Florida* at the time of their liberation. They took divergent paths back home to Charleston—the Johnsons traveling overland and the McCradys traveling by sea. The families paused for several months fifty miles apart, the McCradys at Georgetown and the Johnsons at St. James, Goose Creek, but they were happily reunited after the British evacuated Charleston in December 1782.

The McCradys, like the Johnsons, found their properties intact and their enslaved people waiting. The bustle of the liberated city made it a propitious moment to reap new income from the tavern and other investments. In fact when the sales of the confiscated properties of loyalists finally took place, the ever-industrious McCrady acquired at auction his Wakendaw Plantation across the Cooper River from Charleston, where he bred and trained racehorses. New futures beckoned.

As time passed the Johnson and McCrady families became even more en-twined. Edward McCrady died in 1794, so it was certainly a bittersweet scene when his son John and William Johnson's daughter Jane were united in holy matrimony at St. Philip's Church on March 2, 1797. John McCrady and his new brother-in-law William Johnson Jr. had both attended the College of New Jersey (Princeton), and they now shared a law practice in Charleston. William Johnson Jr. eventually rose to serve as an associate justice of the Supreme Court of the United States.[1]

James Simpson, the man behind the list of troublemakers sent to St. Augustine, returned to England after the war. He died in 1815 at the age of seventy-eight. Whether the Charleston exiles ever became aware of his role in their banishment is doubtful, so it is unlikely that our protagonists ever gave him another thought. Lt. Col. Nisbet Balfour, on the other hand, they surely remembered. Balfour's place in American history was secured as Charleston's malevolent commandant and co-executioner of Col. Isaac Hayne. At home after the war, his actions in America were rewarded with promotion, and he enjoyed a distinguished British army career that culminated in his elevation to the rank of full general in 1803. Balfour died at the age of eighty in 1823.[2]

And alas, poor Cornwallis. He gave the actual order, on Simpson's recom-mendations, to send the Charleston patriots to St. Augustine. After the York-town surrender, South Carolina delegate to Congress and former exile Arthur Middleton looked upon the captured and paroled Cornwallis not as a British general subject to the usual rules of exchange but as a barbarian. To Middleton and others Cornwallis was guilty of a litany of war crimes, not the least of which was "the transportation of [the exiles] to St. Augustine, and the banishment of their wives and children."[3]

Congress failed to impose punitive measures in retaliation for his conduct of the war in the south, but southerners did manage to delay his exchange for almost a year. Upon learning of the eventual exchange of Cornwallis, Edward Rutledge wrote to Middleton that he thought Cornwallis "should have been held a Prisoner for Life as a Rascal, & the World should have known that he was precluded from the Benefits of Freedom, because he was a Monster & an Enemy to Humanity." Cornwallis had a distinguished career in the British army after 1782, yet his name in America is generally synonymous with American victory and British defeat at Yorktown. He died at age sixty-six in 1805.[4]

The chaotic but outwardly stable town of St. Augustine, with its firm English government and purposeful usefulness in contributing to England's war effort (at a safe distance), suddenly found itself without a war. In accordance with the 1783 Treaty of Paris that officially ended the Revolutionary War, and nine months after England abandoned Charleston, the British government returned all of Florida to Spanish control. Great Britain handed over the immense acreage of St. Augustine and all of its difficult peninsula, and in return (among other things) Spain ceased her challenge to Britain's full control of tiny Gibraltar. Once again the history of St. Augustine, that "oldest city," was reset to zero, to begin anew with a new population as it had begun twice before: an uncertain prize—a bewildered Spanish town of dubious function.

Who Were the Patriots Exiled
to St. Augustine in 1780?

The following is a list of patriots exiled to St. Augustine in 1780: sixty South Carolinians, two North Carolinians, and one Georgian.[1] Many of these gentlemen had well-documented lives, but for others there is a paucity of information. Using data that is sometimes incomplete, one can still conclude that of the sixty-three exiles, eleven were not native-born Americans, and of the native-born Americans, nine originally came from other states. There were two brothers, four pairs of brothers-in-law, and one father-in-law/son-in-law combination.

A few were tradesmen and artisans, and others were members of the lowcountry elite. At least seventeen were planters, nineteen were merchants, eight were lawyers, three were doctors, and three were ship captains. Among them were a clergyman, a watchmaker, a painter and glazier, and a gardenist (landscape garden designer). One was a poet, one studied and lectured on electricity, and one was an avid sportsman who owned several prized racehorses. Many were slaveholders to a greater or lesser extent, and eight engaged in the slave trade at some point in time. Socioeconomic differences notwithstanding, they became fellow sufferers in exile.

Fourteen served on one or more of the extralegal councils or committees that functioned as a pre-Revolutionary shadow government of South Carolina prior to the formal rejection of royal authority. Forty served in the military in some capacity during the war. Forty-three had served or would serve in the colonial, provincial, or state legislature. Four had held or would hold the office of lieutenant governor of South Carolina, two had been or would be elected governor of South Carolina but would not serve, and one would be elected governor and die in office. Three of the exiles signed the Declaration of Independence, and one signed the Articles of Confederation. Nine served or would serve in the Continental Congress, the Confederation Congress, or the U.S. Congress. Fifteen would vote to ratify the U.S. Constitution, and three would vote against ratification.

Joseph Bee (1746–1815): arrested November 15, 1780; planter; brother of Thomas Bee, who served as lieutenant governor of South Carolina, 1779–80; supplied provisions to the Continental Army; South Carolina Senate, 1782.[2]

Richard Beresford (1755–1803): arrested November 15, 1780; planter, attorney, and poet; studied law at the Middle Temple in London; served with Brig. Gen. Isaac Huger in the Georgia campaign of 1778; aide-de-camp to Brig. Gen. William Moultrie during the 1780 siege of Charleston; South Carolina House of Representatives, 1782; Privy Council, 1782–83; lieutenant governor of South Carolina, 1783; Confederation Congress, 1783–84; cast the deciding vote for ratification of the Treaty of Paris in 1784; trustee for establishing the College of Charleston, 1785.[3]

John Berwick (d. 1784): arrested November 15, 1780; Charleston cordwainer (shoemaker) and owner of a tanyard (outdoor tannery); Committee of Correspondence, 1774; supplied the militia with funds, provisions, a sailing vessel, and slaves; South Carolina Provincial Congress, 1775–76; South Carolina House of Representatives, 1776–80 and 1782–84; commissioner for the sale of confiscated estates, 1782.[4]

Edward Blake (d. 1795): arrested August 27, 1780; former ship captain employed in the West Indies trade, Charleston merchant, factor, shipowner, and planter (postwar); engaged in the slave trade between 1762 and 1774; Council of Safety, 1775; commissioner of the treasury, 1776–86; first commissioner of South Carolina navy, 1776–80; commissioner of the Continental Loan Office, 1779–80; South Carolina House of Representatives, 1779–80, 1782, and 1787–90; delegate to the South Carolina convention convened to ratify the U.S. Constitution in 1788 (voted in favor); director of the Charleston branch of the Bank of the United States, 1792–93.[5]

Daniel Bourdeaux (d. 1815): arrested November 15, 1780; merchant, planter, and slave trader; co-owner of three trading vessels; brother-in-law of Josiah Smith Jr.; South Carolina Senate, 1783–84 and 1787–88; Privy Council, 1786–88; member of the Charleston Library Society, 1784; trustee for establishing the College of Charleston, 1785; incorporator of the Santee Canal Company in 1786 and the Catawba Canal Company in 1787.[6]

John Budd (1732–91): arrested August 27, 1780; physician; practiced medicine in Salem County, New Jersey, before moving to Charleston in the early 1770s; during the skirmish in Charleston Harbor in November 12, 1775, between the provincial schooner *Defence* and the armed British vessels *Tamar* and *Cherokee*, Doctor Budd paddled a canoe, at the risk of his life, to render aid to his countrymen aboard the *Defence;* he is generally and erroneously attributed with having served as surgeon of the Fourth South Carolina Regiment (Artillery) but instead served in that capacity in Capt. (later Maj.) Joseph Darrell's Cannoneers Company of the Charleston District Militia; member of the Charleston Library Society, 1779; partnered in practice with Dr. David Ramsay after the war; South Carolina House of Representatives, 1785–90; delegate to the South Carolina convention convened to ratify the U.S. Constitution in 1788 (voted in favor); a founding member of the Medical Society of South Carolina, 1789; suggested that the South Carolina legislature stipulate that the streets of the new capital of Columbia be no less than sixty feet wide to prevent the spread of fire and disease.[7]

Robert Cochran (1735–1824): arrested August 30, 1780; former seaman in the Royal Navy; merchant captain; ordnance storekeeper for the Council of Safety; captain of the eighteen-gun South Carolina brig *Notre Dame;* postwar planter and harbormaster of Charleston.[8]

John Splatt Cripps (1754–1811): arrested November 15, 1780; merchant; lieutenant of militia; served as a matross (assistant gunner) in the Fourth South Carolina Regiment (Artillery) in 1780; warden of Charleston (member of the city council) at the time of President George Washington's 1791 visit to Charleston; appointed commissioner of health by the city council in 1808.[9]

Henry Crouch (d. 1783): arrested November 15, 1780; Charleston merchant and planter; furnished provisions for the troops during the war; South Carolina House of Representatives, 1779–80; commissioner for the sale of confiscated estates, 1782.[10]

Benjamin Cudworth (1753–1814): arrested November 15, 1780; a Massachusetts native who resided in Charleston by 1775; served with the Charleston Musketeers Company of the Charleston District Regiment of Militia; a merchant after the war, he divided his residence between Charleston and his Lancaster County plantation; member of the Charleston Library Society; South Carolina House of Representatives, 1787–91; delegate to the South Carolina convention convened to ratify the U.S. Constitution in 1788 (voted against); vendue master in 1783 and deputy supervisor of the U.S. Internal Revenue Service in the District of South Carolina, 1799–1801.[11]

Edward Darrell (1747–97): arrested November 15, 1780; a Bermuda native, ship captain, and shipmaster; resided in Charleston by 1770; brother-in-law of Josiah Smith Jr.; partnered with Josiah Smith Jr. and Daniel DeSaussure in the mercantile business; commissioner of South Carolina navy, 1778–80; member of the Charleston Library Society, 1780; South Carolina House of Representatives, 1782–90; Privy Council, 1789–90; president of the Charleston Chamber of Commerce, 1786–94; delegate to the South Carolina convention convened to ratify the U.S. Constitution in 1788 (voted in favor); gave an address to George Washington on behalf of Charleston's merchants during the president's 1791 southern tour; director of the Santee Canal Company in 1793; director of the Office of Discount and Deposit of the Charleston branch of the Bank of the United States, 1792–96.[12]

Daniel DeSaussure (1736–1798): arrested November 15, 1780; Charleston and Beaufort merchant and importer in partnership with Josiah Smith Jr. and Edward Darrell; Beaufort Council of Safety, 1775; paymaster general, southern district; South

Carolina Provincial Congress, 1775–76; South Carolina House of Representatives, 1776–80; captain in the Beaufort militia; Privy Council, 1783–85; South Carolina Senate, 1785–90, and president of the Senate, 1789–90; delegate to the South Carolina convention convened to ratify the U.S. Constitution in 1788 (voted in favor); treasurer of the College of Charleston, 1791; director, 1792, and president, 1793–98, of the Charleston branch of the Bank of the United States.[13]

John Edwards (1731–81): arrested August 27, 1780; emigrated from Britain to South Carolina ca. 1750; member of the Charleston Library Society, 1770; shipowner and slave trader; Commons House of Assembly, 1772–75; South Carolina Provincial Congress, 1775–76; South Carolina House of Representatives, 1776–80; Privy Council, 1776–80; advanced large sums of money to the revolutionary government of South Carolina; commissioner of South Carolina navy; commissioner of fortifications; died of apoplexy (stroke) in Philadelphia on August 19, 1781, leaving his widow with ten children.[14]

Thomas Ferguson (d. 1786): arrested August 27, 1780; planter; partner in the operation of a large sawmill on the Edisto River; Commons House of Assembly, 1762–75; associated with the radical patriots led by Christopher Gadsden, whose daughter Elizabeth became his fourth wife in 1774; outspoken opponent of the Stamp Act; member of the General Committee of the Non-Importation Association, 1769; member of the committee that persuaded Charleston merchants not to import tea, 1773; South Carolina Provincial Congress, 1775–76; Council of Safety, 1775; South Carolina Senate, 1776; Legislative Council, 1776; South Carolina House of Representatives, 1776–80 and 1782–86; Privy Council, 1776–82; violently opposed the surrender of Charleston and had harsh words for his former father-in-law Christopher Gadsden and Maj. Gen. Benjamin Lincoln; commissioner to purchase an estate for Gen. Nathanael Greene, 1782.[15]

George T. Flagg (1741–1824): arrested August 27, 1780; a native of Boston who resided in Charleston by the mid-1760s working as a painter and glazier; as a mechanic he was a member of the Liberty Tree Party in 1766 and the Palmetto Society in 1777; South Carolina House of Representatives, 1782–88; Charleston warden (member of the city council), 1783–87; served as grand warden, 1799–1800, and deputy grand master, 1808, of the Grand Lodge of Free and Accepted Masons.[16]

Christopher Gadsden (1724–1805): arrested August 27, 1780; Charleston and Georgetown merchant, shipowner, and planter; father-in-law of Thomas Ferguson; educated in England; ship's purser aboard the British man-of-war *Aldborough*, 1745–48; member of the Charleston Library Society, 1750; founding member and captain of the Charleston Artillery Company (later Battalion) in 1756 and participated in the Cherokee campaign of 1761; Royal Council, 1757; Commons House of Assembly, 1757–75; one of three South Carolinians at the Stamp Act Congress in New York in 1765; a leading spokesman for the Sons of Liberty; Continental Congress, 1774–76; colonel in 1775 of the First South Carolina Regiment and brigadier general in 1776, resigned, 1777; helped write South Carolina's Constitution of 1776; South Carolina House of Representatives,1776–78 and 1782; elected vice president of South Carolina (lieutenant governor), 1778–79 and 1780–82; Privy Council, 1778–79 and 1780–82; elected governor in 1782 but declined on account of his health and age; favored leniency for loyalists; delegate to the South Carolina convention convened to ratify the U.S. Constitution in 1788 (voted in favor); presidential elector for John Adams in 1800.[17]

William Hasell Gibbes (1754–1834): arrested August 27, 1780; read law with John Rutledge; entered London's Inner Temple in 1771 but abandoned his law studies when the war began—he subsequently returned home via Bermuda without a passport; was admitted to the South Carolina bar prior to 1783; commissioned captain-lieutenant in the Charleston Battalion of Artillery (militia); after his return from Charleston and Philadelphia, he joined with Francis Marion; South Carolina House of Representatives, 1778–80 and 1782–84; Privy Council, 1783; master of chancery and responsible for the Charleston, Colleton, and Beaufort Districts in the court of equity, 1784–1825.[18]

Thomas Grimball Jr. (1745–83): arrested August 30, 1780; attorney; brother-in-law of Samuel Prioleau Jr.; studied law in Charleston and was admitted to the South Carolina bar in 1765; member of the Charleston Library Society, 1766; captain and major of the Charleston Battalion of Artillery (militia); sheriff of the Charleston District, 1773–75; South Carolina House of Representatives,1776–80 and 1782.[19]

George Abbot Hall (d. 1791): arrested November 15, 1780; shipowner and merchant in the slave and fur trades; member of the Charleston Library Society, 1772; Committee of Ninety-Nine for Charleston, 1774; South Carolina Provincial Congress, 1775–76; South Carolina House of Representatives, 1776–778; collector of the port of Charleston, 1776–91; commissioner of the treasury, 1776; commissioner of South Carolina navy, 1776–80; captain of the True Blue Company of the Charleston District Regiment of Militia; appointed receiver of continental taxes for South Carolina by Robert Morris in 1782.[20]

Thomas Hall (1750–1815): arrested August 30, 1780; captain of the Second South Carolina Regiment (Continental), wounded at the Battle of Sullivan's island on June 28, 1776; original member of the Society of the Cincinnati; justice of the quorum for the Charleston District; justice of the peace for the Charleston District; clerk of court of general sessions for the Charleston District, 1785–1801.[21]

William Hall (1757–1814): arrested August 30, 1780; in merchant service at the onset of the Revolutionary War and detained in England as prisoner; escaped and made his way to Boston in 1776; privateer; lieutenant and captain of the eighteen-gun South Carolina brig *Notre Dame;* postwar merchant captain.[22]

Thomas Heyward Jr. (1746–1809): arrested August 27, 1780; attorney and planter; became a son-in-law of Thomas Savage after the exile; completed his law studies at London's Middle Temple in 1765; admitted to the English bar in 1770 and the

South Carolina bar in 1771; Commons House of Assembly, 1772–75; Committee of Ninety-Nine, 1774; South Carolina Provincial Congress, 1775–76; Council of Safety, 1775–76; South Carolina House of Representatives, 1776–80 and 1782–90; delegate to the Continental Congress and signer of the Declaration of Independence, 1776; elected lieutenant governor in 1779 but declined to serve; captain in the Charleston Battalion of Artillery (militia), wounded at Port Royal Island on February 3, 1779; judge of the Court of General Sessions and Common Pleas, 1779–89; warden of Charleston (member of the city council), 1783–86; trustee of the College of Charleston, 1785; first president of the Agricultural Society of South Carolina, 1785, and member until 1809; delegate to the South Carolina convention convened to ratify the U.S. Constitution in 1788 (voted in favor); retired from public life in 1790; while in Charleston during his 1791 southern tour, President Washington lodged in Heyward's house on Church Street.[23]

Isaac Holmes (1758–1812): arrested August 27, 1780; Charleston merchant; said to have been a militia officer in 1780, but this is unconfirmed; South Carolina House of Representatives, 1779–80, 1785–89, and 1806–8; Privy Council, 1784–90; elected to the South Carolina Senate in 1791 but declined to serve; lieutenant governor of South Carolina, 1791–92; appointed by President George Washington as collector of customs of South Carolina, 1791–97.[24]

Richard Hutson (1747–95): arrested August 27, 1780; attorney and planter; brother-in-law of Col. Isaac Hayne, who was hanged in Charleston by the British on August 4, 1781; graduated from the College of New Jersey (later Princeton University) in 1765 and was admitted to the South Carolina bar; member of the Charleston Library Society, 1772; served in the militia during the Battle of Sullivan's Island on June 28, 1776; South Carolina House of Representatives, 1776–80, 1782–86, and 1789–90; Privy Council, 1780–83; lieutenant governor of South Carolina, 1782–83; delegate to the Continental Congress, 1778–79; signer of the Articles of Confederation on July 9, 1778; first intendant (mayor) of Charleston, 1783; judge of the Court of Chancery, 1784–91 and senior judge, 1791–95; delegate to the South Carolina convention convened to ratify the U.S. Constitution in 1788 (voted in favor); vice president of the board of trustees of the College of Charleston, 1791–93.[25]

Elijah Isaacs (1734–99): captured August 18, 1780; born in Winchester, Virginia; Surrey County, North Carolina Council of Safety, 1775; captain of the Surrey County Regiment of Militia, 1776; captain, major, and lieutenant colonel of the Wilkes County Regiment of North Carolina Militia, 1777–83; wounded and taken prisoner at the Battle of Fishing Creek, South Carolina, on August 18, 1780; North Carolina Senate, 1782–83; promoted to brigadier general of militia in 1782; moved to Anderson County, South Carolina, before 1790.[26]

William Johnson (1741–1818): arrested August 30, 1780; a native of New York who moved to Charleston in the early 1760s; foundry owner; opposed the Stamp Act and helped organize the Liberty Tree Party in 1766; a supporter of Christopher Gadsden's radical politics; Committee of Correspondence, 1774; South Carolina Provincial Congress, 1775–76; South Carolina House of Representatives, 1776–80, 1783–84, and 1787–90; served as a cannoneer in the Charleston Battalion of Artillery (militia), 1780; delegate to the South Carolina convention convened to ratify the U.S. Constitution in 1788 (voted in favor).[27]

Noble Wimberly Jones (1723–1805): arrested November 15, 1780; born near London; served as a cadet in the royal militia under Gen. James Oglethorpe, took part in Oglethorpe's disastrous siege of St. Augustine during the War of Jenkins's Ear in 1740, later promoted to lieutenant with the rank and pay of a surgeon and assigned to a company of rangers; became a physician, and as one of Georgia's first patriots, earned the sobriquet "Morning Star of Liberty"; served in Georgia's colonial and provincial assemblies, Council of Safety, and House of Representatives; elected to the Continental Congress in 1774 but did not attend; elected to the Confederation Congress in 1781; removed to Charleston in 1778 after the British captured Savannah and practiced medicine there until 1780; practiced medicine in Philadelphia, 1781–82, until he returned to Savannah in 1782; Georgia House of Representatives, 1783; president of Georgia's constitutional convention of 1785; received George Washington when the president visited Savannah in 1791; president of the Georgia Medical Society, 1804.[28]

William Lee (1747–1803): arrested November 15, 1780; watchmaker and clockmaker; wartime captain of the True Blue Company of the Charleston District Regiment of Militia; postwar lieutenant colonel of militia; South Carolina House of Representatives, 1782.[29]

John Lewis (ca. 1741–84): arrested August 30, 1780; Anglican clergyman; born in England, educated at Oxford, and came to South Carolina in 1768; rector of St. Paul's Parish, Colleton County.[30]

William Livingston (d. 1791): arrested August 30, 1780; factor; captain of the German Fusiliers Company of the Charleston District Regiment of Militia; died after a fall from his horse.[31]

William Logan (1727–1802): arrested November 15, 1780; merchant, shipowner, slave trader, and planter (postwar); charter member of the Charleston Library Society in 1748; registrar for the court of vice-admiralty, 1765, 1769, 1774; justice of the peace for the Charleston District, 1774; investor in privateering; supplied provisions for Francis Marion's Brigade; South Carolina Senate, 1782; South Carolina House of Representatives, 1783–84; Privy Council, 1783–84.[32]

John Loveday (1744–1804): arrested August 27, 1780; gardenist; messenger of Privy Council, 1776–80; while carrying messages from Gov. John Rutledge, was captured by the British outside of Charleston; powder receiver and arsenal keeper, 1796.[33]

Richard Lushington (d. 1790): arrested August 27, 1780; merchant; lieutenant and captain of the Charleston District Regiment of Militia, 1775–1779; member of the

Charleston Library Society, 1780; lieutenant colonel of the Charleston District Regiment of Militia, 1782; commandant of the militia garrison at Georgetown, 1782; South Carolina House of Representatives, 1782–90; delegate to the South Carolina convention convened to ratify the U.S. Constitution in 1788 (voted in favor).[34]

William Massey (1743–84): arrested August 30, 1780; adjutant of the First South Carolina Regiment (Continental), 1775–77; deputy muster-master general of the Southern District with the rank of lieutenant colonel of Continentals, 1777–80.[35]

Edward McCrady (1750–94): arrested August 27, 1780; born in Ulster, County Antrim, Ireland; entrepreneur and tavern keeper; he was "one of the few of those exiles who occupied no official position—a fact which indicates that it was his personal character and influence which rendered him obnoxious to the British rule"; he was a founding member of the Mt. Zion society, organized to establish a school in the Camden District; also of the Fellowship Society, making the first effort in the United States to establish a lunatic asylum and hospital; the upstairs "Long Room" at McCrady's Tavern on East Bay Street was the site of a formal dinner given on May 4, 1791, hosted by the Society of the Cincinnati, to honor visiting president George Washington.[36]

Arthur Middleton (1742–87): arrested November 15, 1780; planter and politician; brother-in-law of Edward Rutledge; educated in England, studied law at London's Middle Temple; member of the Charleston Library Society, 1765; Commons House of Assembly, 1765–68 and 1772; South Carolina Provincial Congress, 1775–76; Council of Safety, 1775–76; an early supporter of independence from Great Britain; with William Henry Drayton designed the Great Seal of South Carolina in 1776; Continental Congress, 1776–78, and signer of the Declaration of Independence; South Carolina House of Representatives, 1776–80, elected in 1782 and 1783 but did not serve, did serve, 1785–86, reelected in 1787 but died before taking his seat; under the South Carolina constitution of 1778, was elected president of South Carolina but declined the office; delegate to the Confederation Congress, 1781–83; suffered heavy financial losses during the war, including theft by the British and escape of two hundred enslaved persons, but was so wealthy that he was able to continue an elegant lifestyle; trustee of the College of Charleston, 1785.[37]

John Mouat (d. 1787): arrested August 30, 1780; lieutenant in the First South Carolina Regiment (Continental), 1775–80.[38]

Alexander Moultrie (ca. 1750–1807); arrested August 27, 1780; attorney and planter (postwar); half-brother of Brig. Gen. William Moultrie and John Moultrie Jr., royal lieutenant governor of East Florida; entered London's Middle Temple to study law in 1768 and was admitted to the South Carolina bar in 1772; member of the Charleston Library Society, 1772; began militia service as an ensign in 1774, held the rank of captain of the Charleston Musketeers in 1776, and rose to the rank of colonel in the Charleston District Regiment of Militia by 1780;

South Carolina Provincial Congress, 1776; South Carolina House of Representatives, 1776–84; elected attorney general of South Carolina in 1776 and resigned his House seat but was reelected; declined election to the Privy Council in 1783; served as attorney general until 1792, when he was impeached by the House and convicted by the Senate in 1793 for his involvement in the scandalous South Carolina Yazoo Company; Democratic-Republican and supporter of Citizen Genêt's visit to Charleston in 1793.[39]

John Neufville (1727–1804): arrested August 30, 1780; Charleston merchant and shipowner, active in the fur trade and slave trade; charter member of the Charleston Library Society in 1748; an important financier of the revolution in South Carolina; chairman of the Non-Importation Association, 1769; Committee of Ninety-Nine, 1774; South Carolina Provincial Congress, 1775–76; South Carolina House of Representatives, 1776–78 and 1782; Privy Council, 1775–80; commissioner of the Continental Loan Office, 1788–93.[40]

Edward North (1747–98): arrested August 27, 1780; may have had family ties to the Lords North of London; born in Bermuda; a merchant ship captain who operated between Bermuda, Charleston, and the West Indies; moved to Charleston and became a prosperous importer of naval stores, fine linens, and other goods; captured aboard the *Nancy* on December 20, 1777, with a cargo of indigo bound for the West Indies, released on parole to Charleston; made large loans to the state of South Carolina and financed the privateer *Adrianna* in 1778; captain in the Charleston District Regiment of Militia; South Carolina House of Representatives, 1792–94.[41]

Joseph Parker (d. 1785): arrested August 27, 1780; merchant; major of the Charleston District Regiment of Militia.[42]

Christopher Peters (d. 1790): arrested November 15, 1780; planter; South Carolina House of Representatives, 1782.[43]

Benjamin Postell (1759–1801): arrested November 15, 1780; planter; commissioned in 1778 as a second lieutenant in the First South Carolina Regiment (Continental) but resigned in 1779; elected to the South Carolina House of Representatives in 1783 and in 1785 but did not serve, though he did serve, 1778–90; delegate to the South Carolina convention convened to ratify the U.S. Constitution in 1788 (voted against); lieutenant colonel of the Colleton County Cavalry Regiment of the state militia, 1797–1801.[44]

John Ernest Poyas (1730–86): arrested August 27, 1780; Charleston merchant; South Carolina Provincial Congress, 1775; South Carolina House of Representatives, 1776–78 and 1782–84. Poyas is alleged to have been arrested in 1757 for some unrecorded reason, skipped bail, and fled to St. Augustine for a time. Confirmation of this purported sojourn to St. Augustine would cause Poyas to supplant Robert Cochran as the only Charleston exile to have visited St. Augustine prior to being sent there involuntarily.[45]

Samuel Prioleau Jr. (1742–1813): arrested November 15, 1780; Charleston merchant; brother-in-law of Thomas Grimball Jr.; lieutenant in the Charleston District Regiment of Militia; South Carolina House of Representatives, 1776–78 and 1794–95; secretary of the Charleston Chamber of Commerce, 1792.[46]

David Ramsay (1749–1815): arrested August 27, 1780; physician and historian; son-in-law of Henry Laurens; born in Lancaster County, Pennsylvania; attended the College of New Jersey (later Princeton University), graduated class of 1765; studied with Dr. Benjamin Rush and earned his medical degree from the College of Philadelphia (later the University of Pennsylvania) in 1773; established a lucrative medical practice in Charleston in late 1773 or early 1774; member of the Charleston Library Society, 1776; South Carolina House of Representatives, 1776–80, 1782, and 1783–90; Privy Council, 1780–82; Confederation Congress, 1782–86, serving as president pro tempore during his last term; trustee for the College of Charleston, 1785–1815; delegate to the South Carolina convention convened to ratify the U.S. Constitution in 1788 (voted in favor); a founding member and first secretary of the South Carolina Medical Society in 1789, president in 1797; South Carolina Senate, 1791–99, and president of the Senate, 1791–97; made an unsuccessful bid for the U.S. House of Representatives in 1788; director of the Charleston branch of the Bank of the United States, 1792–93; nominated for U.S. senator in 1794 but withdrew his candidacy; Federalist and presidential elector for John Adams in 1796; member of an elected committee in 1795 that unsuccessfully recommended rejection of the Jay Treaty; member of the American Philosophical Society; America's first historian, who contributed thirty-two works to the historical record, beginning with *History of the Revolution of South-Carolina from a British Colony to an Independent State,* a work begun while in St. Augustine, published in 1785; surgeon of the Charleston Regiment of Artillery, 1814; murdered by a deranged man in 1815.[47]

Jacob Read (1752–1816): arrested August 27, 1780; attorney; educated in Savannah, Georgia, and admitted to the South Carolina bar in 1773 but commenced further study of the law at Gray's Inn in London the same year; commissioned captain in the Charleston District Regiment of Militia in 1776; member of the Charleston Library Society, 1777; South Carolina House of Representatives, 1782–94; Privy Council, 1783; Confederation Congress, 1783–85; delegate to the South Carolina convention convened to ratify the U.S. Constitution in 1788 (voted in favor); lost election to the U.S. House of Representatives in 1793; an unsuccessful gubernatorial candidate in 1794 but was elected by the legislature to the U.S. Senate instead, serving 1795–1801; national director of the Bank of the United States, ca. 1797; appointed federal judge by President John Adams in 1801 but never served; lieutenant colonel of the Twenty-Ninth Regiment, ca. 1794–1801, and brigadier general of the Seventh Brigade, ca. 1805–16, of South Carolina militia; military commander of Charleston, 1812–13.[48]

Griffith Rutherford (1721–1805): captured August 16, 1780; surveyor and planter; born in Ireland and immigrated to Philadelphia ca. 1739 with his parents, who died during the voyage; moved to North Carolina in 1753; captain in the British colonial militia during the French and Indian War, 1760; North Carolina House of Burgesses, 1766–71; sheriff of Rowan County, 1767–69; campaigned against the North Carolina Regulators, 1771; colonel and brigadier general of North Carolina militia, 1772, 1776; Committee of Safety for the Salisbury District, 1775; Provincial Congress of North Carolina, 1775–76; participated in the "Snow Campaign" in December 1775; fought against the Cherokees in 1776 and in 1782; North Carolina Senate, 1777–80, 1783–86; part of a court of inquiry against Brig. Gen. John Ashe after the American defeat at Briar Creek on March 3, 1779; participated in the patriot victory at Ramsour's Mill on June 20, 1780; wounded and taken prisoner at the Battle of Camden on August 16, 1780; returned to North Carolina from Philadelphia and resumed field command after his exchange in 1781; occupied Wilmington, N.C., after the British evacuation on November 18, 1781; elected Council of State, 1782–89 and later; unsuccessful North Carolina gubernatorial candidate, 1783; antifederalist delegate to the North Carolina convention convened to ratify the U.S. Constitution in 1788 (voted against); moved in 1786 to an area that later became part of Tennessee; cohosted a dinner at Guilford Court House for George Washington during the president's 1791 southern tour; appointed by Washington to the legislative council of the Southwest Territory in 1793, of which he was elected president in 1794.[49]

Edward Rutledge (1749–1800): arrested August 27, 1780; attorney and planter; brother of Hugh Rutledge and John Rutledge; brother-in-law of Arthur Middleton; studied law under his older brother John before entering London's Middle Temple in 1767; called to the English bar in 1772 and the South Carolina bar in 1773; practiced law in partnership with Charles Cotesworth Pinckney; elected to the Commons House of Assembly, 1773–75, but declined to serve; delegate to the Continental Congress, 1774–77; was at first reluctant to separate from Great Britain but came around to the cause of independence and signed the Declaration of Independence in 1776; served of the first Board of War in 1776; lieutenant in 1774, then captain, 1776–81, in the Charleston Battalion of Artillery (militia); fought at Port Royal Island on February 3, 1779; South Carolina Provincial Congress, 1775–76; Council of Safety, 1775–76; South Carolina House of Representatives, 1776–80, 1782, and 1793–95; Privy Council, 1772–83 and 1787–89; author of the first draft of the Confiscation Act in 1782; member of the Charleston Library Society, 1783; delegate to the South Carolina convention convened to ratify the U.S. Constitution in 1788 (voted in favor); lieutenant colonel of the Regiment of Artillery of the Seventh Brigade of South Carolina militia, 1800; director of the Charleston branch of the Bank of the United States, 1792–93; trustee of the College of Charleston, 1793; director of the Santee Canal Company,

1793; presidential elector in 1788, 1792, and 1796; helped pass a bill in the South Carolina General Assembly in 1788 that extended a ban on slave importation to 1793 and authored an act to ban primogeniture in 1791; declined an offer from President Washington in 1794 to become an associate justice of the Supreme Court; South Carolina Senate, 1796–99; elected governor of South Carolina in 1798 and died in office.[50]

Hugh Rutledge (1745–1811): arrested August 27, 1780; attorney and planter; brother of Edward Rutledge and John Rutledge; admitted to London's Middle Temple in 1765; called to the South Carolina bar, 1768; judge of the Court of Admiralty, 1776; South Carolina House of Representatives, 1776, 1779–80, and 1782–90; Speaker of the House, 1782–84; Legislative Council, 1776; officer in the First Battalion of Charleston militia, 1780; delegate to the South Carolina convention convened to ratify the U.S. Constitution in 1788 (voted in favor); judge of the court of equity of South Carolina, 1791–1811; trustee for establishing the College of Charleston, 1785, 1791, and 1793; trustee of South Carolina College (later the University of South Carolina), 1801–11.[51]

John Sansum (d. 1784): arrested August 27, 1780; constable employed by the Council of Safety, 1775; served in the militia in the Ninety Six District as forage-master general, 1779–80; served as a courier between U.S. superintendent of finance, Robert Morris, and General Greene's army in the southern states, 1782; postwar, deputy marshal to the admiralty court (n.d.).[52]

Thomas Savage (1738–86): arrested November 15, 1780; born in Bermuda and migrated to South Carolina, where he became a successful merchant and planter; owned ships and engaged in the slave trade; militia lieutenant during the Cherokee War, 1760, and captain, 1767; Commons House of Assembly, 1768–71; one of the "Unanimous Twenty-six" who approved the Massachusetts Circular Letter written by Samuel Adams in 1768 that argued against taxation of the colonies by Parliament without representation, particularly via the Townshend Acts, as unconstitutional and a violation of colonial rights; Council of Safety, 1775–76; South Carolina Provincial Congress, 1775–76; commissioner of South Carolina navy, 1776; captain in the Charleston Rangers company of the Charleston District Regiment of Militia and fought at Sullivan's Island on June 28, 1776; South Carolina House of Representatives, 1776–78, 1782–84; warden of Charleston (member of the city council), 1783.[53]

Thomas Singleton (1721–98): arrested August 27, 1780; tavern keeper; served as a private in the Charleston District Regiment of Militia; developed a process to prevent shipworms from penetrating the hulls of ships, 1798.[54]

Josiah Smith Jr. (1731–1826): arrested August 27, 1780; born at Cainhoy in the parish of St. Thomas and moved to Charleston in the mid-1740s; merchant, shipowner, slave trader, and financial agent; one of the principal creditors of his state during the war; commissioner of South Carolina navy, 1776–80; South Carolina House of Representatives, 1776–80 and 1783–86; Privy Council, 1783–84; delegate to the South Carolina convention convened to ratify the U.S. Constitution in 1788 (voted in favor); appointed first cashier of the Office of Discount and Deposit of the Charleston branch of the Bank of the United States and served until 1810.[55]

Philip Smith (1728–96): arrested November 15, 1780; planter; justice of the peace for Colleton County in 1765 and Charleston District in 1774 and 1776; militia captain, 1775; South Carolina Provincial Congress, 1775–76; South Carolina House of Representatives, 1776; justice of the peace for Colleton County in 1765 and Charleston District in 1774 and 1776; lent money and supplied provisions to the military during the war. Smith was the only one of the exiles to defect and take British protection during the banishment. He seems not to have borne the consequences of confiscation or amercement.[56]

James Hamden Thomson (d. 1795): arrested August 30, 1780; tutor, schoolmaster, and sometime Presbyterian preacher; born in Massachusetts; attended the College of New Jersey (later Princeton University), graduated class of 1761; taught at Princeton until 1770, when he began an academy in Charleston; was a gifted schoolmaster "to whom nature had denied every attribute of a soldier."[57]

Peter Timothy (1725–82): arrested August 27, 1780; newspaper owner and editor; born in Holland, emigrated with his Huguenot parents to Philadelphia in 1731; came to Charleston ca. 1733 to establish a family printing business of which Benjamin Franklin was a partner; assumed full editorship and management of the *South-Carolina Gazette* in 1740 (the paper became a vehicle for revolutionary thought); charter member of the Charleston Library Society in 1748; Commons House of Assembly, 1751–54; postmaster general for Charleston, 1756; during the Stamp Act crisis in 1765, was secretary to the deputy postmaster general of the southern colonies and was temporarily in charge of the district in 1766; active in the Sons of Liberty and member of the General Committee of Correspondence in 1774; Committee of Ninety-Nine for Charleston, 1774; clerk of the Council of Safety, 1775; South Carolina Provincial Congress, 1775–76, serving as secretary and official printer; South Carolina House of Representatives, briefly in 1776; clerk of the House of Representatives but not a member, 1776–80; died at sea in 1782 while sailing for Antigua.[58]

John Todd (d. after 1790): arrested August 27, 1780; tavern keeper and merchant; fusilier of the German Fusiliers Company of the Charleston District Regiment of Militia.[59]

Anthony Toomer (1742–98): arrested August 27, 1780; bricklayer and master builder; Committee of Correspondence, 1774; captain in the Charleston Battalion of Artillery (militia), promoted to major after the war; South Carolina Provincial Congress, 1775–77; South Carolina House of Representatives, 1776–80 and 1782–89; delegate to the South Carolina convention convened to ratify the U.S. Constitution in 1788 (voted in favor).[60]

James Wakefield (d. 1794): arrested November 15, 1780; a Charleston merchant who emigrated from London in 1771; in 1774, six months after the Boston Tea Party, he was an intended recipient of a shipment of tea from London of which he refused delivery amid great controversy; ensign and quartermaster of militia; elected to the South Carolina House of Representatives in 1787 but did not serve.[61]

Benjamin Waller (d. after 1801): arrested November 15, 1780; schoolmaster; private in the German Fusiliers Company of the Charleston District Regiment of Militia; commissioner to consider banishment of individuals who refused to take the oath of allegiance to South Carolina in 1778; South Carolina House of Representatives, 1786.[62]

Edward Weyman (1730–93): arrested November 15, 1780; a Pennsylvania-born glass grinder and upholsterer who had moved to Charleston by 1755; messenger of the Commons House of Assembly, 1757–75; Sons of Liberty, 1766; Committee of Correspondence, 1774; secret committee and special committee, 1775; South Carolina Provincial Congress, 1775–76; South Carolina House of Representatives, 1776, 1779–80, and 1782; lieutenant in the Charleston Battalion of Artillery (militia), 1779–80; captain of artillery in Francis Marion's Brigade, 1782; held various port-related offices from 1783 to 1793.[63]

Morton Wilkinson (1745–1890): arrested November 15, 1780; planter; an avid sportsman who owned several prized racehorses; Commons House of Assembly, 1770–71; at the outset of the war, was an ensign in the Willtown Company of the Colleton County Regiment but rose through the ranks to colonel and served with Brig. Gen. Andrew Pickens; South Carolina House of Representatives, 1782; Privy Council, 1782–83; commissioner to purchase an estate for Gen. Nathanael Greene, 1782; South Carolina Senate, 1783–84, declined election in 1785.[64]

How Many Patriots Were
Exiled to St. Augustine?

While it is clear (see appendixes A and C) that a total of sixty-three patriots were exiled to St. Augustine in 1780, an absolutely conclusive primary source or early secondary source listing of patriots exiled to St. Augustine is unavailable. Several sources give actual names for the members of a group or subgroup of exiles, but surprisingly no two sources agree entirely. In other words every account either includes or omits names mentioned in some other account.

The *South-Carolina and American General Gazette* of August 30, 1780, listed twenty-nine prisoners taken on August 27. The *Gazette* of September 6, 1780, listed eleven additional names—those taken on August 30. The *Gazette* of November 18, 1780, named twenty-three gentlemen arrested on November 15. Thus the total number of arrestees named by the *South-Carolina and American General Gazette* is sixty-three.

Josiah Smith Jr., the principal eyewitness whose account was written contemporaneously and later edited, listed twenty-nine exiles for August 27 and eleven for August 30. He named twenty-three in November (including a Georgian with them), plus two North Carolinians, for a total of sixty-five.[1]

The earliest British list outside of the newspapers is an enclosure that accompanied a September 4, 1780, letter from Lt. Col. Nisbet Balfour to Lt. Gen. Charles Cornwallis titled "List of the Names of the Disaffected Inhabitants of Charlestown Who Have Been Sent to [St.] Augustine, 3rd September 1780." The list totals thirty-two and does not stipulate the day of arrest (but it was certainly August 27). Two names are crossed out, and a comment states "in the country" for one (Hugh Swinton) and "in the country on parole" for the other (Peter Bocquet). Another gentleman, Robert Smith, is designated "sick in bed." None of the three seem to have been actually transported.[2]

A list of exiles survives in a manuscript letter from British governor Patrick Tonyn, in a report from him to Lord George Germain dated December 9, 1780, in which names and minimal titles are given for sixty-three "rebel prisoners landed from Charles Town at Saint Augustine[,] East Florida[,] September 15th and November 24th[,] 1780."[3]

Christopher Gadsden said in a letter to George Washington in 1781 that sixty-one arrived in Philadelphia, but he did not name them. This number accounts for Philip Smith, who departed St. Augustine for Charleston on April 23, 1791, and George Abbot Hall, who departed St. Augustine on July 22, 1781.[4]

Eyewitness David Ramsay published an account in 1785 giving a total of sixty-one, twenty-seven for August 27, ten for August 30, twenty-two for November, and two militia officers from North Carolina. He failed to list himself and counted a Georgian with the November South Carolina detainees. In a separate work published in 1809, he gave a total of sixty-three, listing twenty-eight for August 27, ten for August 30, twenty-three for November, adding two (including his own) to the 1785 list and again separately mentioning the two from North Carolina.[5]

Banastre Tarleton's account published in 1787, not eyewitness and clearly using British sources, lists thirty-three as arrested on August 27, including four who are not listed elsewhere. He does not name or number those arrested on August 30, in November, or those from out of state.[6]

Thomas Farr's name appears only on Tarleton's list but has the additional support of a scrapbook, purportedly at the Charleston Library Society, assembled by participant William Hasell Gibbes, in which Farr's clipped signature is included under the brief category of St. Augustine exiles. Gibbes's collection of autographs is too arbitrary to be considered an authoritative roll call. Absence from it does not prove nonparticipation, but inclusion in it certainly witnesses some sort of personal testimony from another exile or from the public understanding at the time.

James Grant Forbes listed sixty-one gentlemen in 1821, some of their names badly misspelled (such as "M'Bready" for McCrady), but all are included elsewhere.[7]

In 1822 Alexander Garden provided a roll call of fifty-eight names, fifty-seven of which are all included elsewhere, adding one additional name that is found in no other list: John Morrall.[8]

Joseph Johnson, writing from his eyewitness father William Johnson's firsthand notes, names a total of sixty-eight without distinguishing on what dates they were arrested. Comparison with other sources clarifies that he gives twenty-eight for August 27, eleven for August 30, twenty-one for November, and eight as out of state (non–South Carolinians) in the November group.[9]

George Rainsford Fairbanks said that the number arrested on August 27 and 30 combined was forty, and the number for November was twenty-three (including a few from North Carolina), giving a total of sixty-three.[10]

In a few cases, being listed among the detainees did not mean that one was necessarily exiled to St. Augustine. Dr. Fayssoux, who is counted as an exile by Johnson, Tarleton, and Smith, was indeed arrested on August 27 and appears on the list Balfour sent to Cornwallis. He was subsequently allowed to remain in Charleston because of his official military-medical status. Thomas Savage was also initially arrested on August 27 but was excused from the first exile on account of his health. However, he was later rearrested, and his name appears in all the lists—including the passenger list of the brigantine that took exiles from St. Augustine to Philadelphia.[11]

The boat lists of those setting out for Philadelphia indicate a total of fifty-nine, which includes twenty-six from August 27, ten from August 30, twenty-one from November, and two from other states.[12]

These figures are represented in the following table:

Published Sources and Numbers of St. Augustine Exiles
(chronologically arranged)

Source	Arrested Aug. 27	Arrested Aug. 30	August subtotal	Arrested Nov. 15	Non-S.C.	Total
Gazette	29	11	40	23	—	63
Smith	29	11	40	23	2	65
Cornwallis	32	—	32	—	—	32
Boat lists	25	10	35	22	2	59
Gadsden	—	—	—	—	—	61
Ramsay '85	27	10	37	22	2	61
Forbes	—	—	—	—	—	61
Garden	—	—	—	—	—	58
Tarleton	33	—	—	—	—	33
Ramsay '09	28	10	38	23	2	63
Johnson	28	11	39	21	8	68
Fairbanks	—	—	40	23	—	63

All names listed (but not all occurring in any one source)

	Arrested Aug. 27	Arrested Aug. 30	August subtotal	Arrested Nov. 15	Non-S.C.	Total
	36	11	48	22	8	77

Appendix C

Source Distribution of the Exiles

Sources

1. *South-Carolina and American General Gazette* (Charleston, S.C.), August 30, 1780, September 6, 1780, and November 18, 1780.

2. "Josiah Smith's "Diary, 1780–81," *South Carolina Historical and Genealogical Magazine* 33, no. 1 (1932): 3–4; and "Josiah Smith's "Diary, 1780–81," *South Carolina Historical and Genealogical Magazine* 33, no. 2 (1932): 87–90, 100.

3. Charles, Earl Cornwallis, *The Cornwallis Papers: The Campaigns of 1780 and 1781 in the Southern Theatre of the American Revolutionary War* (edited by Ian Saberton, 2010), 2:77–78.

4. David Ramsay, *The History of the Revolution of South-Carolina: From a British Province to an Independent State* (1785), 2:161, 458–59.

5. Banastre Tarleton, *A History of the Campaigns of 1780 and 1781, in the Southern Provinces of North America* (1787), 189–90.

6. David Ramsay, *The History of South Carolina: From Its First Settlement in 1670 to the Year 1808* (1809), 1:370–71, 373.

7. Joseph Johnson, *Traditions and Reminiscences, Chiefly of the American Revolution in the South* (1851), 317–19.

8. "Josiah Smith's "Diary, 1780–81," *South Carolina Historical and Genealogical Magazine* 34, no. 1 (1933): 31–32. Smith denoted which exiles were transported on which of two vessels, a brigantine or a schooner, that sailed for Philadelphia. "B" = brigantine; "S" = schooner.

Table 1: The Seventy-nine Names as Compiled from Seven Sources

(Seventy-seven names with two names repeated once.)

Source	1.	2.	3.	4.	5.	6.	7.	8.
	SCAGG	*Smith*	*Cornwallis*	*Ramsay '85*	*Tarleton*	*Ramsay '90*	*Johnson*	*Smith*
Total each source	**63**	**65**	**32**	**61**	**33**	**63**	**68**	**59**
Arrested August 27, 1780	*29*	*29*	*32*	*27*	*33*	*28*	*28*	*25*
1. Atkinson, Joseph	—	—	—	—	✓	—	—	—
2. Blake, Edward	✓	✓	✓	✓	✓	✓	✓	B
3. Bocquet, Peter*	—	—	✓	—	—	—	—	—
4. Budd, John	✓	✓	✓	✓	✓	✓	✓	B
5. Edwards, John	✓	✓	✓	✓	✓	✓	✓	—
6. Farr, Thomas*	—	—	—	—	✓	—	—	—
7. Fayssoux, Peter*	✓	✓	✓	—	✓	—	✓	—
8. Ferguson, Thomas	✓	✓	✓	✓	✓	✓	✓	B
9. Flagg, George	✓	✓	✓	✓	✓	✓	✓	S
10. Floyd, John*	—	—	—	—	✓	—	—	—
11. Gadsden, Christopher	✓	✓	✓	✓	✓	✓	✓	B
12. Gibbes, William Hasell	✓	✓	✓	✓	✓	✓	✓	B
13. Heyward, Thomas, Jr.	✓	✓	✓	✓	✓	✓	✓	S
14. Holmes, Isaac	✓	✓	✓	✓	✓	✓	✓	B
15. Hutson, Richard	✓	✓	✓	✓	✓	✓	✓	B
16. Loveday, John	✓	✓	✓	✓	✓	✓	✓	B
17. Lushington, Richard	✓	✓	✓	✓	✓	✓	✓	B
18. McCrady, Edward	✓	✓	✓	✓	✓	✓	✓	S
19. Moultrie, Alexander	✓	✓	✓	✓	✓	✓	✓	S
20. North, Edward	✓	✓	✓	✓	✓	✓	✓	B
21. Parker, Joseph	✓	✓	✓	✓	✓	✓	✓	S
22. Poyas, John Ernest	✓	✓	✓	✓	✓	✓	✓	B
23. Price, William*	—	—	—	—	✓	—	—	—
24. Ramsay, David	✓	✓	✓	—	✓	✓	✓	S
25. Read, Jacob	✓	✓	✓	✓	✓	✓	✓	B
26. Rutledge, Edward	✓	✓	✓	✓	✓	✓	✓	S
27. Rutledge, Hugh	✓	✓	✓	✓	✓	✓	✓	S
28. Sansum, John	✓	✓	✓	✓	✓	✓	✓	S
29. Savage, Thomas†	✓	✓	✓	✓	✓	✓	—	—
30. Singleton, Thomas	✓	✓	✓	✓	✓	✓	✓	S

Source	1. SCAGG	2. Smith	3. Cornwallis	4. Ramsay '85	5. Tarleton	6. Ramsay '90	7. Johnson	8. Smith
31. Smith, Josiah, Jr.	✓	✓	✓	✓	✓	✓	✓	B
32. Smith, Robert*	—	—	✓	—	—	—	—	—
33. Swinton, Hugh*	—	—	✓	—	—	—	—	—
34. Timothy, Peter	✓	✓	✓	✓	✓	✓	✓	B
35. Todd, John	✓	✓	✓	✓	✓	✓	✓	B
36. Toomer, Anthony	✓	✓	✓	✓	✓	✓	✓	—
Arrested August 30, 1780	*11*	*11*	*0*	*10*	*0*	*10*	*11*	*10*
37. Cochran, Robert	✓	✓	—	✓	—	✓	✓	B
38. Grimball, Thomas, Jr.†	✓	✓	—	—	—	—	✓	S
39. Hall, Thomas	✓	✓	—	✓	—	✓	✓	—
40. Hall, William	✓	✓	—	✓	—	✓	✓	B
41. Johnson, William	✓	✓	—	✓	—	✓	✓	S
42. Lewis, John	✓	✓	—	✓	—	✓	✓	B
43. Livingston, William	✓	✓	—	✓	—	✓	✓	B
44. Massey, William	✓	✓	—	✓	—	✓	✓	S
45. Mouat, John	✓	✓	—	✓	—	✓	✓	B
46. Neufville, John	✓	✓	—	✓	—	✓	✓	S
47. Thomson, James Hamden	✓	✓	—	✓	—	✓	✓	B
Arrested November 15, 1780	*23*	*23*	*0*	*22*	*0*	*23*	*21*	*22*
48. Bee, Joseph	✓	✓	—	✓	—	✓	✓	S
49. Beresford, Richard	✓	✓	—	✓	—	✓	✓	S
50. Berwick, John	✓	✓	—	✓	—	✓	✓	B
51. Bourdeaux, Daniel	✓	✓				✓	✓	S
52. Cripps, John Splatt	✓	✓	—	✓	—	✓	✓	S
53. Crouch, Henry	✓	✓	—	✓	—	✓	✓	S
54. Cudworth, Benjamin	✓	✓	—	✓	—	✓	✓	S
55. Darrell, Edward	✓	✓	—	✓	—	✓	✓	B
56. DeSaussure, Daniel	✓	✓	—	✓	—	✓	✓	B
57. Grimball, Thomas, Jr.†	—	—	—	✓	—	✓	—	—
58. Hall, George Abbot	✓	✓	—	✓	—	✓	✓	—
59. Jones, Noble Wimberly (Ga.)§	✓	✓	—	✓	—	✓	✓	S
60. Lee, William	✓	✓	—	✓	—	✓	✓	B
61. Logan, William	✓	✓	—	✓	—	✓	—	B
62. Middleton, Arthur	✓	✓	—	✓	—	✓	✓	S

Table 1 continued

Source	1. SCAGG	2. Smith	3. Cornwallis	4. Ramsay '85	5. Tarleton	6. Ramsay '90	7. Johnson	8. Smith
Arrested November 15, 1780	23	23	0	22	0	23	21	22
63. Peters, Christopher	✓	✓	—	✓	—	✓	✓	S
64. Postell, Benjamin	✓	✓	—	✓	—	✓	✓	S
65. Prioleau, Samuel, Jr.	✓	✓	—	✓	—	✓	—	S
66. Savage, Thomas†	✓	✓	—	—	—	—	✓	B
67. Smith, Philip	✓	✓	—	✓	—	✓	✓	—
68. Wakefield, James	✓	✓	—	✓	—	✓	✓	S
69. Waller, Benjamin	✓	✓	—	✓	—	✓	✓	S
70. Weyman, Edward	✓	✓	—	✓	—	✓	✓	S
71. Wilkinson, Morton	✓	✓	—	✓	—	✓	✓	S
Non–South Carolinians‡	0	2	0	2	0	2	8	2
72. Clarke (Ga.)*	—	—	—	—	—	—	✓	—
73. Henderson (N.C.)	—	—	—	—	—	—	✓	—
74. Isaacs, Elijah (N.C.)	—	✓	—	✓	—	✓	✓	S
75. Jackson (Ga.)*	—	—	—	—	—	—	✓	—
76. McCall (Ga.)*	—	—	—	—	—	—	✓	—
77. Moore, Stephen (N.C.)	—	—	—	—	—	—	✓	—
78. Rutherford, Griffith (N.C.)	—	✓	—	✓	—	✓	✓	B
79. Twiggs (Ga.)*	—	—	—	—	—	—	✓	—

Notes

* Peter Bocquet, Thomas Farr, John Floyd, William Price, Robert Smith, and Hugh Swinton are included in certain listings but do not seem to have been arrested or exiled to St. Augustine. Dr. Peter Fayssoux was arrested but released. Only Johnson lists the Georgians Clarke, Jackson, McCall, and Twiggs.

† Thomas Grimball Jr. and Thomas Savage are listed twice. Grimball is listed on August 30 (correct) and November 15, 1780. Savage is listed on August 27 and November 15, 1780 (correct).

§ Noble Wimberly Jones's name is printed in the *South-Carolina and American General Gazette* notice of November 18, 1780, of "persons alluded to in our last" who "sailed yesterday" for St. Augustine. This list has twenty-three names, including Daniel Bourdeaux, Noble Wimberly Jones, and Thomas Savage.

‡ Also counted as November arrests but not sailing together with the South Carolina patriots: five Georgian and four North Carolinian prisoners added to November group, according to Johnson. Noble Wimberly Jones is generally listed among the South Carolinians and is therefore counted with them.

Table 2: Reduction of Table 1

The following are named in all six sources as arrested on August 27, 1780:

Blake, Edward	Loveday, John	Rutledge, Hugh
Budd, John	Lushington, Richard	Sansum, John
Ferguson, Thomas	McCrady, Edward	Savage, Thomas
Flagg, George	Moultrie, Alexander	Singleton, Thomas
Gadsden, Christopher	North, Edward	Smith, Josiah, Jr.
Gibbes, William Hasell	Parker, Joseph	Timothy, Peter
Heyward, Thomas, Jr.	Poyas, John Ernest	Todd, John
Holmes, Isaac	Read, Jacob	
Hutson, Richard	Rutledge, Edward	

The following are named as arrested on August 27, 1780, only in the sources checked:

	Johnson Acc't	Ramsay 1809	Tarleton 1787	Ramsay 1785	Smith diary	Philadelphia boats
Atkinson, Joseph	—	—	✓	—	—	—
Bourdeaux, Daniel	✓	✓	—	—	—	✓
Edwards, John	—	✓	✓	✓	✓	—
Farr, Thomas	—	—	✓	—	—	—
Fayssoux, Peter	✓	—	✓	—	✓	—
Floyd, John	—	—	✓	—	—	—
Price, William	—	—	✓	—	—	—
Ramsay, David	✓	✓	✓	—	✓	✓
Toomer, Anthony	✓	✓	✓	✓	✓	—

The following were arrested on August 30, 1780, and (with one exception), are cited in five sources: Johnson's account, Ramsay 1809, Ramsay 1785, Smith's diary, and Smith's Philadelphia boat lists

Cochran, Robert
Hall, Capt. Thomas—named in first four sources but not in the
    Philadelphia boat lists
Hall, Capt. William
Johnson, William
Lewis, Rev. John
Livingston, Capt. William
Massey, William
Mouat, John
Neufville, John
Thomson, Rev. James Hamden

The following were arrested in November 1780, and are named in four sources: Johnson's account, Ramsay 1785, Ramsay 1809, and Smith's Philadelphia boat lists

Bee, Joseph
Beresford, Richard
Berwick, John
Cripps, John Splatt
Crouch, Henry
Cudworth, Benjamin
Darrell, Edward
DeSaussure, Daniel
Grimball, Thomas, Jr.—listed by Smith as having been arrested August 30th
Lee, William
Middleton, Arthur
Peter, Christopher
Postell, Benjamin
Wakefield, James
Waller, Benjamin
Weyman, Edward
Wilkinson, Morton

The following were arrested in November 1780 but are named only in the sources checked:

	Johnson Acc't	Ramsay 1809	Ramsay 1785	Boat lists
Hall, George Abbot	✓	✓	✓	—
Logan, William	—	✓	✓	✓
Prioleau, Samuel	—	✓	✓	✓
Smith, Philip	✓	✓	✓	—

Five Georgian and four North Carolinian prisoners were added to the November group, according to Johnson; three of these are also named in Ramsay 1785, and on the boat lists:

Clarke (Ga.)	only in Johnson
Henderson (NC)	only in Johnson
Isaacs, Colonel Elijah (NC)	in Johnson, in Ramsay 1785, and on the boat list
Jackson (Ga.)	only in Johnson
Jones, Dr. Noble Wimberly (Ga.)	in Johnson, in Ramsay 1785, the boat list, and Forbes
McCall (Ga.)	only in Johnson
Moore, Stephen (NC)	only in Johnson
Rutherford, General Griffith (NC)	in Johnson, in Ramsay 1785, and on the boat list
Twiggs (Ga.)	only in Johnson

Notes

Preface

1. Smith, "Diary," *South Carolina Historical and Genealogical Magazine* (henceforth *SCHGM*) 33, no. 1: 1–2; Salley, *Journal of the Commissioners of the Navy of South Carolina,* 1:3, 246, and 2:4, 79.

2. Smith, "Diary," *SCHGM* 33, no. 1: 1–2.

3. Morgan and Rushton, *Banishment in the Early Atlantic World,* 153–82; *Royal Gazette* (Charleston, S.C.), June 30, 1781; *Royal Gazette* (Charleston, S.C.), August 15, 1781.

4. Holcomb, *South Carolina Deed Abstracts, 1783–1788, Books I-5 through Z-5,* 151 (Books O-5, pp. 301–6), 472 (Z-5, pp. 479–82). At the time of McCrady's purchase, this property was empty "lot number 19" on East Bay Street. It was later recorded as No. 153 East Bay. Johnson's address was No. 140 East Bay.

5. "Long room" was an established term in Charleston and in eighteenth-century England for an assembly room in a private house or public building, occasionally (as here) serving even as a private reception hall and theater. The *Royal Gazette* of Saturday, July 14, 1781, carries a notice for a long room on Church Street that, unlike McCrady's, was not used in conjunction with a tavern. McCrady's Long Room, in its original structure and location, is still in operation in 2019.

6. Bailey and Cooper, *Biographical Directory of the South Carolina House,* 3:383–85.

7. Johnson's family had been cheated out of valuable Manhattan land by state lawyers working for the established church. McCrady's reason for leaving the old country was his rejection of class snobbery. His fiancée's aristocratic family disapproved of him for not having a title, but the couple was sponsored in marriage by her near relative Alexander McDougall, who later became a major general in the Continental Army. Johnson would also have been considered a rebel simply for being a member of the prewar Provincial Congress. Both men were interred in the graveyard at St. Philip's Church in Charleston. Entry for June 3, 1775, *Extracts from the Journals of the Provincial Congresses of South Carolina,* 71.

Prologue

1. Memorial of James Simpson, February 12, 1784, AO 12: American Loyalist Claims, fol. 720.

2. Moultrie, *Memoirs,* 2:109–11; Uhlendorf, *Siege of Charleston,* 89.

3. James Simpson to Henry Clinton, July 1, 1780, *Report on the American Manuscripts in the Royal Institution of Great Britain,* 2:149–50.

4. James Simpson to Henry Clinton, May 15, 1780, "James Simpson's Reports on the Carolina Loyalists, 1779–1780," 518–19.

Introduction—Two Towns at Odds

1. The town was called Charles Town or Charlestown until 1783.

2. Reynolds, *Old St. Augustine,* 138. Reynolds provides a concise chronology of St. Augustine from 1512 to 1845.

3. Solís de Méras, *Pedro Menéndez de Avilés,* 255.

4. Weir, *Colonial South Carolina,* 3–9.

5. Hanna and Hanna, *Florida's Golden Sands,* 232; Tebeau, *History of Florida,* 58; Weir, *Colonial South Carolina,* 50; Wright, *British St. Augustine,* 2.

6. Edgar, "Notable Libraries of Colonial South Carolina," 105.

7. Manucy and Johnson, "Castle St. Mark and the Patriots of the Revolution," 1; Waterbury, *Oldest City,* 71 (quoted).

8. Waterbury, *Oldest City,* 64–67.

9. Moultrie, *Memoirs,* 1:205.

10. Bennett and Lennon, *Quest for Glory,* 46–84.

11. Wright, *Florida in the American Revolution,* 106.

Chapter 1—A Loyalist Embarks on a Secret Mission

1. Hill, "Exercise in Futility," iii, 1, 21; Woods, *Register of Burials at the Temple Church,* 81; Memorial of James Simpson, February 12, 1784, and evidence supporting James Simpson's memorial, January 27, 1786, AO 12/48, American Loyalist Claims, fols. 71r, 780; Smith, *South Carolina as a Royal Province,* 413; McCrady, *History of South Carolina under the Royal Government,* 465; Strozier, *Report of the Georgia Bar Association,* 186.

2. Hill, "Exercise in Futility," 7–12.

3. Memorial of James Simpson, February 12, 1784, and evidence supporting James Simpson's memorial, January 27, 1786, AO 12/48, American Loyalist Claims, fols. 71r, 780; Hill, "Exercise in Futility," 13, 23–25; James Simpson to Court of Chancery, December 20, 1764, South Carolina Court of Chancery, Petitions to Practice Law, 1752–1778, Series 2142004, box 1, item 12, SCDAH (quoted); McCrady, *History of South Carolina under the Royal Government,* 481.

4. Memorial of James Simpson, February 12, 1784, and evidence supporting James Simpson's memorial, January 27, 1786, AO 12/48, American Loyalist Claims, fols. 71r, 780; Hill, "Exercise in Futility," 19, 38; Affidavit of William Bull II, July 28, 1777, AO 13/135, American Loyalist Claims, fol. 3060; *South-Carolina Gazette* (Charleston, S.C.), December 31, 1763; Smith, *South Carolina as a Royal Province,* 73–90; Whitney, *Government of the Colony of South Carolina,* 38–46.

5. *New-York Journal,* June 22, 1769; Memorial of James Simpson, February 12, 1784, and evidence supporting James Simpson's memorial, January 27, 1786, AO 12/48, American Loyalist Claims, fols. 71r, 780; Whitney, *Government of the Colony of South Carolina,* 86–90; Ubbelohde, *Vice-Admiralty Courts and the American Revolution,* 104–19.

6. Affidavit of William Bull II, July 28, 1777, AO 13/135, American Loyalist Claims, fol. 3060; Hill, "Exercise in Futility," 37; Smith, *South Carolina as a Royal Province,* 412–14.

7. Memorial of James Simpson, February 12, 1784, and evidence supporting James Simpson's memorial, January 27, 1786, AO 12/48, American Loyalist Claims, fols. 71r, 78o; Drayton, *Memoirs,* 1:257–58.

8. McCrady, *Revolution 1775–1780,* 2, 53–62, 66–68; Moultrie, *Memoirs,* 1:59–60.

9. Deposition of Elizabeth Simpson, July 11, 1775, "Journal of the Council of Safety," 69–70.

10. Peter Timothy to William Henry Drayton, August 13, 1775, and Arthur Middleton to William Henry Drayton, August 22, 1775, "Correspondence of Hon. Arthur Middleton," *SCHGM* 27, no. 3: 129, 135 (quoted).

11. Memorial of James Simpson, February 12, 1784 (first quote), and evidence supporting James Simpson's memorial, January 27, 1786, AO 12/48, American Loyalist Claims, fols. 71r, 78o; entry for June 3, 1775, *Extracts from the Journals of the Provincial Congresses of South Carolina,* 35–36; William Campbell to Earl of Dartmouth, July 23, 1775, *Documents of the American Revolution,* 11:55 (second quote); Piecuch, *Three Peoples, One King,* 47 (third quote), 347n74.

12. Memorial of James Simpson, February 12, 1784, and evidence supporting James Simpson's memorial, January 27, 1786, AO 12/48, American Loyalist Claims, fols. 71r, 78o; *South-Carolina Gazette,* September 7, 1775.

13. Memorial of James Simpson, February 12, 1784, AO 12/48, American Loyalist Claims, fols. 71r–72o; Memorial of James Simpson, July 28, 1777, AO 13/135, American Loyalist Claims, fols. 312o–r; Hill, "Exercise in Futility," 64–66.

14. Simpson, "British View of the Siege of Charleston, 1776," 93n1.

15. Ibid., 95 (first quote), 97 (second quote).

16. Ibid., 98–100.

17. Ibid., 103.

18. Memorial of James Simpson, February 12, 1784, AO 12/48, American Loyalist Claims, fol. 72o; Henry Laurens to John Laurens, August 14, 1776, *Papers of Henry Laurens,* 11:232, 232n16; Hill, "Exercise in Futility," 70; Memorial of James Simpson, August 5, 1782, AO 13/135, American Loyalist Claims, fol. 312o (quoted).

19. Salley, *Journal of the General Assembly of South Carolina, September 17, 1776–October 20, 1776,* 121; Cooper *Statutes at Large,* 1:135–36; Memorial of James Simpson, February 12, 1784, AO 12/48, American Loyalist Claims, fol. 72o; Coldham, *American Migrations,* 736–37; *South-Carolina and American General Gazette* (Charleston, S.C.), March 13, 1777; Hill, "Exercise in Futility," 71.

20. Memorial of James Simpson, February 12, 1784, and evidence supporting James Simpson's memorial, January 27, 1786, AO 12/48, American Loyalist Claims, fols. 72o–78r; Edward Stanley to William Knox, September 30, 1778, *Documents of the American Revolution,* 13:355.

21. Sturgess, *Register of Admissions to the Honourable Society of the Middle Temple,* 195, 385; Chesney, *Journal of Alexander Chesney,* 100.

22. Memorial of James Simpson, July 28, 1777, William Bull testimonial letter, July 28, 1777, Charles G. Montagu testimonial letter, March 12, 1778, AO 13/135, American Loyalist Claims, fols. 316o, 319r; Hill, "Exercise in Futility," vi, 42, 45, 74–75, 82.

23. George Germain to Archibald Campbell, January 16, 1779, *Documents of the American Revolution,* 17:32.

24. Ibid.

25. Memorial of James Simpson, July 28, 1777, George Germain to James Simpson, January 19, 1779, AO 13/135, American Loyalist Claims, fol. 3170; Germain to Henry Clinton, March 31, 1779, *Documents of the American Revolution,* 17:89–90.

26. James Simpson to George Germain, August 28, 1779, "James Simpson's Reports on the Carolina Loyalists," 515; Germain to Clinton, March 31, 1779, *Documents of the American Revolution,* 17:89–90; Bragg, *Crescent Moon over Carolina,* 125–49.

27. Simpson to Germain, August 28, 1779, "James Simpson's Reports on the Carolina Loyalists," 515–16; Piecuch, *Three Peoples, One King,* 166–70.

28. Simpson to Germain, August 28, 1779, "James Simpson's Reports on the Carolina Loyalists," 515–16.

29. Ibid.

30. Memorial of James Simpson, February 12, 1784 (quoted), and evidence supporting James Simpson's memorial, January 27, 1786, AO 12/48, American Loyalist Claims, fols. 72r–730, 810; Hill, "Exercise in Futility," 43–44; Chesney, *Journal of Alexander Chesney,* 100.

31. Memorial of James Simpson, February 12, 1784, and evidence supporting James Simpson's memorial, January 27, 1786, AO 12/48, American Loyalist Claims, fols. 72r–730, 810.

32. *New-York Gazette, and the Weekly Mercury,* August 23, 1779; Simpson to Germain, August 28, 1779, "James Simpson's Reports on the Carolina Loyalists," 516.

33. Simpson to Germain, August 28, 1779, "James Simpson's Reports on the Carolina Loyalists," 516–17.

34. Ibid., 517.

35. Ibid. (first quote); Henry Clinton to George Germain, August 21, 1779, *Documents of the American Revolution* 17:189–90 (second quote).

36. Moultrie, *Memoirs,* 2:41–43.

37. Henry Clinton to George Germain, March 9, 1780, *Documents of the American Revolution* 16:279; Clinton to Germain, May 16, 1780, *Documents of the American Revolution,* 16:327.

38. James Simpson to Henry Clinton, May 15, 1780, "James Simpson's Reports on the Carolina Loyalists, 1779–1780," 518–19.

39. Ibid.

40. James Simpson to Henry Clinton, July 1, 1780, *Report on the American Manuscripts in the Royal Institution of Great Britain,* 2:149–50; Simpson to George Germain, June 9, 1780, *Documents of the American Revolution,* 18:104–5 (quoted); Simpson to Clinton, July 16, 1780, *Report on the American Manuscripts in the Royal Institution of Great Britain,* 2:158.

41. Simpson to Germain, June 9, 1780, *Documents of the American Revolution,* 18:104–5; Simpson to Germain, August 13, 1780, *Documents of the American Revolution,* 18:137–39.

42. James Simpson to Charles Cornwallis, July 10, 1780, *Documents of the American Revolution,* 16:381; Simpson to George Germain, August 13, 1780, *Documents of the American Revolution,* 18:137–39; Cornwallis to Simpson, July 10, 1780, *Documents of the American Revolution,* 16:381.

43. Simpson to Germain, June 9, 1780, *Documents of the American Revolution,* 18:104–5 (quoted); Calhoon, *Loyalists in Revolutionary America,* 487–90; Simpson to Henry Clinton,

August 13, 1780, *Report on the American Manuscripts in the Royal Institution of Great Britain,*
2:169–70.

44. Simpson to Germain, June 9, 1780, *Documents of the American Revolution,* 18:104–5
(quoted); Simpson to Clinton, August 13, 1780, *Report on the American Manuscripts in the
Royal Institution of Great Britain,* 2:169–70.

45. Simpson to Clinton, August 13, 1780, *Report on the American Manuscripts in the Royal
Institution of Great Britain,* 2:169–70; Simpson to Germain, August 13, 1780, *Documents of
the American Revolution,* 18:138; Simpson to Germain, August 30, 1780, *Documents of the
American Revolution,* 18:155.

46. Simpson to Germain, August 30, 1780, *Documents of the American Revolution,*
18:155–56.

47. Ibid.; Stedman, *History of the Origin, Progress, and Termination of the American War,*
214 (quoted).

48. Tarleton, *History of the Campaigns of 1780 and 1781,* 159–60 (quoted), 189–90.

49. Simpson to Germain, August 30, 1780, *Documents of the American Revolution,*
18:155–56.

Chapter 2—A Rude Awakening

1. Ramsay, *History of the Revolution of South-Carolina,* 2:405–7; Johnson, *Traditions and
Reminiscences,* 267.

2. Johnson, *Traditions and Reminiscences,* 267; Borick, *Relieve Us of This Burthen,* 86–88;
Moultrie, *Memoirs,* 2:164 (quoted).

3. Clinton, *American Rebellion,* 181; Tarleton, *History of the Campaigns of 1780 and 1781,*
70–78.

4. Moultrie, *Memoirs,* 2:210–11.

5. James Simpson to Henry Clinton, May 15, 1780, "James Simpson's Reports on the
Carolina Loyalists," 519; McCrady, *Revolution 1775–1780,* 712–14; Ramsay, *History of the Revolution of South-Carolina,* 2:118–21, 445–47; Johnson, *Traditions and Reminiscences,* 267.

6. Garden, *Anecdotes of the Revolutionary War* (1822), 266; Moultrie, *Memoirs,* 1:295.

7. McCrady, *Revolution 1775–1780,* 714–17; Ramsay, *History of the Revolution of South-
Carolina,* 2:121–22, 161 (quoted), 448; Smith, "Diary," *SCHGM* 33, no. 1: 25.

8. Garden, *Anecdotes of the American Revolution* (1828), 411.

9. Charles Cornwallis to Nisbet Balfour, August 31, 1780, *Cornwallis Papers,* 2:65 (first
quote); Balfour to Cornwallis, August 31, 1780, *Cornwallis Papers,* 2:67; Cornwallis to Henry
Clinton, September 3, 1780, *Cornwallis Papers,* 2:43 (second quote).

10. Bragg, *Martyr of the American Revolution,* 17–20; Stephen and Lee, *Dictionary of
National Biography,* 1:976–77.

11. Bragg, *Martyr of the American Revolution,* 20–27; Henry Clinton to Charles Cornwallis, May 20, 1780, *Cornwallis Papers,* 1:48–49, 49n14; Cornwallis to Nisbet Balfour, July 17,
1780, *Cornwallis Papers,* 1:250.

12. Moultrie, *Memoirs,* 2:115, 126, 131, 132, 252 (quoted), 300.

13. Stoesen, "British Occupation of Charleston," 74.

14. Cornwallis to Clinton, September 3, 1780, *Cornwallis Papers,* 2:43.

15. Ibid. (quoted); Proclamation, August 4, 1780, in Tarleton, *History of the Campaigns
of 1780 and 1781,* 144–46.

16. Garden, *Anecdotes of the American Revolution* (1828), 112.

17. Ibid.

18. Ramsay, *History of the Revolution of South-Carolina*, 2:161; Smith, "Diary," *SCHGM* 33, no. 1: 2–3; *Cornwallis Papers*, 1:172n25; Ford, *British Officers Serving in the American Revolution*, 26.

19. Garden, *Anecdotes of the Revolutionary War* (1822), 265.

20. Huish, *Memoirs of George the Fourth*, 1:404–7; Ford, *British Officers Serving in the American Revolution*, 121.

21. Huish, *Memoirs of George the Fourth*, 1:407–8.

22. Ibid., 409, 567–68.

23. Ramsay, *History of South-Carolina*, 1:370–71; Smith, "Diary," *SCHGM* 33, no. 1: 2–3; Cornwallis to Clinton, September 3, 1780, *Cornwallis Papers*, 2:43; Ramsay, *History of South Carolina*, 1:371; Christopher Gadsden to George Washington, August 10, 1781, *Writings of Christopher Gadsden*, 170.

24. Fludd, *Biographical Sketches of the Huguenot Solomon Legaré*, 108–9.

25. Smith, "Diary," *SCHGM* 33, no. 1: 3–4. *The South-Carolina and American General Gazette*, August 30, 1780, published twenty-nine names as "a correct list of the persons sent on board the *Lord Sandwich* on Sunday morning last." The public was offered no editorial comment or explanation of why the arrests were made. For the names see appendix C. See also "List of the Names of the Disaffected Inhabitants of Charlestown Who Have Been Sent to [St.] Augustine, 3rd September 1780," *Cornwallis Papers*, 2:77–78.

26. Gen. Edward McCrady (the historian), "The McCrady Family," unpublished typescript, ca. 1890, 1, McCrady Family Papers.

27. Miller and Andrus, *Charleston's Old Exchange Building*, 25–37.

28. Rev. Edward McCrady (1868–1944), unpublished manuscript notes, ca. 1903, McCrady Family Papers, James Waring McCrady, Sewanee, Tenn.; Josiah Smith Jr. to George Smith, December 5, 1780, and Josiah Smith Jr. to James Poyas, December 5, 1780, Josiah Smith Letter Book, fols. 408, 411.

29. Rev. Edward McCrady (1868–1944), unpublished manuscript notes, ca. 1903. Reverend McCrady was the great-grandson of the lady in question. The passage quoted was based on conversations he had had with his uncle, Edward McCrady the historian. The same source preserves the memory of Eliza's indignant reaction to appearing hatless in public.

30. McCrady, *Revolution 1775–1780*, 717; Smith, "Diary," *SCHGM* 33, no. 1: 3; Winfield, *British Warships in the Age of Sail*, 289.

31. Smith, "Diary," *SCHGM* 33, no. 1: 3; McCrady, *Revolution 1775–1780*, 717.

32. Smith, "Diary," *SCHGM* 33, no. 1: 3; McCrady, *Revolution 1775–1780*, 717, 724.

33. Smith, "Diary," *SCHGM* 33, no. 1: 4–5.

34. Ibid.

35. Ibid., 5.

36. Ibid.

37. Ibid., 5–6.

38. Moultrie, *Memoirs*, 2:115–16, 115n.

39. Ibid., 138; *South-Carolina and American General Gazette*, August 30, 1780.

40. Moultrie, *Memoirs*, 2:138–39.

41. Ibid., 2:139 (quoted); McCrady, *Revolution 1775–1780*, 723–24; Smith, "Diary," *SCHGM* 33, no. 1: 6–7; Balfour to Cornwallis, August 31, 1780, *Cornwallis Papers*, 2:67.

42. Johnson, *Traditions and Reminiscences*, 316; *South-Carolina and American General Gazette*, September 6, 1780.

43. Johnson, *Traditions and Reminiscences*, 316 (first quote); Ramsay, *History of the Revolution of South-Carolina*, 2:164 (second quote).

44. Johnson, *Traditions and Reminiscences*, 316; Kane and Askwith, *List of Officers of the Royal Regiment of Artillery*, 19.

45. Johnson, *Traditions and Reminiscences*, 316; Mary Cochran to Charles Cochran, March 27, 1781, Cochran Family Papers, 1752–1814 (1004.03.01), South Carolina Historical Society, Charleston.

46. McCrady, *Revolution 1775–1780*, 719–20; Charles Cornwallis to George Germain, September 19, 1780, in Stevens, *Campaign in Virginia*, 1:267; Clinton, *American Rebellion*, 226; Stedman, *History of the Origin, Progress, and Termination of the American War*, 214; Tarleton, *History of the Campaigns of 1780 and 1781*, 159–60.

47. McCrady, *Revolution 1775–1780*, 720; Charles Cornwallis to John Harris Cruger, August 18, 1780, *Correspondence of Charles, First Marquis Cornwallis*, 1:56–57.

48. McCrady, *Revolution 1775–1780*, 720; Ramsay, *History of South Carolina*, 1:372; Smith, "Diary," *SCHGM* 33, no. 1: 5–6; Johnson, *Traditions and Reminiscences*, 267 (quoted); Charles Cornwallis to George Germain, September 19, 1780, in Stevens, *Campaign in Virginia*, 1:267.

49. Smith, "Diary," *SCHGM* 33, no. 1: 7; Davidson, *Friend of the People*, 7, 26–27, 34, 37.

50. Davidson, *Friend of the People*, 34, 37–49.

51. Smith, "Diary," *SCHGM* 33, no. 1: 7; Park, *Major Thomas Savage of Boston and His Descendants*, 30–31; Salley, *Journal of the Commissioners of the Navy of South Carolina*, 1:3; Smith, "Diary," *SCHGM* 33, no. 2: 100; Edgar and Bailey, *Biographical Directory of the South Carolina House*, 2:596–97.

52. Smith, "Diary," *SCHGM* 33, no. 1: 7; Moultrie, "Moultries, Part II," 260; *City Gazette* (Charleston, S.C.), November 5, 1790; Hemphill and Wates, *Extracts from the Journals of the Provincial Congresses of South Carolina, 1775–1776*, 6, 71, 266.

53. John Moultrie to Alexander Moultrie, July 8, 1780, in Gubbins, Transcripts and abstracts of Moultrie family papers, 1746–1965, Letters (43/36).

54. Smith, "Diary," *SCHGM* 33, no. 1: 6–7; McCrady, *Revolution 1775–1780*, 724; Johnson, *Traditions and Reminiscences*, 316 (quoted).

55. Smith, "Diary," *SCHGM* 33, no. 1: 6–7; McCrady, *Revolution 1775–1780*, 724.

56. Smith, "Diary," *SCHGM* 33, no. 1: 7–8.

57. Ibid.

58. Nisbet Balfour to Charles Cornwallis, September 4, 1780, *Cornwallis Papers*, 2:75; Smith, "Diary," *SCHGM* 33, no. 1: 8; *The Remembrancer, or, Impartial Repository of Public Events for the Year 1781*, part 2, 201 (quoted). The author of the quoted passage is not given.

59. Smith, "Diary," *SCHGM* 33, no. 1: 8.

Chapter 3—The Reception at St. Augustine

1. Houston, *Documents Illustrative of the Canadian Constitution*, 63; Smith, "Façade of Unity," 20.

2. Smith, "Façade of Unity," 20.

3. Mowat, "St. Augustine under the British Flag," 131, 133–35, 144–47. Refugees from Georgia and South Carolina more than tripled the population of St. Augustine in 1782–83.

4. Siebert, "Port of St. Augustine during the British Regime, Part I," 247–53.

5. Ibid.

6. Ibid., 134–35; Wright, *British St. Augustine*, 10, 12.

7. Smith, "Diary," *SCHGM* 33, no. 1: 8; Wright, *Florida in the American Revolution*, 6.

8. Smith, "Diary," *SCHGM* 33, no. 1: 8–9; Siebert, "Port of St. Augustine during the British Regime, Part I," 265.

9. Smith, "Diary," *SCHGM* 33, no. 1: 8–9.

10. Jahoda, *Florida*, 38; Barbour, *Florida for Tourists, Invalids, and Settlers*, 101, 106 (quoted).

11. Smith, "Diary," *SCHGM* 33, no. 1: 8–9.

12. Ibid.

13. Ibid., 9.

14. Wright, *British St. Augustine*, 4, 8; Fairbanks, *History and Antiquities of the City of St. Augustine*, 130; Jefferys, *Plan of the town of St. Augustine, the Capital of East Florida*, USF Tampa Library.

15. Smith, "Diary," *SCHGM* 33, no. 1: 9.

16. Fairbanks, *History and Antiquities of the City of St. Augustine*, 166–67.

17. Ibid.

18. Wright, *British St. Augustine*, 7–9.

19. Smith, "Diary," *SCHGM* 33, no. 1: 9; Schafer, *St. Augustine's British Years*, 178; Cannon, *Historical Record of the Sixth, or Inniskilling Regiment of Dragoons*, 96; Baldry and White, "Disbanded Regiments," 92.

20. Schafer, *St. Augustine's British Years*, 178; Cashin, *King's Ranger*, 41; Waterbury, *Oldest City*, 108–9; Wright, *Florida in the American Revolution*, 15, 20, 22, 25–30, 40–42, 55–56, 95–96, 103, 107.

21. Mowat, *East Florida as a British Province*, 83–106; Waterbury, *Oldest City*, 109; Mowat, "Enigma of William Drayton," 15–16.

22. Patrick Tonyn to Charles Cornwallis, September 8, 1780, *Cornwallis Papers*, 2:312 (first quote); Tonyn to Nisbet Balfour, September 9, 1780, *Cornwallis Papers*, 2:313 (all other quotes).]

23. Tonyn to Balfour, September 9, 1780, *Cornwallis Papers*, 2:313.

24. Smith, "Diary," *SCHGM* 33, no. 1: 9; Garden, *Anecdotes of the Revolutionary War* (1822), 169 (quoted).

25. Newton, "Three Patterns of Local History," 146.

26. Smith, "Diary," *SCHGM* 33, no. 1: 9–10; Garden, *Anecdotes of the Revolutionary War* (1822), 169–70 (quoted).

27. Edgar and Bailey, *Biographical Directory of the South Carolina House*, 2:259–61; Godbold and Woody, *Christopher Gadsden and the American Revolution*, 9–10, 23–29.

28. Edgar and Bailey, *Biographical Directory of the South Carolina House*, 2:261–62; Godbold and Woody, *Christopher Gadsden and the American Revolution*, 147–54; entry for September 16, 1776, *Journals of the Continental Congress*, 5:761.

29. Smith, "Diary," *SCHGM* 33, no. 1: 10; Garden, *Anecdotes of the Revolutionary War*

(1822), 169 (quoted); Godbold and Woody, *Christopher Gadsden and the American Revolution,* 202.

30. Smith, "Diary," *SCHGM* 33, no. 1: 10; Manucy and Johnson, "Castle St. Mark and the Patriots of the Revolution," 8–9. The square footage of the cell is derived from the author's calculations based on a measured drawing of Castle St. Mark: "Castillo de San Marcos, 1 Castillo Drive, Saint Augustine, St. Johns County, FL," HABS FLA, 55-SAUG, 1- (sheet 2 of 9), Historic American Buildings Survey, Library of Congress, Washington, D.C.

31. Garden, *Anecdotes of the Revolutionary War* (1822), 170 (first quote); Manucy and Johnson, "Castle St. Mark and the Patriots of the Revolution," 8–9; Patrick Tonyn to George Germain, December 9, 1780, *Documents of the American Revolution,* 18:254 (second quote).

32. Gadsden to Washington, August 10, 1781, *Writings of Christopher Gadsden,* 170.

33. Ibid.

34. Garden, *Anecdotes of the Revolutionary War* (1822), 170 (quoted), 172.

35. Smith, "Diary," *SCHGM* 33, no. 1: 10 (quoted); Johnson, *Traditions and Reminiscences,* 317.

36. Smith, "Diary," *SCHGM* 33, no. 1: 10.

37. Wright, *British St. Augustine,* 12; Smith, "Diary," *SCHGM* 33, no. 3: 199–201.

38. Smith, "Diary," SCHGM 33, no. 1: 10.

Chapter 4—The Exiles Settle In

1. Smith, "Diary," *SCHGM* 33, no. 1: 10–11; Rabb, *Spain, Britain, and the American Revolution in Florida,* 125–26.

2. Smith, "Diary," *SCHGM* 33, no. 1: 12; Outland, *Tapping the Pines,* 45; Dewhurst, *History of St. Augustine, Florida,* 125. Dewhurst says that these gallows were erected by the British at the northeast corner of the courtyard in the fort. It is safe to say that a gesture that dramatic could not have been made without at least the tacit approval of the British.

3. Smith, "Diary," *SCHGM* 33, no. 1: 12.

4. Ibid., 12–13.

5. Ibid., 11–12.

6. Ibid.; Johnson, *Traditions and Reminiscences,* 319 (quoted).

7. Smith, "Diary," *SCHGM* 33, no. 1: 12.

8. Edgar and Bailey, *Biographical Directory of the South Carolina House,* 2:323–25, 573–76; Haw, *John and Edward Rutledge,* 91–92.

9. Edgar and Bailey, *Biographical Directory of the South Carolina House,* 2:323–25, 573–76; Haw, *John and Edward Rutledge,* 82, 98, 118, 133; Moultrie, *Memoirs,* 1:14, 90, 292–95; 2:100.

10. Haw, *John and Edward Rutledge,* 143, 314n18; Webber, "Dr. John Rutledge and His Descendants," 24; Eliza Lucas Pinckney to Elizabeth Motte (Mrs. Thomas) Pinckney, September 12, 1780, *Papers of Eliza Lucas Pinckney and Harriott Pinckney Horry Digital Edition,* http://rotunda.upress.virginia.edu/PinckneyHorry/ELP0139 (accessed 2018–05–17); Wheeler and Neblett, *Chosen Exile,* 17 (quoted).

11. Siebert, *Loyalists in East Florida,* 2:311–12, 354–55; Wallace, *Regimental Chronicle and List of Officers of the 60th,* 101, 106; *Cornwallis Papers,* 1:355n24; Mowat, *East Florida as a British Province,* 123.

12. Manucy and Johnson, "Castle St. Mark and the Patriots of the Revolution," 12.

13. Wright, *Florida in the American Revolution*, 5, 10, 106 (quoted); Manucy and Johnson, "Castle St. Mark and the Patriots of the Revolution," 12.

14. Manucy, "Changing Traditions in St. Augustine Architecture," 103.

15. Ibid., 103–4; Wright, *British St. Augustine*, 5.

16. Siebert, *Loyalists in East Florida*, 2:17n14–15, 311–12.

17. Lewis V. Fuser to Henry Clinton, September 25, 1779, *Report on American Manuscripts in the Royal Institution of Great Britain*, 2:38.

18. Spencer Man[n] to James Grant, October 4, 1775, in Force, *American Archives*, ser. 4, 4:335 (first quote); *Report on American Manuscripts in the Royal Institution of Great Britain*, 2:127 (second quote); Siebert, *Loyalists in East Florida*, 2:17n15.

19. Smith, "Diary," *SCHGM* 33, no. 1: 13–14.

20. Ibid., 14.

21. Ibid., 13

22. Ibid., 14; Wright, *British St. Augustine*, 40; McCord, *Statutes at Large*, 9:704.

23. Ramsay, *History of the Revolution of South-Carolina*, 2:169; Smith, "Diary," *SCHGM* 33, no. 1: 14–15.

24. Smith, "Diary," *SCHGM* 33, no. 1: 15.

25. Ibid., 16–17.

26. Ibid., 17–18.

27. Ibid., 11, 21; Ravenel, *Charleston, the Place and the People*, 290.

28. Wright, *British St. Augustine*, 41. Much of the information found here and the following paragraph was obtained by Waring McCrady at the St. Augustine History Museum.

29. Ibid.

30. Tonyn to Germain, December 9, 1780, *Documents of the American Revolution*, 18:253–54 (quoted); McCrady, *Revolution 1780–1783*, 371.

31. McCrady, *Revolution 1780–1783*, 371.

32. Smith, "Fourteenth Colony," 267–68; Smith, "Diary," *SCHGM* 34, no. 1: 32.

33. McCrady, *Revolution 1780–1783*, 372; Wright, *British St. Augustine*, 32–35.

34. Smith, "Diary," *SCHGM* 33, no. 1: 18; Moultrie, "Moultries, Part II," 248–49.

35. Smith, "Diary," *SCHGM* 33, no. 1: 18.

36. Townsend, *John Moultrie, Junior, M.D.*, 99–108; Moultrie, "Moultries, Part II," 248–49.

37. Moultrie, "Moultries, Part II," 248–49; Bragg, *Crescent Moon over Carolina*, 6–7, 178.

38. Smith, "Diary," *SCHGM* 33, no. 1: 19; Josiah Smith Jr. to George Appleby, December 2, 1780, Josiah Smith Letter Book, fol. 408.

39. Wright, *British St. Augustine*, 38; Wright, "British East Florida," 9.

40. Entry for September 23, 1780, *Journals of the Continental Congress, 1774–1789*, 18:851 (quoted); George Washington to Henry Clinton, October 6, 1780, *Writings of George Washington* (ed. Fitzpatrick), 20:128.

41. Henry Clinton to George Washington, October 9, 1780, *Writings of George Washington* [Sparks], 7:552–53.

42. George Washington to Henry Clinton, October 16, 1780, *Writings of George Washington* (ed. Sparks), 7:553 (quoted); Cornwallis to Clinton, September 3, 1780, *Cornwallis Papers*, 2:43.

43. Charles Cornwallis to Henry Clinton, December 4, 1780, *Cornwallis Papers*, 3:27–28.

44. John André to George Washington, September 24, 1780, George Washington Papers, Library of Congress.

Chapter 5—A Rather Dull Life of Restricted Routine

1. Wright, *British St. Augustine,* 31–32; Doggett, *Dr. Andrew Turnbull,* 15–16; Rasico, *Minorcans of Florida,* 1.

2. Doggett, *Dr. Andrew Turnbull,* 15–20, 25–26, 29–31, 33–36, 39; Jahoda, *Florida, a Bicentennial History,* 39; Tebeau, *History of Florida,* 82–83; Rasico, *Minorcans of Florida,* 14–29; Abbey, *Florida: Land of Change,* 79–80 (quoted).

3. Reynolds, *Old St. Augustine,* 84–89; Doggett, *Dr. Andrew Turnbull,* 36–39, 159–63, 171; Abbey, *Florida: Land of Change,* 80–81; Tebeau, *History of Florida,* 82–83; Reynolds, *Old St. Augustine,* 84–89.

4. Doggett, *Dr. Andrew Turnbull,* 157; Dewhurst, *History of St. Augustine, Florida,* 125; Quinn, *Minorcans in Florida,* 85; Smith, "Diary," *SCHGM* 33, no. 1: 21; Corbett, "Problem of the Household in the Second Spanish Period," 69.

5. Abbey, *Florida: Land of Change,* 82.

6. Johnson, *Traditions and Reminiscences,* 316–17; Smith, "Diary," *SCHGM* 33, no. 1: 19. Fortunately for Thomas Buckel, after the war had been settled in the Americans' favor and his holdings taken by the state, the story of this generosity so impressed the South Carolina legislature that they returned to him his sequestered properties.

7. Edgar and Bailey, *Biographical Directory of the South Carolina House,* 2:672–75.

8. *South-Carolina and American General Gazette,* September 20, 1780.

9. McCowen, *British Occupation of Charleston,* 93, 153–54.

10. Nash, *Forgotten Fifth,* 42–45.

11. Ramsay, *History of the Revolution of South-Carolina,* 2:169–71; "Cruden's Commission Concerning the Sequestration of Property, 16th September 1780," *Cornwallis Papers,* 2:320–23; "Preliminary Sketch of the Sequestration Proclamation Made on 16th September 1780," *Cornwallis Papers,* 2:323–24; John Cruden to Charles Cornwallis, September 29, 1780, *Cornwallis Papers,* 2:324–25; "Queries from Cruden to Cornwallis about Sequestration, undated," *Cornwallis Papers,* 2:325–28; *South-Carolina and American General Gazette,* October 4, November 22, and December 30, 1780.

12. "America, Charles-Town, September 11, 1780," *Lady's Magazine,* January 1781, 55; McCowen, *British Occupation of Charleston,* 153–54

13. Ramsay, *History of the Revolution of South-Carolina,* 2:167 (quoted); Corbett, "Problem of the Household in the Second Spanish Period," 72.

14. Dewhurst, *History of St. Augustine, Florida,* 125.

15. Smith, "Diary," *SCHGM* 33, no. 1: 11; Strock, *By Faith, with Thanksgiving,* 1–2; Waterbury, "John Forbes," 18–19, 23–24 (quoted); Coleman, "Commentary," 93–94.

16. Coleman, "Commentary," 94.

17. Waterbury, "John Forbes," 16–19, 21.

18. Ibid., 17.

19. Smith, "Diary," *SCHGM* 33, no. 1: 12, 19–20, 24.

20. Ibid., 22; Ramsay, *History of the Revolution of South-Carolina,* 2:168.

21. Manucy and Johnson, "Castle St. Mark and the Patriots of the Revolution," 18–19; Fairbanks, *Florida, Its History And Its Romance,* 160.

22. Garden, *Anecdotes of the Revolutionary War* (1822), 172–73; Reynolds, *Old St. Augustine*, 96 (quoted).

23. Gadsden to Washington, August 10, 1781, *Writings of Christopher Gadsden*, 170.

24. Smith, "Diary," *SCHGM* 33, no. 1: 20.

25. Ibid.

26. Ibid., 25–27.

27. Ibid.

28. Ibid., 26, 27–28 (quoted).

29. Smith, "Diary," *SCHGM* 34, no. 1: 32; Fairbanks, "Florida during the English Occupation," 25.

30. Wright, *Florida in the American Revolution*, 101; Wright, *British St. Augustine*, 38.

31. Patrick Tonyn to Charles Cornwallis, November 24, 1780, *Cornwallis Papers*, 3:433–34; Tonyn to Nisbet Balfour, November 24, 1780, *Cornwallis Papers*, 3:434–35 (quoted).

32. Smith, "Diary," *SCHGM* 33, no. 1: 20–21, 23.

33. Ibid., 21.

34. Ibid., 22–23; Tebeau, *History of Florida*, 83–84.

35. Smith, "Diary," *SCHGM* 33, no. 1: 7, 23; Johnson, *Traditions and Reminiscences*, 320–21 (both quotes); McLachlan, *Princetonians, 1748–1768*, 361–62.

36. Johnson, Traditions and Reminiscences, 320–21, 321n (first quote); Smith, "Diary," SCHGM 33, no. 1: 23 (all other quotes).

37. Romans, *Concise Natural History of East and West Florida*, 9. Actually this observation was in the context of praising the overall healthiness of St. Augustine, about which, Romans said, "I do not think that on all the continent there is a more healthy spot; burials have been less frequent here than any where else . . . the Spanish inhabitants live here to a great age."

38. Smith, "Diary," *SCHGM* 33, no. 1: 24.

39. Ibid.

Chapter 6—Robbery, Religious Differences, and New Arrivals

1. Smith, "Diary," *SCHGM* 33, no. 1: 24 (quoted); Waterbury, "John Forbes," 8.

2. Smith, "Diary," *SCHGM* 33, no. 1: 24 (quoted); Wright, *Florida in the American Revolution*, 107.

3. Smith, "Diary," *SCHGM* 33, no. 1: 24–25.

4. Smith, "Diary," *SCHGM* 33, no. 2: 99.

5. Ibid., 81.

6. Smith, "Diary," *SCHGM* 33, no. 1: 25.

7. Smith, "Diary," *SCHGM* 33, no. 2: 79–81.

8. Ibid., 82.

9. John Rutledge to the [Hon'ble Delegates of So. Carolina to Congress], December 30, 1780, "Letters of John Rutledge," *SCHGM* 18, no. 2: 62, 64.

10. Smith, "Diary," *SCHGM* 33, no. 2: 80–83; Siebert, "Port of St. Augustine during the British Regime, Part 2," 87.

11. Smith, "Diary," *SCHGM* 33, no. 2: 80–83.

12. Ibid., 83.

13. McCrady, *Revolution 1780–1783*, 372 (quoted); Manucy and Johnson, "Castle St. Mark and the Patriots of the Revolution," 15–16; Smith, "Diary," *SCHGM* 33, no. 2: 84.

14. Smith, "Diary," *SCHGM* 33, no. 2: 84; Manucy and Johnson, "Castle St. Mark and the Patriots of the Revolution," 15–16.

15. Smith, "Diary," *SCHGM* 33, no. 2: 84.

16. Ibid., 85 (first, third, and fourth quotes); "A Prayer for the King's Majesty," *Book of Common Prayer* (1779), 27 (second quote).

17. Smith, "Diary," *SCHGM* 33, no. 2: 85–86.

18. Ibid., 86.

19. Ibid., 91; Hanna and Hanna, *Florida's Golden Sands,* 234; Gold, "That Infamous Floridian, Jesse Fish," 6.

20. Gold, "That Infamous Floridian, Jesse Fish," 1.

21. Ibid.

22. Lawson, "Luciano de Herrera"; Wright, *Florida in the American Revolution,* 107 (quoted), Johnson, *Traditions and Reminiscences,* 320.

23. Smith, "Diary," *SCHGM* 33, no. 2: 86.

24. Ibid.

25. Ibid. (quoted); Papers of the Continental Congress, NA microfilm series M247, roll 175 (vol. 2), fols. 351–53; Colcock, "Case of Colonel Hayne."

26. George Germain to Henry Clinton, November 9, 1780, *Documents of the American Revolution,* 18:224 (quoted); William Knox to James Simpson, November 9, 1780, Boehm, *Records of the British Colonial Office, Class 5, Part 5,* reel 12, 847–48.

27. Nisbet Balfour to Charles Cornwallis, November 15, 1780, *Cornwallis Papers,* 3:76.

28. Charles Cornwallis to Nisbet Balfour, November 18, 1780, *Cornwallis Papers,* 3:78; Smith, "Diary," *SCHGM* 33, no. 2: 87; Ramsay, *History of South-Carolina,* 1:374.

29. *South-Carolina and American General Gazette,* November 15, 1780.

30. *South-Carolina and American General Gazette,* November 18, 1780; Smith, "Diary," *SCHGM* 33, no. 2: 87 (quoted).

31. Smith, "Diary," *SCHGM* 33, no. 2: 89; Fairbanks, *History and Antiquities of the City of St. Augustine, Florida,* 172.

32. Smith, "Diary," *SCHGM* 33, no. 2: 89; Nisbet Balfour to Charles Cornwallis, September 1, 1780, *Cornwallis Papers,* 2:70 (quoted).

33. *South-Carolina and American General Gazette,* November 22, 1780.

34. Smith, "Diary," *SCHGM* 33, no. 2: 89.

35. Ibid., 89 90, 100.

36. Ibid., 88.

37. Ibid., 88–89.

38. Ibid., 90.

39. Ibid., 90–91.

40. Ibid., 91, 96–97; Alured Clarke to Nisbet Balfour, December 29, 1780, *Cornwallis Papers,* 3: 426 (quoted).

41. Smith, "Diary," *SCHGM* 33, no. 2: 91; *South-Carolina and American General Gazette,* December 2, 1780.

42. Johnson, *Traditions and Reminiscences,* 321–22.

43. Smith, "Diary," *SCHGM* 33, no. 2: 90–92; Manucy and Johnson, "Castle St. Mark and the Patriots of the Revolution," 17–18; Tonyn to Germain, December 9, 1780, *Documents of the American Revolution,* 18:253–54 (quoted).

Chapter 7—A Charge of Haughty and Arrogant Behavior

1. Josiah Smith Jr. to George Appleby, December 2, 1780, Josiah Smith Letter Book, fols. 404–7.

2. Ibid.

3. Josiah Smith Jr. to George Smith, December 5, 1780, Josiah Smith Letter Book, fols. 408–9, 412–13.

4. Josiah Smith Jr. to James Poyas, December 5, 1780, Josiah Smith Letter Book, fols. 410–11, 413–14.

5. Ibid.

6. *South-Carolina and American General Gazette,* December 9, 1780.

7. *South-Carolina and American General Gazette,* December 16 and 30 (quoted), 1780.

8. Samuel Huntington to Nathanael Greene, September 24, 1780, *Papers of General Nathanael Greene,* 6:311; Greene to Charles Cornwallis, December 17, 1780, *Papers of General Nathanael Greene,* 6:591–93.

9. Smith, "Diary," *SCHGM* 33, no. 2: 92.

10. Ibid., 92–93.

11. Ramsay, *History of the Revolution of South-Carolina,* 2:157–58; McCrady, *Revolution 1775–1780,* 730 (quoted).

12. *Charleston Evening Post* (Charleston, S.C.), December 22, 1927; Smith, "Diary," *SCHGM* 33, no. 2: 94 (quoted).

13. Shaffer, *To Be an American,* 9–19, 26–29, 30–31, 37–50.

14. Ibid., 58–59; Moultrie, *Memoirs,* 1:viii; Johnson, "David Ramsay," 189–91; Olson, "Dr. David Ramsay and Lt. Colonel Thomas Brown," 257 (quoted).

15. Shaffer, *To Be an American,* 58, 302–3; Moultrie, *Memoirs,* 1:viii.; Ramsay, *History of the Revolution of South-Carolina,* 2:168; John Laurens, "Account of the Operations in South Carolina, Respecting Capitulation, May 1779," Henry Laurens Papers, 1747–1860, Manuscripts (37/45B oversize), SCHS, fol. 2; and McCrady, *Revolution 1775,* 371–72. See also Haw, "Broken Compact," 43–44, 50. Ramsay would go on to publish a single-volume biography of George Washington in 1807, a two-volume history of South Carolina in 1809, and two volumes on the American Revolution in 1811. His extensive three-volume history of the United States, published in 1816, comprised the first three volumes of the twelve-volume *Universal History Americanized* published posthumously in 1819. He produced a number of shorter works as well.

16. Smith, "Diary," *SCHGM* 33, no. 2: 93, 94.

17. Ibid., 93–94 (first and second quotes); entry for April 25, 1781, *Journals of the Continental Congress,* 20:437–38; Lincoln, *Naval Records of the American Revolution,* 261; affidavit of Thomas Johnson, January 29, 1781, Papers of the Continental Congress, NA microfilm series M247, roll 177 (vol. 2), fols. 493–94 (third quote).

18. William Moultrie to John Mathews, March 21, 1781 (quoted), Thomas Heyward to Moultrie, January 31, 1781, and affidavits of Thomas Johnson and James McQueen, January 29, 1781, Papers of the Continental Congress, NA microfilm series M247, roll 177 (vol. 2), fols. 489–95; entry for April 25, 1781, *Journals of the Continental Congress,* 20:437–38.

19. Smith, "Diary," *SCHGM* 33, no. 2: 94–95, 102.

20. Ibid., 95.

21. Ibid., 91, 92, 95–96.

22. Ibid., 97.

23. Ibid.; Moultrie, *Memoirs,* 2:49 (quoted). The smallpox cases described by Moultrie were aboard prison ships in Charleston Harbor.

24. Smith, "Diary," *SCHGM* 33, no. 2: 98.

25. Ibid.

26. Ibid.

27. Ibid., 98–99.

28. Ibid., 99–100.

29. Ibid., 101.

30. Ibid., 86, 103, 111, 115.

31. Edward Rutledge to George Washington, August 14, 1781, George Washington Papers, Series 4, General Correspondence, 1697–1799, MSS 44693: reel 080, Manuscript Division, Library of Congress, Washington, D.C.

32. Josiah Smith Jr. to John Dart, January 31, 1781, Josiah Smith Letter Book, fol. 423.

33. Smith, "Diary," *SCHGM* 33, no. 2: 102.

34. Ibid., 103–4; William McIntosh to Alured Clarke, December 12, 1780, *Cornwallis Papers,* 3:428.

35. Smith, "Diary," *SCHGM* 33, no. 2: 104–5; Alured Clarke to Charles Cornwallis, January 2, 1781, *Cornwallis Papers,* 3:429–30.

36. Wright, *Florida in the American Revolution,* 100.

37. Ibid.; Patrick Tonyn to George Germain, November 10, 1780, *Documents of the American Revolution,* 21:435; Tonyn to Germain, November 10, 1780, Public Records Office, Colonial Office, class 5, part 5, vol. 560, 53–56 (hereinafter PRO CO 5/560).

38. Smith, "Diary," *SCHGM* 33, no. 2: 105.

Chapter 8—The Winter and Spring of 1781

1. Smith, "Diary," *SCHGM* 33, no. 2: 105 (quoted); Dodge, *Biographical Directory of the United States Congress,* 1789; Force, *American Archives,* 4th ser., 1:58–60. Several biographies include Read among Americans in London in 1774 who signed a petition against the Boston Port Act, but this is not supported by the evidence. When General Washington returned his commission to the Continental Congress at Annapolis, Maryland, on December 23, 1783, Read was present as a witness to the poignant event.

2. Reynolds, *Old St. Augustine,* 129n; Johnson, *Traditions and Reminiscences,* 217 (both quotes).

3. Smith, "Diary," *SCHGM* 33, no. 2: 106.

4. Ibid., 107.

5. Ibid., 107–8. An interesting side note to Lushington's South Carolina militia service is that his company included nearly all of the Jews of Charleston who fought in the Revolution. They were engaged at Port Royal Island in February 1779, participated in the attempt to retake Savannah in October of that same year, and were in the siege lines of Charleston at the time of surrender in May 1780. Elzas, *Jews of South Carolina,* 87–90.

6. Smith, "Diary," *SCHGM* 33, no. 2: 108–9.

7. Mary Cochran to Charles March 27, 1781, Cochran Family Papers, 1752–1814 (1004.03.01), South Carolina Historical Society, Charleston; Josiah Smith Jr. to George Smith, February 28, 1781, Josiah Smith Letter Book, fols. 426–27 (quoted).

8. "Biographical Sketch of Capt. Robt Cochran," Cochran Family Papers, 1752–1814 (1004.03.01), South Carolina Historical Society, Charleston [typescript], fols. 1–2; Coker, *Charleston's Maritime Heritage,* 52; Morgan, *Naval Documents,* 3:143, 221, 248.

9. "Biographical Sketch of Capt. Robt Cochran," Cochran Family Papers, fol. 2; Morgan, *Naval Documents,* 3:143, 221, 248, 326–28, 647–48, 862, 887, 1045–46.

10. "Biographical Sketch of Capt. Robt Cochran," Cochran Family Papers, fol. 3; Coker, *Charleston's Maritime Heritage,* 77; Morgan, *Naval Documents,* 3:326–28, 647–48, 862, 887, 1045–46; Charles Lee to William Moultrie, June 21 and 23, 1776, *Lee Papers,* 2:79–81.

11. "Biographical Sketch of Capt. Robt Cochran," Cochran Family Papers, fols. 2–3; Coker, *Charleston's Maritime Heritage,* 86–87; Salley, *Journal of the Commissioners of the Navy of South Carolina,* 1:43–44; Morgan, *Naval Documents,* 7:1150, 1150n2, 1251, 1311–14; "East Florida," in Force, *American Archives,* 4th ser., 3:705–7.

12. Salley, *Journal of the Commissioners of the Navy of South Carolina,* 1:112; Johnson, *Traditions and Reminiscences,* 117–28; Crawford, *Naval Documents,* 12:478.

13. Crawford, *Naval Documents,* 11:576; Wickes and Dickinson, *History of Medicine in New Jersey,* 176.

14. Borick, *Relieve Us of This Burthen,* 70–72, 74–79.

15. John Mathews to George Washington, February 15, 1781, *Letters of Delegates to Congress,* 16:715; George Washington to John Mathews, February 26, 1781, *Writings of George Washington* (ed. Fitzpatrick), 21:303 (quoted).

16. John Mathews to George Washington, March 6, 1781, *Letters of Delegates to Congress,* 17:26.

17. George Washington to John Mathews, March 23, 1781, *Writings of George Washington* (ed. Fitzpatrick), 21:303, 365 (quoted).

18. Smith, "Diary," *SCHGM* 33, no. 2: 109–10; Smith, "Diary," *SCHGM* 33, no. 1: 11–12.

19. Wright, *Florida in the American Revolution,* 18.

20. Ibid.; Mowat, *East Florida as a British Province,* 124; Patrick Tonyn to George Germain, December 9, 1780, *Documents of the American Revolution,* 18:253–54.

21. Smith, "Diary," *SCHGM* 33, no. 2: 110–11; Mowat, *East Florida as a British Province,* 124; Tebeau, *History of Florida,* 84; Wright, *British St. Augustine,* 40–41.

22. Smith, "Diary," *SCHGM* 33, no. 2: 110–11; Patrick Tonyn to George Germain, July 30, 1781, PRO CO 5/560, 247–49.

23. Garden, *Anecdotes of the American Revolution* (1828), 229–30. The butt of the waggery was discreetly left anonymous, presumably out of respect for his dignity.

24. Ibid.

25. Ibid.

26. *Pennsylvania Evening Post* (Philadelphia), February 9, 1781.

27. Johnson, *Traditions and Reminiscences,* 322.

28. Ibid., 322.

29. Ibid., 322–23.

30. Ibid., 111–112; Tuchman, *First Salute,* 5–6, 12, 14–15.

31. Smith, "Diary," *SCHGM* 33, no. 2: 112, 114 (quoted); Tuchman, *First Salute,* 89–93, 219, 243; Patrick Tonyn to Henry Clinton, January 31, 1781, PRO CO 5/560, 207–10.

32. Smith, "Diary," *SCHGM* 33, no. 2: 112, 116; Bailey and Cooper, *Biographical Directory of the South Carolina House,* 2:163.

33. Smith, "Diary," *SCHGM* 33, no. 2: 113, 115, 116 (quoted).

34. Ibid., 112–13; Wallace, *Regimental Chronicle and List of Officers of the 60th,* 100.

35. Smith, "Diary," *SCHGM* 33, no. 2: 113–14.

36. Moultrie, *Memoirs,* 2:210–11, 325–26 (quoted).

37. Smith, "Diary," *SCHGM* 33, no. 3: 197, 202–3; Alured Clarke to Nisbet Balfour, January 24, 1781, *Report on American Manuscripts in the Royal Institution of Great Britain,* 2:238.

38. Smith, "Diary," *SCHGM* 33, no. 3: 202.

39. Ibid.

40. Ibid., 203.

41. Garden, *Anecdotes of the Revolutionary War* (1822), 224–25.

42. Ibid., 224.

43. Ibid., 227.

44. Ibid.

45. Ibid., 227–28; Eastman, *Remembering Old Charleston,* 31.

46. Garden, *Anecdotes of the Revolutionary War* (1822), 228; Webber, "Death Notices," 158; *Royal Gazette,* May 19, 1781; Eastman, *Remembering Old Charleston,* 32.

47. Fenhagen, "John Edwards," 15–17, 18–19.

48. Ibid., 17–18; Garden, *Anecdotes of the Revolutionary War* (1822), 228–29.

49. Wilkinson and Gilman, *Letters of Eliza Wilkinson,* 95–100. See also C. P. Seabrook Wilkinson, "Eliza Yonge Wilkinson," in *American Women Prose Writers to 1820,* 405–8.

Chapter 9—All Fortunes Reverse

1. Nisbet Balfour to Henry Clinton, May 6, 1781, Letterbook of Lieut. Col. Nisbet Balfour, Society of the Cincinnati.

2. Ibid.

3. Haarmann, "Spanish Conquest of British West Florida," 107–8, 112–13, 132–33.

4. Smith, "Diary," *SCHGM* 33, no. 4: 284–86; *Royal Gazette,* June 27, 1781.

5. Nisbet Balfour to Nathanael Greene, June 12, 1781, *Papers of General Nathanael Greene,* 8:383; Balfour to Charles Cornwallis, June 7, 1781, *Cornwallis Papers,* 5:278–79.

6. Balfour to Clinton, May 6, 1781, Letterbook of Lieut. Col. Nisbet Balfour, Society of the Cincinnati.

7. Smith, "Diary," *SCHGM* 33, no. 2: 116; Balfour to Clinton, May 6, 1781, Letterbook of Lieut. Col. Nisbet Balfour, Society of the Cincinnati; Nisbet Balfour to the militia prisoners of war, May 17, 1781, Smith, "Diary," *SCHGM* 33, no. 3: 205–6 (quoted); Stoesen, "British Occupation of Charleston," 75–76; Borick, *Relieve Us of This Burthen,* 99–101.

8. Smith, "Diary," *SCHGM* 33, no. 4: 284.

9. Smith, "Diary," *SCHGM* 33, no. 3: 204; *Royal Gazette,* May 12, 1781 (quoted).

10. Josiah Smith Jr. to George Smith, June 8, 1781, Josiah Smith Letter Book, fol. 441; Smith, "Diary," *SCHGM* 33, no. 2: 116; Fenhagen, "John Edwards," 17–18; Gibbes,

Documentary History, 75–76; Smith, "Diary," *SCHGM* 33, no. 4: 282–83; Moultrie, *Memoirs,* 2:140, 142, 149, 398, 400–401, 403; Borick, *Relieve Us of This Burthen,* 99–100.

11. Samuel Prioleau Jr. to Catherine Prioleau, June 19, 1781, William Ravenel Papers (1130.02.01), South Carolina Historical Society.

12. Balfour to the militia prisoners, May 17, 1781, Smith, "Diary," *SCHGM* 33, no. 3: 205.

13. Samuel Prioleau Jr. to Catherine Prioleau, June 19, 1781, William Ravenel Papers (1130.02.01), South Carolina Historical Society.

14. Manucy and Johnson, "Castle St. Mark and the Patriots of the Revolution," 21; Reynolds and Faunt, *Biographical Directory of the Senate of the State of South Carolina,* 204–5; Gibbes, *Documentary History,* 76; Harper, *Memoir of the Life, Character, and Public Services, of the Late Hon. Henry Wm. De Saussure,* 9–11, 12–13.

15. Smith, "Diary," *SCHGM* 33, no. 4: 284.

16. Garden, *Anecdotes of the American Revolution* (1828), 227–8.

17. Ibid., 228.

18. Ibid.

19. Committee report, June 11, 1781, *Journals of the Continental Congress,* 20:620–23.

20. Ibid.; Papers of the Continental Congress, NA microfilm series M247, roll 38 (vol. 2), fol. 371–2a. The report of the committee to which this matter was referred is listed among postponed reports.

21. Smith, "Diary," *SCHGM* 33, no. 3: 197.

22. Ibid., 197–98.

23. Balfour to Clinton, May 6, 1781, Letterbook of Lieut. Col. Nisbet Balfour, Society of the Cincinnati.

24. Cashin, *King's Ranger,* 126–37. Earlier Brown had suffered a fractured skull, burns, scalping, and tarring and feathering at the hands of the patriot Sons of Liberty, only to recover and become one of the most intrepid and infamous loyalist leaders in the South.

25. Ibid., 28–29, 136–38.

26. Ibid., 136–37, 140–41; Ramsay, *History of South Carolina,* 1:372–73; Manucy and Johnson, "Castle St. Mark and the Patriots of the Revolution," 18–19.

27. Johnson, *Traditions and Reminiscences,* 324. Johnson relates this episode as happening in the aftermath of the hanging by the British of Col. Isaac Hayne in Charleston on August 4, 1781. This is impossible; the St. Augustine exiles would not learn of Hayne's fate until after they reached Philadelphia.

28. Smith, "Diary," *SCHGM* 33, no. 3: 198; Webber, "Death Notices," 158; *Royal Gazette,* May 19, 1781; Garden, *Anecdotes of the Revolutionary War* (1822), 228; Eastman, *Remembering Old Charleston,* 32.

29. Smith, "Diary," *SCHGM* 33, no. 4: 284–86; *Royal Gazette,* June 27, 1781 (quoted).

30. Johnson, *Traditions and Reminiscences,* 320; Manucy and Johnson, "Castle St. Mark and the Patriots of the Revolution," 17; Reynolds, *Old St. Augustine,* 96–97.

31. Johnson, *Traditions and Reminiscences,* 320.

32. Smith, "Diary," *SCHGM* 33, no. 3: 199–200.

33. Ibid., 200.

34. Ibid., 200–201.

35. Ibid., 201; Johnson, *Traditions and Reminiscences,* 319.

36. Smith, "Diary," *SCHGM* 33, no. 3: 201.

37. Ibid., 199; Johnson, *Traditions and Reminiscences,* 330. William Johnson says this day was July 9, 1781. Smith is correct.

38. *Royal Gazette,* June 27, 1781 (first quote); Smith, "Diary," *SCHGM* 33, no. 3: 199 (second quote); Smith, "Diary," *SCHGM* 33, no. 4: 284–86; *Royal Gazette,* June 30, 1781.

39. Smith, "Diary," *SCHGM* 33, no. 4: 288.

40. Ibid.; Johnson, *Traditions and Reminiscences,* 330.

41. Smith, "Diary," *SCHGM* 33, no. 4: 288; Johnson, *Traditions and Reminiscences,* 330; Smith, "Diary," *SCHGM* 33, no. 2: 98.

42. Smith, "Diary," *SCHGM* 33, no. 4: 288.

43. Ibid.

44. Ibid., 288–89; Smith, "Diary," *SCHGM* 34, no. 1: 32.

45. Smith, "Diary," *SCHGM* 33, no. 4: 287; *Royal Gazette,* June 30, 1781 (quoted).

46. Smith, "Diary," *SCHGM* 33, no. 4: 287; *Royal Gazette,* June 30, 1781 (quoted).

47. Smith, "Diary," *SCHGM* 33, no. 4: 287; *Royal Gazette,* May 12, 1781 (quoted).

48. *Royal Gazette,* May 12, 1781 (quoted); *Royal Gazette,* June 30, 1781.

49. *Royal Gazette,* July 14, 1781.

50. Johnson, *Traditions and Reminiscences,* 331–32.

51. Ibid.

52. *Royal Gazette,* July 11, 1781.

53. Smith, "Diary," *SCHGM* 33, no. 4: 287.

54. Smith, "Diary," *SCHGM* 34, no. 2: 78–83; McCrady, *Revolution 1780–1783,* 379; Mary Cochran to Benjamin Franklin, July 6, 1781, *Papers of Benjamin Franklin,* 35:229–31. Ramsay's account rounds this number up to "more than a thousand." Ramsay, *History of South Carolina,* 1:464.

55. McCrady, *Revolution 1780–1783,* 379.

Chapter 10—Freedom Bound

1. Smith, "Diary," *SCHGM* 34, no. 1: 32.

2. Ibid.

3. Ibid., 32–33.

4. Ibid., 31–32, 33; Smith, "Diary," *SCHGM* 33, no. 4: 289. Comparing the number of persons Smith states were aboard with the number of individuals listed by name reveals that his accounting is not completely accurate.

5. Johnson, *Traditions and Reminiscences,* 386–87.

6. Ibid.

7. Smith, "Diary," *SCHGM* 34, no. 1: 32; Mary Cochran to Charles Cochran, March 27, 1781, Cochran Family Papers (quoted).

8. Smith, "Diary," *SCHGM* 34, no. 1: 31–33.

9. Ibid., 33.

10. Ibid., 33–34.

11. Ibid. Thirty-eight shillings in 1781 were worth roughly three hundred dollars in 2019. For the historical value of money, see: https://www.measuringworth.com/calculators /ppoweruk/.

12. Smith, "Diary," *SCHGM* 34, no. 1: 33–34.

13. Ibid., 34–35.

14. Ibid., 35.

15. Ibid., 35–36.

16. Ibid., 36–37; Wayne E. McFee, the National Centers for Coastal Ocean Science, correspondence with C. L. Bragg, August 12, 2019. *Grampus griseus,* known as "Risso's dolphin," is the largest species called "dolphin." *Grampus* was also a common term for the orca. According to McFee, the fact that Smith states that the aquatic mammals were spouting like porpoises increases the likelihood they were indeed referring to *Grampus griseus.*

17. Ibid., 37–38; Navy Records Society, *Naval Miscellany,* 1:197.

18. Smith, "Diary," *SCHGM* 34, no. 1: 38

19. Ibid., 39.

20. Ibid.; Smith, "Diary," *SCHGM* 34, no. 2: 67 (quoted).

21. Smith, "Diary," *SCHGM* 34, no. 2: 67.

22. Ibid., 68.

23. Johnson, *Traditions and Reminiscences,* 330–31.

24. Ibid.

25. Ibid., 332–33 (quoted); Smith, "Diary," *SCHGM* 34, no. 2: 67.

26. Johnson, *Traditions and Reminiscences,* 332–33.

27. Smith, "Diary," *SCHGM* 34, no. 2: 78–84; Godbold and Woody, *Christopher Gadsden and the American Revolution,* 214; Mary Sansum to the South Carolina General Assembly, October 9, 1788, in Kierner, *Southern Women in Revolution,* 39–41 (quoted); *Royal Gazette,* August 11, 1781; Moultrie, *Memoirs,* 2:200.

28. Gadsden to Washington, August 10, 1781, *Writings of Christopher Gadsden,* 170 (quoted); Smith, "Diary," *SCHGM* 34, no. 2: 84; Smith, "Diary," *SCHGM* 34, no. 3: 138.

29. Smith, "Diary," *SCHGM* 34, no. 2: 68–69.

30. John Mathews to Nathanael Greene, August 14, 1781, *Papers of General Nathanael Greene,* 9:266; David Ramsay to Benjamin Lincoln, August 13, 1781, quoted in *Papers of General Nathanael Greene,* 9:268n3; Smith, "Diary," *SCHGM* 34, no. 2: 78–83; McCrady, *Revolution 1780–1783,* 379; Resolution, July 13, 1781, *Journals of the Continental Congress,* 20:748–49.

31. Robert Morris to Thomas McKean, July 20, 1781, *Papers of Robert Morris,* 1:344–46; order, July 23, 1781, *Journals of the Continental Congress,* 21:781.

32. Resolutions, July 23 and 24, 1781, *Journals of the Continental Congress,* 21:782–83, 786; Mathews to Greene, August 14, 1781, *Papers of General Nathanael Greene,* 9:266 (quoted).

33. Resolution, July 23, 1781, *Journals of the Continental Congress,* 21:782–83; Smith, "Diary," *SCHGM* 34, no. 3: 138–46.

34. Smith, "Diary," *SCHGM* 34, no. 3: 138–46. One hundred dollars in 1781 are worth roughly twenty-three hundred dollars in 2019. Thirty dollars in 1781 are worth roughly seven hundred dollars in 2019. For the historical value of money, see https://www.measuringworth .com/calculators/uscompare/.

35. Johnson, *Traditions and Reminiscences,* 369.

36. Ibid.

37. Smith, "Diary," *SCHGM* 34, no. 2: 68–69.

38. Johnson, *Traditions and Reminiscences,* 390.

39. Ibid., 390–91.

40. Ibid., 370.

41. Smith, "Diary," *SCHGM* 34, no. 2: 69.

42. Ibid., 69, 69n4.

43. Ibid.

44. *Royal Gazette,* July 11, 1781; Bragg, *Martyr of the American Revolution,* 43–51.

45. Bragg, *Martyr of the American Revolution,* 51–58; Ramsay, *History of the Revolution of South-Carolina,* 2:280.

46. Bragg, *Martyr of the American Revolution,* 51–58; copy of Charles Fraser to Isaac Hayne, July 29, 1781, Papers of the Continental Congress, NA microfilm series M247, roll 175 (vol. 2), 351–52 (quoted).

47. Bragg, *Martyr of the American Revolution,* 43–51; *Royal Gazette,* August 8, 1781.

48. Nathanael Greene to Francis Marion, August 10, 1781, *Papers of General Nathanael Greene,* 9:159; Greene to Thomas McKean, August 25, 1781, *Papers of General Nathanael Greene,* 9:242; Greene to Nisbet Balfour, August 26, 1781, *Papers of General Nathanael Greene,* 9:249–51; affidavit of Isaac Neufville, August 30, 1781, *Journals of the Continental Congress,* 21:927; *Parliamentary Register,* 8:81–82, 89–100.

49. Christopher Gadsden to the South Carolina delegates to the Continental Congress, September 17, 1781, *Writings of Christopher Gadsden,* 177 (first quote); Tench Tilghman to George Washington, October 27, 1781, in Sparks, *Correspondence of the American Revolution,* 3:434–35; entries for October 24 and 25, 1781, *Journals of the Continental Congress,* 21:1071, 1073–74 (second quote).

50. Boudinot, *Journal or Historical Recollections,* 59.

Chapter 11—Homecoming

1. Dunkerly and Boland, *Eutaw Springs,* 109–11; Bragg, *Martyr of the American Revolution,* 73, 77. Rawdon sailed for England not long after the execution of Col. Isaac Hayne on August 4, 1781.

2. Lumpkin, *From Savannah to Yorktown,* 222–35, 307–12.

3. Ibid., 236–45, 277.

4. Johnson, *Traditions and Reminiscences,* 370 (quoted); Ramsay, *History of the American Revolution,* 2:349n; entry for December 3, 1781, *Journals of the Continental Congress,* 21:1149.

5. Johnson, *Traditions and Reminiscences,* 372–73.

6. Fludd, *Biographical Sketches of the Huguenot Solomon Legaré,* 131; Johnson, *Traditions and Reminiscences,* 377.

7. Johnson, *Traditions and Reminiscences,* 386–87.

8. Ibid., 377; Fludd, *Biographical Sketches of the Huguenot Solomon Legaré,* 131.

9. Johnson, *Traditions and Reminiscences,* 377–78.

10. Ibid., 378–80.

11. Ibid., 380 (quoted). See also Moultrie, *Memoirs,* 2:355–56.

12. Johnson, *Traditions and Reminiscences,* 387–88.

13. Ibid., 380–81.

14. Ibid., 384–85.

15. Ibid.

16. Louis-Casimir, Baron de Holtzendorff, to Robert Cochran, March 25, 1782, Cochran Family Papers, 1752–1814 (1004.03.01), South Carolina Historical Society, Charleston.

17. Benjamin Franklin to Robert Cochran, June 12, 1779, *Papers of Benjamin Franklin,*

29:675 (first quote); Mary Cochran to Franklin, July 6, 1781, *Papers of Benjamin Franklin*, 35:229–31 (second quote).

18. Holtzendorff to Cochran, March 25, 1782, Cochran Family Papers.

19. Pension file for Ann Hall, widow of William Hall, pension number W. 21,255, Revolutionary War Pension and Bounty-Land Warrant Application Files, NA microfilm series M804, roll 1166, 14–34.

20. John Rutledge to the South Carolina delegates to the Continental Congress, August 6, 1781, *Russell's Magazine* 3, no. 1 (1858): 33–34.

21. Aedanus Burke to Arthur Middleton, October 9, 1781, "Correspondence of Hon. Arthur Middleton," *SCHGM* 26, no. 4: 184–85.

22. Christopher Gadsden to Thomas McKean, August 25, 1781, *Writings of Christopher Gadsden*, 172–73; diary entry for August 29, 1781, *Papers of Robert Morris*, 2:150.

23. Christopher Gadsden to Thomas McKean, August 25, 1781, *Writings of Christopher Gadsden*, 172–73; Robert Morris to Nathanael Greene, September 10, 1781, Greene to Francis Marion, October 23, 1781, Gadsden to Greene, November 4, 1781, and Greene to Morris, November 21, 1781, *Papers of General Nathanael Greene*, 9:316, 316–17n2, 469, 526, 602 (quoted); Godbold and Woody, *Christopher Gadsden and the American Revolution*, 216.

24. *Pennsylvania Packet* (Philadelphia), August 21, 1781; Smith, "Diary," *SCHGM* 34, no. 2: 70 (quoted); Fenhagen, "John Edwards," 18.

25. South Carolina delegates to John Ross, December 29, 1781, *Letters of Delegates to Congress*, 18:264, 264–65n1; John Rutledge to the South Carolina delegates to the Continental Congress, November 22, 1781, "Letters of John Rutledge," *SCHGM* 18, no. 4: 163–65. In 1793 the South Carolina attorney general was directed to recoup principal and interest from the recipients. Stevens, *Journals of the House of Representatives, 1792–1794*, 280, 344–45, 379, 379n38.

26. Rutledge to the South Carolina delegates, November 22, 1781, "Letters of John Rutledge," *SCHGM* 18, no. 4: 163; Johnson, *Sketches of the Life and Correspondence of Nathanael Greene*, 2:278; Aedanus Burke to Arthur Middleton, January 25, 1782, "Correspondence of Hon. Arthur Middleton," *SCHGM* 26, no. 4: 191; Edward Rutledge to Middleton, February 26, 1782, "Correspondence of Hon. Arthur Middleton," *SCHGM* 27, no. 1: 6.

27. Rutledge to the South Carolina delegates, January 29, 1782, "Letters of John Rutledge," *SCHGM* 18, no. 4: 166–67; Salley, *Journal of the House of Representatives of South Carolina, January 8, 1782–February 26, 1782*, 3, 5–6, 130–34; McCrady, *Revolution 1780–1783*, 560–61, 739–42.

28. Heyward, "Heyward Family of S.C.," 153–54.

29. Salley, *Journal of the House of Representatives of South Carolina, January 8, 1782–February 26, 1782*, 33, 34–36, 38; Garden, *Anecdotes of the American Revolution* (1822), 173; McCrady, *Revolution 1780–1783*, 570, 572.

30. David Ramsay to Benjamin Rush, February 9, 1782, "David Ramsay, 1749–1815: Selections from His Writings," 68.

31. Cooper, *Statutes at Large*, 4:xxvi–xxvii, 508–28 (quoted).

32. Ibid., 4:516–23 (quoted); Salley, *Journal of the House of Representatives of South Carolina, January 8, 1782–February 26, 1782*, 21–23, 32.

33. McCord, *Statutes at Large*, 6:629–32, 633; Salley, *Journal of the House of Representatives*

of South Carolina, January 8, 1782–February 26, 1782, 61–62, 91; Cooper, *Statutes at Large,* 4:523–25.

34. McCord, *Statutes at Large,* 6:629–33; Ramsay, *History of the Revolution of South-Carolina,* 2:280; James Simpson to William Knox, January 16, 1781, *Documents of the American Revolution,* 20:32; Cooper, *Statutes at Large,* 1:135–36; Simpson to Knox, February 21, 1781, *Documents of the American Revolution,* 19:45; Memorial of James Simpson, August 5, 1782, AO 13/135, American Loyalist Claims, fol. 311r.

35. Cooper, *Statutes at Large,* 4:517; Haw, *John and Edward Rutledge,* 164; McCrady, *Revolution 1780–1783,* 581, 582–89; Edward Rutledge to Arthur Middleton, February 14 and 26, 1782, "Correspondence of Hon. Arthur Middleton," *SCHGM* 27, no. 1: 5, 6, 8 (quoted).

36. McCrady, *Revolution 1780–1783,* 581, 582–89; Arthur Middleton to Aedanus Burke, April 7, 1782, "Correspondence of Hon. Arthur Middleton," *SCHGM* 27, no. 1: 29 (quoted).

37. Moultrie, *Memoirs,* 2:210–11 (first quote), 325–26 (second quote); Nadelhaft, "Ending South Carolina's War," 50–51, 51n3; Cooper, *Statutes at Large,* 4:624–26.

38. Christopher Gadsden to Morton Wilkinson, September [n.d.] 1781, *Writings of Christopher Gadsden,* 174–75.

39. McCrady, *Revolution 1780–1783,* 580–81; Garden, *Anecdotes of the American Revolution* (1822), 170 (quoted).

40. Christopher Gadsden to Francis Marion, November 17, 1782, *Writings of Christopher Gadsden,* 194–97.

41. Ibid.

42. Ibid., 195–96, 196n4; Godbold and Woody, *Christopher Gadsden and the American Revolution,* 218–20.

43. Smith, "Diary," *SCHGM* 34, no. 4: 206; resolution, February 14, 1782, *Journal of the House of Representatives of South Carolina, January 8, 1782–February 26, 1782,* 82; resolution, April 3, 1782, *Journals of the Continental Congress,* 22:161; George Washington to Guy Carleton, May 21, 1782, *Writings of George Washington* (ed. Fitzpatrick), 24:270 (quoted).

44. George Washington to Benjamin Lincoln, May 28, 1782, *Writings of George Washington* (ed. Fitzpatrick), 24:296 (first quote); Washington to John Morin Scott, June 10, 1782, *Writings of George Washington* (ed. Fitzpatrick), 24:326–27 (second quote).

45. David Ramsay to Nathanael Greene, June 9, 1782, *Letters of Delegates to Congress,* 18:566–67 (quoted); report and resolutions, June 14, 1782, *Journals of the Continental Congress,* 22:330–32; George Washington to Guy Carleton, July 4, 1782, *Writings of George Washington* (ed. Fitzpatrick), 24:400; diary entry for July 30, 1782, *Papers of Robert Morris,* 6:89–90nn10–11; Smith, "Diary," *SCHGM* 34, no. 4: 206.

46. Brook Watson to Maurice Morgann, July 9, 1782, and Morgann to Watson, July 12, 1782, *Report on American Manuscripts in the Royal Institution of Great Britain,* 3:15, 17; Robert Morris to John Cruden, August 5, 1782, *Papers of Robert Morris,* 6:137–38; Smith, "Diary," *SCHGM* 34, no. 4: 206–8.

47. Smith, "Diary," *SCHGM* 34, no. 4: 207.

48. Johnson, *Traditions and Reminiscences,* 386 (quoted); Smith, "Diary," *SCHGM* 34, no. 4: 207; George Washington to Guy Carleton, September 3, 1782, *Writings of George Washington* (ed. Fitzpatrick), 25:114; list, August 28, 1782, *Report on American Manuscripts in the Royal Institution of Great Britain,* 3:96.

49. Moultrie, *Memoirs,* 2:359. The dragoons were those formerly commanded by Lt. Col. "Light Horse Harry" Lee.

50. Ibid., 359–60.

51. Ibid., 385.

52. Ibid., 385–86.

53. Ibid., 386.

Epilogue

1. McCrady and Ashe, *Cyclopedia,* 1:150–51, 510–11; *City Gazette,* March 4, 1797.

2. Chesney, *Journal of Alexander Chesney,* 99–100; Stephen and Lee, *Dictionary of National Biography,* 1:976–77; Charles Cornwallis to Henry Clinton, September 3, 1780, *Cornwallis Papers,* 2:43; Stephen and Lee, *Dictionary of National Biography,* 4:1161–66.

3. Cornwallis to Clinton, September 3, 1780, *Cornwallis Papers,* 2:43; entry for February 23, 1782, *Journals of the Continental Congress,* 22:93–95 (quoted).

4. Edward Rutledge to Arthur Middleton, April 23, 1782, "Correspondence of Hon. Arthur Middleton," *SCHGM* 27, no. 1: 15 (quoted); Stephen and Lee, *Dictionary of National Biography,* 4:1161–66.

Appendix A—Who Were the Patriots Exiled to St. Augustine in 1780?

1. The starting points for all of the names listed in this appendix are Smith, "Diary," *SCHGM* 33, no. 1: 3–4, 6–7; Johnson, *Traditions and Reminiscences,* 317–19; and Manucy and Johnson, "Castle St. Mark and the Patriots of the Revolution," 21–22.

2. Bailey, Morgan, and Taylor, *Biographical Directory of the South Carolina Senate,* 1:119–20.

3. Moss, *Roster of South Carolina Patriots in the American Revolution,* 65; *Columbia Record,* December 1, 1960; Bailey and Cooper, *Biographical Directory of the South Carolina House,* 3:67–68.

4. Salley, "Historical Notes," 104; Bailey and Cooper, *Biographical Directory of the South Carolina House,* 3:68–69.

5. Bailey and Cooper, *Biographical Directory of the South Carolina House,* 3:70–72.

6. Ibid., 79–81.

7. Ibid., 105–6; indented certificate issued by South Carolina to John Budd on August 22, 1785, *Accounts Audited,* SCDAH, series S108092, roll 16, frame 50 (file no. 881); Moss, *Roster of South Carolina Patriots in the American Revolution,* 120; Armstrong, *Pioneer Families of Northwestern New Jersey,* 260–61; Webber, "Marriage and Death Notices from the *City Gazette,*" 83; Waring, *History of Medicine in South Carolina,* 119, 181, 286, 341, 347; Moore, *Columbia and Richland County,* 43.

8. "Biographical Sketch of Capt. Robt Cochran," Cochran Family Papers, fol. 2–3; Hagy and Hagy, *Charleston, South Carolina City Directories: For the Years 1816, 1819, 1822, 1825, and 1829,* 5.

9. Moss, *Roster of South Carolina Patriots in the American Revolution,* 217; Salley, *President Washington's Tour,* 15; *Charleston Courier,* April 6, 1808.

10. Bailey and Cooper, *Biographical Directory of the South Carolina House,* 3:162–63.

11. Ibid., 163–64; Moss, *Roster of South Carolina Patriots in the American Revolution,* 222.

12. Bailey and Cooper, *Biographical Directory of the South Carolina House,* 3:169–70;

Woodward and Craven, *Princetonians, 1784–1790,* 357–58; *City Gazette* (Charleston, S.C.), May 14, 1791.

13. Bailey and Cooper, *Biographical Directory of the South Carolina House,* 3:182–84.

14. Fenhagen, "John Edwards," 15–21; Edgar and Bailey, *Biographical Directory of the South Carolina House,* 2:214–16.

15. Edgar and Bailey, *Biographical Directory of the South Carolina House,* 2:248–51.

16. Bailey and Cooper, *Biographical Directory of the South Carolina House,* 3:235–36.

17. Edgar and Bailey, *Biographical Directory of the South Carolina House,* 2:259–63.

18. Bailey and Cooper, *Biographical Directory of the South Carolina House,* 3:258–61; Moss, *Roster of South Carolina Patriots in the American Revolution,* 352.

19. Bailey and Cooper, *Biographical Directory of the South Carolina House,* 3:289.

20. Ibid., 296–98; Moss, *Roster of South Carolina Patriots in the American Revolution,* 401.

21. Heitman, *Historical Register of Officers of the Continental Army,* 268; Moss, *Roster of South Carolina Patriots in the American Revolution,* 402; Wilson, *Year Book of the Society, Sons of the Revolution, in the Commonwealth of Kentucky,* 314.

22. Johnson, *Traditions and Reminiscences,* 121–27.

23. Edgar and Bailey, *Biographical Directory of the South Carolina House,* 2:323–25.

24. Bailey and Cooper, *Biographical Directory of the South Carolina House,* 3:342–43.

25. Ibid., 3:364–66.

26. Isaacs, "Lt.-Col. Elijah Isaacs," April 2017, http://www.carolana.com/NC/Revolution/Elijah_Isaacs_Biography_Barry_Isaacs_April_2017.pdf, accessed July 12, 2018; Clark, *Colonial Records of North Carolina,* 16:168; Wheeler, *Historical Sketches of North Carolina,* 1:465.

27. Moss, *Roster of South Carolina Patriots in the American Revolution,* 504; Bailey and Cooper, *Biographical Directory of the South Carolina House,* 3:383–85.

28. Allen, *American Biographical Dictionary,* 484; Jones, "Noble Wymberley Jones," 207–18.

29. Bailey and Cooper, *Biographical Directory of the South Carolina House,* 3:423–24; Moss, *Roster of South Carolina Patriots in the American Revolution,* 590; *City Gazette* (Charleston, S.C.), December 5, 1803; Read, *Descendants of Thomas Lee of Charleston, South Carolina,* 83–84.

30. Johnson, *Traditions and Reminiscences,* 317, 321n; Weis, *Colonial Clergy of Virginia, North Carolina, and South Carolina,* 83; Dalcho, *Historical Account of the Protestant Episcopal Church in South Carolina,* 357–58, 363; *South-Carolina Gazette and Public Advertiser* (Charleston, S.C.), August 21, 1784.

31. Moss, *Roster of South Carolina Patriots in the American Revolution,* 574; *City Gazette* (Charleston, S.C.), July 6, 1791.

32. Bailey and Cooper, *Biographical Directory of the South Carolina House,* 3:439–40; Logan, *Record of the Logan Family,* 18–24.

33. Christopher Gadsden to George Washington, August 10, 1781, *Writings of Christopher Gadsden,* 170; Henry Laurens to Lachlan McIntosh, November 28, 1776, *Papers of Henry Laurens,* 11:280n1.

34. Moss, *Roster of South Carolina Patriots in the American Revolution,* 587; Bailey and Cooper, *Biographical Directory of the South Carolina House,* 3:444–45.

35. Heitman, *Historical Register of Officers of the Continental Army,* 384; Moss, *Roster of South Carolina Patriots in the American Revolution,* 663; O'Kelley, *Unwaried Patience and*

Fortitude, 19, 610n120; *South-Carolina Gazette and General Advertiser* (Charleston, S.C.), November 6, 1784.

36. McCrady and Ashe, *Cyclopedia of Eminent and Representative Men of the Carolinas,* 1:150; *City Gazette* (Charleston, S.C.), May 14, 1791.

37. Bailey, Morgan, and Taylor, *Biographical Directory of the South Carolina Senate,* 2:1099–100.

38. O'Kelley, *Unwaried Patience and Fortitude,* 1; Moss, *Roster of South Carolina Patriots in the American Revolution,* 708; McCrady, *Revolution 1775–1780,* 14; *State Gazette of South-Carolina* (Charleston, S.C.), September 24, 1787.

39. Bailey and Cooper, *Biographical Directory of the South Carolina House,* 3:515–17; Moss, *Roster of South Carolina Patriots in the American Revolution,* 708.

40. Bailey and Cooper, *Biographical Directory of the South Carolina House,* 3:525–26; Moss, *Roster of South Carolina Patriots in the American Revolution,* 724.

41. Otto, *Family of Captain Edward North and His Wife,* 1–3, 71–72nn16–25; Edgar and Bailey, *Biographical Directory of the South Carolina House,* 4:425; Moss, *Roster of South Carolina Patriots in the American Revolution,* 733; *City Gazette* (Charleston, S.C.), August 22, 1798; Colonial Dames of America, *Ancestral Records and Portraits,* 2:577–78.

42. Moss, *Roster of South Carolina Patriots in the American Revolution,* 753; *South-Carolina Gazette and General Advertiser* (Charleston, S.C.), June 8, 1785.

43. Bailey and Cooper, *Biographical Directory of the South Carolina House,* 3:548.

44. Ibid., 3:573–74.

45. Ibid., 3:583; Manigault and Prioleau, *Register of Carolina Huguenots,* 3:1449; Riley, "Michael Kalteisen and the Founding of the German Friendly Society in Charleston," 34, 34n16; John Ernest Poyas, assignee of P.M. [provost marshal] vs Adam Shekell and Michael Kalteison, October 26, 1757, South Carolina Court of Common Pleas, Judgment Rolls, 1703–1790, Series 136002, box 44A, item 111A (microfilm roll ST 212, frames 47–58), South Carolina Department of Archives and History.

46. Bailey and Cooper, *Biographical Directory of the South Carolina House,* 3:588–89; Moss, *Roster of South Carolina Patriots in the American Revolution,* 789.

47. Bailey and Cooper, *Biographical Directory of the South Carolina House,* 3:590–94.

48. Ibid., 597–99; Moss, *Roster of South Carolina Patriots in the American Revolution,* 803.

49. Powell, *Dictionary of North Carolina Biography,* 5:275–76; Long, *General Griffith Rutherford and Allied Families,* 6–70.

50. Edgar and Bailey, *Biographical Directory of the South Carolina House,* 2:573–76; Haw, *John and Edward Rutledge,* 164; Moss, *Roster of South Carolina Patriots in the American Revolution,* 839.

51. Bailey and Cooper, *Biographical Directory of the South Carolina House,* 3:627–28.

52. *South-Carolina Gazette and Public Advertiser* (Charleston, S.C.), October 16, 1784; Moss, *Roster of South Carolina Patriots in the American Revolution,* 844; John Mathews to Arthur Middleton, August 25, 1782, "Correspondence of Hon. Arthur Middleton," *SCHGM* 27, no. 2: 70, 70n34; diary entry for June 19, 1782, *Papers of Robert Morris,* 5:447, 447n8.

53. Edgar and Bailey, *Biographical Directory of the South Carolina House,* 2:596–98; Moss, *Roster of South Carolina Patriots in the American Revolution,* 847.

54. Moss, *Roster of South Carolina Patriots in the American Revolution,* 868; *City Gazette* (Charleston, S.C.), October 6, 1798.

55. Smith, "Diary," *SCHGM* 33, no. 1: 1–2; *Charleston Courier,* February 20, 1826; Bailey and Cooper, *Biographical Directory of the South Carolina House,* 3:665–67.

56. Bailey and Cooper, *Biographical Directory of the South Carolina House,* 3:670–71; Smith, "Diary," *SCHGM* 33, no. 2: 113–14.

57. McLachlan, *Princetonians, 1748–1768,* 339, 361–62; Salley, "Daniel Trezevant, Huguenot, and Some of His Descendants," 35nccc; Hamilton, "Extracts from a Private Manuscript," *Year Book—1898, City of Charleston,* 299–300 (quoted).

58. Edgar and Bailey, *Biographical Directory of the South Carolina House,* 2:672–75.

59. Moss, *Roster of South Carolina Patriots in the American Revolution,* 934.

60. Bailey and Cooper, *Biographical Directory of the South Carolina House,* 3:716–18.

61. Ibid., 735; James Laurens to Henry Laurens, July 22, 1774, *Papers of Henry Laurens,* 9:524–28, 525n7, 527n2.

62. Bailey and Cooper, *Biographical Directory of the South Carolina House,* 3:737; Moss, *Roster of South Carolina Patriots in the American Revolution,* 963; *City Gazette* (Charleston, S.C.), January 16, 1801.

63. Bailey and Cooper, *Biographical Directory of the South Carolina House,* 3:759–61; Moss, *Roster of South Carolina Patriots in the American Revolution,* 981.

64. Bailey, Morgan, and Taylor, *Biographical Directory of the South Carolina Senate,* 3:1724–25; Moss, *Roster of South Carolina Patriots in the American Revolution,* 992.

Appendix B—How Many Patriots Were Exiled to St. Augustine?

1. Smith, "Diary," *SCHGM* 33, no. 1: 3–4; Smith, "Diary," *SCHGM* 33, no. 2: 87–90.

2. "List of the Names of the Disaffected Inhabitants of Charlestown Who Have Been Sent to [St.] Augustine, 3rd September 1780," *Cornwallis Papers,* 2:77–78.

3. "Alphabetical Return of the Names and Titles of the Rebel Prisoners Landed from Charles Town at Saint Augustine[,] East Florida[,] September 15th and November 24th[,] 1780," PRO CO 5/560, 115–18.

4. Christopher Gadsden to George Washington, August 10, 1781, *Writings of Christopher Gadsden,* 170; Smith, "Diary," *SCHGM* 33, no. 2: 113–14; Smith, "Diary," *SCHGM* 33, no. 3: 198.

5. Ramsay, *History of the Revolution of South-Carolina,* 2:161, 458–59; Ramsay, *History of South Carolina,* 1:370–71, 373.

6. Tarleton, *History of the Campaigns of 1780 and 1781,* 189–90.

7. Forbes, *Sketches of the Floridas, Historical and Topographical,* 32.

8. Garden, *Anecdotes of the American Revolution* (1822), 165.

9. Johnson, *Traditions and Reminiscences,* 317–19.

10. Fairbanks, *Florida, Its History and Its Romance,* 160.

11. Smith, "Diary," *SCHGM* 33, no. 1: 7; "List of the Names of the Disaffected Inhabitants of Charlestown Who Have Been Sent to [St.] Augustine, 3rd September 1780," *Cornwallis Papers,* 2:77–78.

12. Smith, "Diary," *SCHGM* 34, no. 1: 31–32.

Bibliography

Primary Sources

Manuscripts and Original Documents

Balfour, Nisbet. Letterbook of Lieut. Col. Nisbet Balfour, British Commandant of Charleston, S.C.: Charleston, S.C., 1 Jan.–1 Dec. 1781. MSS L2001F617. Robert Charles Lawrence Fergusson Collection. Archives and Library Collections of the Society of the Cincinnati at Anderson House, Washington, D.C.

Cochran Family. Cochran Family Papers, 1752–1814. Call no. 1004.03.01. Bacot Family Collection, 1752–1973, call no. 1004.00. South Carolina Historical Society, Charleston.

Colcock, John, 1744–82. "Case of Colonel Hayne, 1781." Call no. 43/0083. South Carolina Historical Society, Charleston.

Continental Congress. Papers of the Continental Congress, 1774–1789. Record Group 360: Records of the Continental and Confederation Congresses and the Constitutional Convention, 1765–1821. Microfilm series M247, rolls 175 and 177. National Archives and Records Administration, Washington, D.C.

Gubbins, M. C. B. Transcripts and abstracts of Moultrie family papers, 1746–1965. Letters (43/36). South Carolina Historical Society, Charleston.

Laurens, John. "Account of the Operations in South Carolina, Respecting Capitulation, May 1779," Henry Laurens Papers, 1747–1860, Manuscripts (37/45B oversize), South Carolina Historical Society, Charleston.

McCrady Family Papers. James Waring McCrady. Sewanee, Tenn.

Ravenel, William, 1806–88. William Ravenel Papers, 1746–1886. Mss. 1130.02.01. South Carolina Historical Society, Charleston.

Revolutionary War Pension and Bounty-Land Warrant Application Files. Record Group 15. Microfilm series M804, roll 1166. National Archives and Records Administration, Washington, D.C.

Smith, Josiah, Jr. Josiah Smith Letter Book, 1771–1784, Charleston and Georgetown Districts, South Carolina. Frederick, Md.: University Publications of America, 1990. Microfilm. [#3018, Southern Historical Collection, Wilson Library, University of North Carolina at Chapel Hill.]

South Carolina Court of Common Pleas. Judgment Rolls, 1703–1790. Series 136002. South Carolina Department of Archives and History, Columbia. Microfilm.

South Carolina Department of Archives and History, Archives and Publications Division. *Accounts Audited of Claims Growing Out of the Revolution in South Carolina, 1775–1856*

(Microcopy no. 8), 1985. Series: S108092. South Carolina Department of Archives and History, Columbia.

Washington, George. Papers, 1592–1943. Series 4, General Correspondence, Library of Congress, Washington, D.C.

Published Sources and Personal Accounts

Boehm, Randolph, ed. *Records of the British Colonial Office, Class 5. Part 5: The American Revolution, 1772–1784.* Frederick, Md.: University Publications of America, 1981. Microfilm.

Boudinot, Elias. *Journal or Historical Recollections of American Events during the Revolutionary War.* Philadelphia: Frederick Bourquin, 1894.

Chesney, Alexander. *The Journal of Alexander Chesney, a South Carolina Loyalist in the Revolution and After.* Edited by E. Alfred Jones, with an introduction by Wilbur Henry Siebert. *Ohio State University Bulletin* 26, no. 4 (1921).

Church of England. *The Book of Common Prayer, and Administration of the Sacraments, and Other Rites and Ceremonies of the Church, According to the Use of the Church of England: Illustrated and Explained by the Full and Comprehensive Paraphrase at the Bottom of Each Page: With the Psalter or Psalms of David, and Practical Observations Thereon.* Carlisle, England: J. Harrison, 1779.

Clark, Walter, ed. *The Colonial Records of North Carolina.* Vol. 16. Goldsboro, N.C.: Nash Brothers, 1899.

Clark, William Bell, William James Morgan, and Michael J. Crawford, eds. *Naval Documents of the American Revolution.* 12 vols. Washington, D.C.: Naval History Division, Department of the Navy; Government Printing Office, 1964–2013.

Clinton, Henry. *The American Rebellion: Sir Henry Clinton's Narrative of His Campaigns, 1775–1782, with an Appendix of Original Documents.* Edited by William B. Willcox. New Haven: Yale University Press, 1954.

Coldham, Peter Wilson. *American Migrations, 1765–1799.* Baltimore: Genealogical Pub. Co., 2000.

Continental Congress. *Journals of the Continental Congress, 1774–1789.* 34 vols. Edited by Worthington C. Ford et al. Washington, D.C.: Government Printing Office, 1904–37.

Cooper, Thomas, ed. *The Statutes at Large of South Carolina.* Vols. 1 and 4. Columbia: A. S. Johnston, 1836, 1838.

Cooper, Thomas, and David James McCord, eds. *The Statutes at Large of South Carolina.* 9 vols. Columbia: A. S. Johnston, 1836–39.

Cornwallis, Charles Earl. *An Answer to That Part of the Narrative of Lieutenant-General Sir Henry Clinton, K.B.: Which Relates to the Conduct of Lieutenant-General Earl Cornwallis during the Campaign in North-America in in the Year 1781.* London: J. Debrett, 1783.

———. *Correspondence of Charles, First Marquis Cornwallis.* 3 vols. Edited by Charles Ross. London: John Murray, 1859.

———. *The Cornwallis Papers: The Campaigns of 1780 and 1781 in the Southern Theatre of the American Revolutionary War.* 6 vols. Edited by Ian Saberton. East Sussex, England: Naval & Military Press, 2010.

Davies, K. G. *Documents of the American Revolution, 1770–1783.* 21 vols. Shannon: Irish University Press, 1972–81.

Drayton, John, *Memoirs of the American Revolution, from Its Commencement to the Year 1776,*

Inclusive; as Relating to the State of South-Carolina: and Occasionally Referring to the States of North-Carolina and Georgia. 2 vols. Charleston: A. E. Miller, 1821.

Force, Peter, ed. and comp. *American Archives.* Series 4, vols. 3 and 4. Washington, D.C.: M. St. Clair Clark & Peter Force, 1837–1846.

Franklin, Benjamin. *The Papers of Benjamin Franklin.* 42 vols. Edited by Leonard W. Lebaree et al. New Haven: Yale University Press, 1959–2017.

Gadsden, Christopher. *The Writings of Christopher Gadsden, 1746–1805.* Edited by Richard Walsh. Columbia: University of South Carolina Press, 1966.

Gibbes, Robert Wilson, ed. *Documentary History of the American Revolution, Consisting of Letters and Papers Relating to the Contest for Liberty, Chiefly in South Carolina, in 1781 and 1782.* Columbia: Banner Steam-Power Press, 1853.

Great Britain. Parliament. *The Parliamentary Register; or, History of the Proceedings and Debates of the House of Lords.* Fifteenth Parliament, Second Session, vol. 8. London: J. Debrett, 1782.

———. Public Records Office, London. Colonial Office. Class 5, part 5: The American Revolution, 1772–1784. Vol. 560: East Florida, Correspondence of Governor Tonyn with the Secretary of State, 1780 to 1783, and additional papers to 1785. Microfilm, reel 66-D. Special and Area Studies Collections, George A. Smathers Library, University of Florida, Gainesville, Fla.

———. Public Records Office, London. Audit Office. Papers of the American Loyalist Claims Commission. American Loyalist Claims, 1776–1835. PRO Refs. AO 12–13 (fols. 71–86) (fols. 308–78). The National Archives of the United Kingdom, Kew, Surrey, England.

Greene, Nathanael. *The Papers of General Nathanael Greene.* 13 vols. Edited by Richard K. Showman et al. Chapel Hill: University of North Carolina Press, 1976–2005.

Hemphill, William Edwin, and Wylma Anne Wates, eds. *Extracts from the Journals of the Provincial Congresses of South Carolina, 1775–1776.* Columbia: South Carolina Archives Department, 1960.

Historic American Buildings Survey. Prints and Photographs Division, Library of Congress, Washington, D.C.

Houston, William. *Documents Illustrative of the Canadian Constitution.* Toronto: Carswell, 1891.

Jefferys, Thomas. *Plan of the Town of St. Augustine, the Capital of East Florida; The Bay of Espiritu Santo, on the Western Coast of East Florida.* London: William Faden 1777. Florida Map Collection. USF Tampa Library. University of South Florida, Tampa.

Laurens, Henry. *The Papers of Henry Laurens.* 16 vols. Edited by David R. Chestnut et al. Columbia: University of South Carolina Press, 1968–2002.

Lee, Charles. *The Lee Papers, 1754–1811. Vol. 2, 1776–1778.* Edited by Henry Edward Bunbury. *Collections of the New-York Historical Society for the Year 1872.* New York: New-York Historical Society, 1783.

Lincoln, Charles Henry Lincoln. *Naval Records of the American Revolution, 1775–1788.* Washington, D.C.: Government Printing. Office, 1906.

Middleton, Arthur. "Correspondence of Hon. Arthur Middleton, Signer of the Declaration of Independence." Annotated by Joseph W. Barnwell. *South Carolina Historical and Genealogical Magazine* 26, no. 4 (1925): 183–213.

————. "Correspondence of Hon. Arthur Middleton (Continued)." Annotated by Joseph W. Barnwell. *South Carolina Historical and Genealogical Magazine* 27, no. 1 (1926): 1–29.

————. "Correspondence of Hon. Arthur Middleton (Continued)." Annotated by Joseph W. Barnwell. *South Carolina Historical and Genealogical Magazine* 27, no. 2 (1926): 51–80.

————. "Correspondence of Hon. Arthur Middleton (Continued)." Annotated by Joseph W. Barnwell. *South Carolina Historical and Genealogical Magazine* 27, no. 3 (1926): 107–55.

Morris, Robert. *The Papers of Robert Morris, 1781–1784.* 8 vols. Edited by E. James Ferguson and John Catanzariti. Pittsburgh: University of Pittsburgh Press, 1973.

Moultrie, William. *Memoirs of the American Revolution So Far as It Related to the States of North and South-Carolina, and Georgia.* 2 vols. New York: David Longworth, 1802.

Navy Records Society (Great Britain). *Publications of the Navy Records Society.* Vol. 20: *The Naval Miscellany.* Vol. 1. Edited by John Knox Laughton. London: Navy Records Society, 1902.

O'Kelley, Patrick, ed. *Unwaried Patience and Fortitude: Francis Marion's Orderly Book.* West Conshohocken, Pa.: Infinity Publishing.com., 2006.

Ramsay, David. "David Ramsay, 1749–1815: Selections from His Writings." Edited by Robert L. Brunhouse. Transactions of the American Philosophical Society 55, no. 4 (1965).

————. *A Sermon on Tea.* Lancaster, Pa.: Francis Bailey, 1774.

Rutledge, John. "Letters of John Rutledge (Continued)." Edited by Joseph W. Barnwell. *South Carolina Historical and Genealogical Magazine* 18, no. 2 (1917): 59–69.

Salley, Alexander S., Jr., ed. *Journal of the Commissioners of the Navy of South Carolina.* 2 vols. Columbia: Historical Commission of South Carolina, 1912–13.

————. *Journal of the General Assembly of South Carolina, September 17, 1776–October 20, 1776.* Columbia: Historical Commission of South Carolina, 1909.

————. *Journal of the House of Representatives of South Carolina, January 8, 1782–February 26, 1782.* Columbia: Historical Commission of South Carolina, 1916.

Schulz, Constance, ed. *The Papers of Eliza Lucas Pinckney and Harriott Pinckney Horry Digital Edition.* Charlottesville: University of Virginia Press, Rotunda, 2012 (http://rotunda.upress.virginia.edu/PinckneyHorry/).

Simpson, James. "A British View of the Siege of Charleston, 1776." Edited by Frances Reece Kepner. *Journal of Southern History* 11, no. 1 (1945): 93–103.

————. "James Simpson's Reports on the Carolina Loyalists, 1779–1780." Edited by Alan S. Brown. *Journal of Southern History* 21, no. 4 (1955): 513–19.

Smith, Josiah, Jr. "Josiah Smith's Diary, 1780–1781." Annotated by Mabel L. Webber. *South Carolina Historical and Genealogical Magazine* 33, no. 1 (1932): 1–28; 33, no. 2 (1932): 79–116; 33, no. 3 (1932): 197–207; 33, no. 4 (1932): 281–89; 34, no. 1 (1933): 31–39; 34, no. 2 (1933): 67–84; 34, no. 3 (1933): 138–48; 34, no. 4 (1933): 194–210.

Smith, Paul H., et al., eds. *Letters of Delegates to Congress, 1774–1789.* 25 vols. Washington, D.C.: Library of Congress, 1976–2000.

South Carolina Historical Society. "Journal of the Council of Safety of the Province of South Carolina, 1775." *Collections of the South-Carolina Historical Society* 2 (1858).

Stevens, Michael E., ed. *Journals of the House of Representatives, 1792–1794.* Columbia: University of South Carolina Press, 1988.

Tarleton, Banastre. *A History of the Campaigns of 1780 and 1781, in the Southern Provinces of*

North America. Dublin: Colles, Exshaw, White, H. Whitestone, Burton, Byrne, Moore, Jones & Dornin, 1787.

The Remembrancer, or, Impartial Repository of Public Events for the Year 1781. Pt. 2. London: J. Debrett, 1781.

Royal Commission on Historical Manuscripts. *Report on American Manuscripts in the Royal Institution of Great Britain*. 4 vols. London: H. M. Stationery Office, 1904–9.

Rutledge, John. "Letters to the Delegates." *Russell's Magazine* 3, no. 1 (1858): 33–34.

Sparks, Jared. *Correspondence of the American Revolution: Being Letters of Eminent Men to George Washington, from the Time of His Taking Command of the Army to the End of His Presidency.* Volume 3. Boston: Little, Brown, 1853.

Uhlendorf, Bernhard A., trans. and ed. *The Siege of Charleston, with an Account of the Province of South Carolina: Diaries and Letters of Hessian Officers from the von Jungkenn Papers in the William L. Clements Library.* Ann Arbor: University of Michigan Press, 1938.

Washington, George. *The Writings of George Washington.* 12 vols. Edited by Jared Sparks. Boston: Hilliard, Gray, 1834–39.

———. *The Writings of George Washington from the Original Manuscript Sources, 1745–1799.* 39 vols. Edited by John C. Fitzpatrick. Washington, D.C.: Government Printing Office, 1931–44.

Webber, Mabel L., comp. "Death Notices from *The South Carolina and American General Gazette,* and Its Continuation *The Royal Gazette:* May 1766–June 1782 (Continued)." *South Carolina Historical and Genealogical Magazine* 17, no. 4 (1916): 147–66.

———. "Marriage and Death Notices from *The City Gazette.*" *South Carolina Historical and Genealogical Magazine* 21, no. 2 (1920): 77–87.

Wilkinson, Eliza, and Caroline Howard Gilman. *Letters of Eliza Wilkinson, during the Invasion and Possession of Charlestown, S.C., by the British in the Revolutionary War.* New York: Samuel Colman, 1839.

Newspapers

Charleston Courier (Charleston, S.C.)

Charleston Evening Post (Charleston, S.C.)

City Gazette (Charleston, S.C.)

Columbia Record (Columbia, S.C.)

New-York Gazette, and the Weekly Mercury (New York, N.Y.)

New-York Journal (New York, N.Y.)

Pennsylvania Evening Post (Philadelphia, Pa.)

Pennsylvania Packet (Philadelphia, Pa.)

Royal Gazette (Charleston, S.C.)

Royal Georgia Gazette (Savannah, Ga.)

South-Carolina and American General Gazette (Charleston, S.C.)

South-Carolina Gazette (Charleston, S.C.)

South-Carolina Gazette and General Advertiser (Charleston, S.C.)

South-Carolina Gazette and Public Advertiser (Charleston, S.C.)

State Gazette of South-Carolina (Charleston, S.C.)

Secondary Sources

Books and Pamphlets

Abbey, Kathryn Trimmer. *Florida: Land of Change.* Chapel Hill: University of North Carolina Press, 1941.

Allen, William. *The American Biographical Dictionary: Containing an Account of the Lives, Characters, and Writings of the Most Eminent Persons Deceased in North America from Its First Settlement.* Boston: Jewett, 1857.

Armstrong, William C. *Pioneer Families of Northwestern New Jersey.* Baltimore: Genealogical Publishing, 2002.

Bailey, N. Louise, and Elizabeth Ivey Cooper. *Biographical Directory of the South Carolina House of Representatives, Volume III: 1775–1790.* Columbia: University of South Carolina Press, 1981.

Bailey, N. Louise, Mary L. Morgan, and Carolyn R. Taylor. *Biographical Directory of the South Carolina Senate, 1776–1985.* 3 vols. Columbia: University of South Carolina Press, 1986.

Barbour, George M. *Florida for Tourists, Invalids, and Settlers.* New York: Appleton, 1882.

Baule, Steven M., and Stephen Gilbert. *British Army Officers Who Served in the American Revolution, 1775–1783.* Westminster, Md.: Heritage Books, 2004.

Bennett, Charles E., and Donald R. Lennon. *A Quest for Glory: Major General Robert Howe and the American Revolution.* Chapel Hill: University of North Carolina Press, 1991.

Borick, Carl P. *Relieve Us of This Burthen: American Prisoners of War in the Revolutionary South, 1780–1782.* Columbia: University of South Carolina Press, 2012.

Bragg, C. L. *Crescent Moon over Carolina: William Moultrie and American Liberty.* Columbia: University of South Carolina Press, 2013.

———. *Martyr of the American Revolution: The Execution of Isaac Hayne, South Carolinian.* Columbia: University of South Carolina Press, 2016.

Calhoon, Robert M. *The Loyalists in Revolutionary America, 1760–1781.* New York: Harcourt Brace Jovanovich, 1973.

Cannon, Richard. *Historical Record of the Sixth, or Inniskilling Regiment of Dragoons: Containing an Account of the Formation of the Regiment in 1689, and of Its Subsequent Services to 1846.* London: Parker, Furnivall & Parker, 1984.

Cashin, Edward J. *The King's Ranger: Thomas Brown and the American Revolution on the Southern Frontier.* New York: Fordham University Press, 1999.

Colonial Dames of America. *Ancestral Records and Portraits: A Compilation from the Archives of Chapter I, the Colonial Dames of America.* Vol. 2. New York: Grafton, 1910.

Coker, P. C. *Charleston's Maritime Heritage, 1670–1865: An Illustrated History.* Charleston: CokerCraft, 1987.

Coleman, Kenneth. "Commentary." In *Eighteenth-Century Florida: The Impact of the American Revolution.* Edited by Samuel Proctor, 93–98. Gainesville: University Presses of Florida, 1978.

Commager, Henry Steele, and Richard B. Morris, eds. *The Spirit of Seventy-Six: The Story of the American Revolution as Told by the Participants.* 1975. Rpt., New York: De Capo, 1995.

Corbett, Theodore G. "The Problem of the Household in the Second Spanish Period." In *Eighteenth-Century Florida: The Impact of the American Revolution.* Edited by Samuel Proctor, 49–75. Gainesville: University Presses of Florida, 1978.

Dalcho, Frederick. *An Historical Account of the Protestant Episcopal Church in South Carolina, from the First Settlement of the Province to the War of the Revolution.* Charleston: E. Thayer, 1820.

Davidson, Chalmers G. *Friend of the People: The Life of Dr. Peter Fayssoux of Charleston, South Carolina.* Columbia: Medical Association of South Carolina, 1950.

Dewhurst, William W. *The History of St. Augustine, Florida.* New York: Putnam, 1881.

Dodge, Andrew R. *Biographical Directory of the United States Congress: 1774–2005; the Continental Congress, Sept. 5, 1774 to Oct. 21, 1788, and the Congress of the United States from the First through the One Hundred Eighth Congresses, March 4, 1789 to Jan. 3, 2005 Inclusive.* Washington, D.C.: U.S. Government Printing Office, 2005.

Doggett, Carita. *Dr. Andrew Turnbull and the New Smyrna Colony of Florida.* Jacksonville: Drew, 1919.

Dunkerly, Robert M., and Irene B. Boland. *Eutaw Springs: The Final Battle of the American Revolution's Southern Campaign.* Columbia: University of South Carolina Press, 2017.

Eastman, Margaret M. R. *Remembering Old Charleston: A Peek behind Parlor Doors.* Charleston, S.C.: History Press, 2008.

Edgar, Walter, and N. Louise Bailey. *Biographical Directory of the South Carolina House of Representatives, Volume II: The Commons House of Assembly, 1692–1775.* Columbia: University of South Carolina Press, 1977.

Edgar, Walter, and N. Louise Bailey. *Biographical Directory of the South Carolina House of Representatives, Volume IV: 1791–1815.* Columbia: University of South Carolina Press, 1989.

Elzas, Barnett A. *The Jews of South Carolina from the Earliest Times to the Present Day.* Philadelphia: Lippincott, 1905.

Fairbanks, George R. "Florida during the English Occupation." In *Library of Southern Literature*, vol. 16, edited by Lucian Lamar Knight, 22–28. Atlanta: Martin & Hoyt, 1909.

———. *Florida, Its History And Its Romance.* 2nd rev. ed. Jacksonville: Drew, 1901.

———. *The History and Antiquities of the City of St. Augustine, Florida.* New York: Drew, 1858.

———. *History of Florida from Its Discovery by Ponce de Leon, in 1512, to the Close of the Florida War, in 1842.* Philadelphia: Lippincott, 1871.

Fludd, Eliza C. K. *Biographical Sketches of the Huguenot Solomon Legaré and of His Family: Extending Down to the Fourth Generation of Descendants.* Charleston, S.C.: Perry, 1886.

Forbes, James Grant. *Sketches of the Floridas, Historical and Topographical.* New York: Van Winkle, 1821.

Ford, Worthington Chauncey. *British Officers Serving in the American Revolution, 1774–1783.* Brooklyn, N.Y.: Historical Print. Club, 1897.

Garden, Alexander. *Anecdotes of the American Revolution Illustrative of the Talents and Virtues of the Heroes and Patriots, Who Acted the Most Conspicuous Parts Therein.* 2nd ser. Charleston, S.C.: Miller, 1828.

———. *Anecdotes of the Revolutionary War in America: With Sketches of Character of Persons the Most Distinguished, in the Southern States, for Civil and Military Services.* 1st ser. Charleston, S.C.: Miller, 1822.

Godbold, E. Stanly, and Robert H. Woody. *Christopher Gadsden and the American Revolution.* Knoxville: University of Tennessee Press, 1982.

Hagy, James William, and James William Hagy. *Charleston, South Carolina City Directories: For the Years 1816, 1819, 1822, 1825, and 1829.* Baltimore: Clearfield, 1996.

Hamilton, Paul. "Extracts from a Private Manuscript During the Period of the Revolutionary War, from 1776–1780." In *Year Book—1898, City of Charleston, So. Ca.,* 299–327. Charleston: Lucas & Richardson, 1898.

Hanna, Alfred Jackson, and Kathryn Abbey Hanna. *Florida's Golden Sands.* New York: Dobbs-Merrill, 1950.

Harper, William. *Memoir of the Life, Character, and Public Services, of the Late Hon. Henry Wm. De Saussure.* Charleston: W. Riley, 1841.

Haw, James. *John and Edward Rutledge of South Carolina.* Athens: University of Georgia Press, 1997.

Heitman, Francis Bernard. *Historical Register of Officers of the Continental Army during the War of the Revolution, April 1775, to December, 1783.* Washington, D.C.: Rare Book Shop and Publishing, 1914.

Hill, James Riley, III. "An Exercise in Futility: The Pre-revolutionary Career and Influence of Loyalist James Simpson." M.A. thesis, University of South Carolina, 1992.

Holcomb, Brent H. *South Carolina Deed Abstracts, 1783–1788, Books I-5 through Z-5.* Columbia: SCMAR, 1996.

Huish, Robert. *Memoirs of George the Fourth: Descriptive of the Most Interesting Scenes of His Private and Public Life, and the Important Events of His Memorable Reign: With Characteristic Sketches of All the Celebrated Men Who Were His Friends and Companions as a Prince and His Ministers and Counsellors as a Monarch.* 2 vols. London: T. Kelly, 1830.

Isaacs, Barry. "Lt.-Col. Elijah Isaacs," April 2017, http://www.carolana.com/NC/Revolution/Elijah_Isaacs_Biography_Barry_Isaacs_April_2017.pdf.

Jahoda, Gloria. *Florida, a Bicentennial History.* New York: Norton, 1976.

Johnson, Joseph. *Traditions and Reminiscences, Chiefly of the American Revolution in the South.* Charleston, S.C.: Walker & James, 1851.

Johnson, William. *Sketches of the Life and Correspondence of Nathanael Greene, Major General of the Armies of the United States, in the War of the Revolution.* 2 vols. Charleston, S.C.: Miller, 1822.

Jones, Charles Colcock. "Noble Wymberley Jones." In *Men of Mark in Georgia,* vol. 1, edited by William J. Northen, 208–18. Atlanta: Caldwell, 1907.

Kane, John, and William Harrison Askwith. *List of Officers of the Royal Regiment of Artillery from the Year 1716 to the Year 1899.* London: Royal Artillery Institution, 1900.

Kierner, Cynthia A. *Southern Women in Revolution, 1776–1800: Personal and Political Narratives.* Columbia: University of South Carolina Press, 1998.

Logan, G. William. *A Record of the Logan Family of Charleston, South Carolina.* Sacramento, Cal.: Record Book and Job Printing Office, 1874.

Long, Minnie Rutherford Harsh. *General Griffith Rutherford and Allied Families: Harsh, Graham, Cathey, Locke, Holeman, Johnson, Chambers.* Milwaukee: Wisconsin Cuneo, 1942.

Lumpkin, Henry. *From Savannah to Yorktown: The American Revolution in the South.* Columbia: University of South Carolina Press, 1981.

Manigault, Edward Lining, and Horry Frost Prioleau. *Register of Carolina Huguenots: Partial listing of 81 Refugee Families,* vol. 3, *Marion–Villepontoux.* N.p.: CreateSpace Independent Publishing Platform, 2007.

Manucy, Albert. "Changing Traditions in St. Augustine Architecture." In *Eighteenth-Century Florida: The Impact of the American Revolution.* Edited by Samuel Proctor, 99–132. Gainesville: University Presses of Florida, 1978.

McCowen, George Smith, Jr. *The British Occupation of Charleston, 1780–1782.* Columbia: University of South Carolina Press, 1972.

McCrady, Edward. *The History of South Carolina in the Revolution, 1775–1780.* New York: Macmillan, 1901.

———. *The History of South Carolina in the Revolution, 1780–1783.* New York: Macmillan, 1902.

———. *The History of South Carolina under the Royal Government, 1719–1776.* New York: Macmillan, 1899.

McCrady, Edward, and Samuel A. Ashe, eds. *Cyclopedia of Eminent and Representative Men of the Carolinas of the Nineteenth Century.* Vol. 1. Madison, Wis.: Brant & Fuller, 1892.

McLachlan, James. *Princetonians, 1748–1768: A Biographical Dictionary.* Princeton, N.J.: Princeton University Press, 1976.

Miller, Ruth M., and Ann Taylor Andrus. *Charleston's Old Exchange Building: A Witness to American History.* Charleston, S.C.: History Press, 2005.

Moore, John Hammond. *Columbia and Richland County: A South Carolina Community, 1740–1990.* Columbia: University of South Carolina Press, 1993.

Morgan, Gwenda, and Peter Rushton. *Banishment in the Early Atlantic World: Convicts, Rebels and Slaves.* New York: Bloomsbury, 2013.

Moss, Bobby Gilmer. *Roster of South Carolina Patriots in the American Revolution.* Baltimore: Genealogical Publishing, 1983.

Mowat, Charles L. *East Florida as a British Province, 1763–84.* Berkeley: University of California Press, 1943.

Nash, Gary B. *Forgotten Fifth: African Americans in the Age of Revolution.* Cambridge, Mass.: Harvard University Press, 2009.

Otto, Olaf North. *The Family of Captain Edward North and His Wife, Elizabeth Tucker: In Bermuda, America, England, Canada, British India, New Zealand, Australia, and South Africa.* [Adana, Turkey]: O. N. Otto, 1996.

Outland, Robert B., III. *Tapping the Pines: The Naval Stores Industry in the American South.* Baton Rouge: Louisiana State University Press, 2004.

Park, Lawrence. *Major Thomas Savage of Boston and His Descendants.* Boston: Clapp, 1914.

Piecuch, Jim. Three Peoples, One King: Loyalists, Indians, and Slaves in the Revolutionary South, 1775–1782. Columbia: University of South Carolina Press, 2008.

Powell, William S. *Dictionary of North Carolina Biography,* vol. 5, *P–S.* Chapel Hill: University of North Carolina Press,1994.

Quinn, Jane. *Minorcans in Florida: Their History and Heritage.* St. Augustine: Mission, 1975.

Raab, James W. *Spain, Britain, and the American Revolution in Florida, 1763–1783.* Jefferson, N.C.: McFarland, 2008.

Ramsay, David. *The History of the American Revolution.* 2 vols. Trenton, N.J.: Wilson, 1811.

———. *The History of the Revolution of South-Carolina: From a British Province to an Independent State.* 2 vols. Trenton, N.J.: Collins, 1785.

———. *The History of South Carolina: From Its First Settlement in 1670 to the Year 1808.* 2 vols. Charleston, S.C.: Longworth, 1809.

Rasico, Philip D. *The Minorcans of Florida: Their History, Language, and Culture.* New Smyrna Beach, Fla.: Luther's, 1990.

Ravenel, Harriott Horry. *Charleston, the Place and the People.* New York: Macmillan, 1912.

Read, Thomas Carpenter. *The Descendants of Thomas Lee of Charleston, South Carolina, 1710–1769: A Genealogical-Biographical-Compilation.* Columbia: Bryan, 1964.

Reynolds, Charles B. *Old St. Augustine: A Story of Three Centuries.* St. Augustine: Reynolds, 1886.

Reynolds, Emily Bellinger, and Joan Reynolds Faunt. *Biographical Directory of the Senate of the State of South Carolina, 1776–1964.* Columbia: S.C. Archives Dept., 1964.

Romans, Bernard. *A Concise Natural History of East and West Florida.* New York: Aitken, 1776.

Salley, Alexander S., Jr. *President Washington's Tour through South Carolina in 1791.* Columbia: Crowson-Stone, 1950.

Schafer, Daniel L. *St. Augustine's British Years, 1763–1784.* El Scribano no. 38. St. Augustine: St. Augustine Historical Society, 2001.

Shaffer, Arthur H. *To Be an American: David Ramsay and the Making of the American Consciousness.* Columbia: University of South Carolina Press, 1991.

Siebert, Wilbur Henry. *Loyalists in East Florida, 1774–1785.* 2 vols. Deland, Fla.: Florida State Historical Society, 1929.

Smith, Roger. "The Façade of Unity British East Florida's War for Dependence." M.A. thesis, University of Florida, 2008.

Smith, Roger. "The Fourteenth Colony: Florida and the American Revolution in the South." Ph.D. diss., University of Florida, 2011.

Smith, William Roy. *South Carolina as a Royal Province, 1710–1776.* New York: Macmillan, 1903.

Solís de Méras, Gonzalo. *Pedro Menéndez de Avilés, Adelantado, Governor and Captain-General of Florida.* Translated and edited by Jeannette Thurber Conner. Deland, Fla.: Florida Historical Society, 1923.

Strozier, Harry S., ed. *Report of the Thirty-Eighth Annual Session of the Georgia Bar Association.* Macon, Ga.: Burke, 1922.

Stedman, Charles. *The History of the Origin, Progress, and Termination of the American War.* London: Murray, Debrett & Kerby, 1794.

Stephen, Leslie, and Sidney Lee, eds. *Dictionary of National Biography.* 22 vols. New York: Macmillan, 1908–9.

Strock, G. Michael. *By Faith, with Thanksgiving: A History of Trinity Episcopal Parish 1821–1996.* St. Augustine: Trinity Episcopal Parish, 1996.

Sturgess, H. A. C., comp. *Register of Admissions to the Honourable Society of the Middle Temple, from the Fifteenth Century to the Year 1944.* Vol. 1. London: Butterworth, 1949.

Tebeau, Charlton W. *A History of Florida.* Coral Gables: University of Miami Press, 1971.

Tuchman, Barbara W. *The First Salute: A View of the American Revolution.* New York: Knopf, 1988.

Ubbelohde, Carl. *The Vice-Admiralty Courts and the American Revolution.* Chapel Hill: University of North Carolina Press, 1960.

Wallace, Nesbit Willoughby. *A Regimental Chronicle and List of Officers of the 60th, or the King's Royal Rifle Corps, Formerly the 62nd, or the Royal American Regiment of Foot.* London: Harrison, 1879.

Waterbury, Jean Parker, ed. *The Oldest City: St. Augustine, Saga of Survival.* St. Augustine: St. Augustine Historical Society, 1983.

Weir, Robert M. *Colonial South Carolina, a History.* Columbia: University of South Carolina Press, 1997.

Weis, Frederick Lewis. *The Colonial Clergy of Virginia, North Carolina, and South Carolina.* Baltimore: Genealogical Publishing, 1955.

Wheeler, Mary Bray, and Genon Hickerson Neblett. *Chosen Exile: The Life and Times of Septima Sexta Middleton Rutledge, American Cultural Pioneer.* Nashville: Rutledge Hill, 1980.

Whitney, Edson Leone. *Government of the Colony of South Carolina.* Baltimore: Johns Hopkins Press, 1895.

Wickes, Stephen, and Jonathan Dickinson. *History of Medicine in New Jersey and of Its Medical Men, from the Settlement of the Province to A.D. 1800.* Newark: Dennis, 1879.

Wilkinson, C. P. Seabrook "Eliza Yonge Wilkinson." In American Women Prose Writers to 1820. Edited by Carla Mulford, with Angela Vietto and Amy E. Winans. Detroit: Gale Research, 1999.

Wilson, Samuel M. comp. *Year Book of the Society, Sons of the Revolution, in the Commonwealth of Kentucky, 1894–1913: And Catalogue of Military Land Warrants Granted by the Commonwealth of Virginia to Soldiers and Sailors of the Revolution.* Lexington: [Kentucky Society of the Sons of the Revolution], 1913.

Winfield, Rif. *British Warships in the Age of Sail, 1793–1817: Design, Construction, Careers and Fates.* Barnsley, England: Seaforth, 2007.

Woods, Henry George, ed. *Register of Burials at the Temple Church, 1628–1853.* London: Sotheran, 1905.

Woodward, Ruth L., and Wesley Frank Craven. *Princetonians, 1784–1790: A Biographical Dictionary.* Princeton, N.J.: Princeton University Press, 1991.

Wright, J. Leitch, Jr. "British East Florida: Loyalist Bastion." In *Eighteenth-Century Florida: The Impact of the American Revolution,* edited by Samuel Proctor, 1–13. Gainesville: University Presses of Florida, 1978.

———. *British St. Augustine.* St. Augustine: Historic St. Augustine Preservation Board, 1975.

———. *Florida in the American Revolution.* Gainesville: University Presses of Florida, 1975.

Articles from Journals, Magazines, and Periodicals

"America, Charles-Town, September 11, 1780," *Lady's Magazine,* January 1781, 55.

Baldry, W. Y., and A. S. White. "Disbanded Regiments." *Journal of the Society for Army Historical Research* 1, no. 3 (1922): 90–92.

Edgar, Walter B. "Notable Libraries of Colonial South Carolina." *South Carolina Historical Magazine* 72, no. 2 (1971): 105–10.

Fenhagen, Mary Pringle. "John Edwards and Some of His Descendants." *South Carolina Historical Magazine* 55, no. 1 (1954): 15–27.

Gold, Robert L. "That Infamous Floridian, Jesse Fish." *Florida Historical Quarterly* 52, no. 1 (1973): 1–17.

Haarmann, Albert W. "The Spanish Conquest of British West Florida, 1779–1781." *Florida Historical Quarterly* 39, no. 2 (1960): 107–34.

Haw, James. "A Broken Compact: Insecurity, Union, and the Proposed Surrender of Charleston, 1779." *South Carolina Historical Magazine* 96, no. 1 (1995): 30–53.

Johnson, Elmer Douglass. "David Ramsay: Historian or Plagiarist?" *South Carolina Historical Magazine* 57, no. 4 (1956): 189–98.

Lawson, Katherine S. "Luciano de Herrera, Spanish Spy in British St. Augustine." *Florida Historical Quarterly* 23, no. 3 (1945): 170–76.

Moultrie, James. "The Moultries, Part II: The Moultries of South Carolina." Annotated by Alexander S. Salley Jr. *South Carolina Historical and Genealogical Magazine* 5, no. 4 (1904): 247–60.

Manucy, Albert, and Alberta Johnson. "Castle St. Mark and the Patriots of the Revolution." *Florida Historical Quarterly* 21, no. 1 (1942): 3–24.

Mowat, Charles L. "The Enigma of William Drayton." *Florida Historical Quarterly* 22, no. 1 (1943): 3–33.

———. "St. Augustine under the British Flag, 1763–1775." *Florida Historical Quarterly* 20, no. 2 (1941): 131–50.

Nadelhaft, Jerome. "Ending South Carolina's War: Two 1782 Agreements Favoring the Planters." *South Carolina Historical Magazine* 80, no. 1 (1979): 50–64.

Newton, Craig A. "Three Patterns of Local History: South Carolina Historians, 1779–1830." *South Carolina Historical Magazine* 65, no. 3 (1964): 145–57.

Olson, Gary D. "Dr. David Ramsay and Lt. Colonel Thomas Brown: Patriot Historian and Loyalist Critic." *South Carolina Historical Magazine* 77, no. 4 (1976): 257–67.

Riley, Helen M. "Michael Kalteisen and the Founding of the German Friendly Society in Charleston." *South Carolina Historical Magazine* 100, no. 1 (1999): 29–48.

Salley, Alexander S., Jr. "Daniel Trezevant, Huguenot, and Some of His Descendants." *South Carolina Historical and Genealogical Magazine* 3, no. 1 (1902): 24–56.

———, ed. "Historical Notes." *South Carolina Historical and Genealogical Magazine* 7, no. 2 (1906): 99–113.

Siebert, Wilbur H. "The Port of St. Augustine during the British Regime. Part I." *Florida Historical Quarterly* 24, no. 4 (1946): 247–65.

———. "The Port of St. Augustine during the British Regime. Part II." *Florida Historical Quarterly* 25, no. 1 (1946): 76–93.

Stoesen, Alexander R. "The British Occupation of Charleston, 1780–1782." *South Carolina Historical Magazine* 63, no. 1 (1962): 71–82.

Waterbury, Jean Parker. "John Forbes: Man of the Cloth, of His Times, and of St. Augustine." *El Escribano* 18 (1981): 1–32.

Webber, Mabel L. "Dr. John Rutledge and His Descendants." *South Carolina Historical and Genealogical Magazine* 31, no. 1 (1930): 7–25.